PARENTING
WITH AN
ACCENT

PARENTING
WITH AN
ACCENT

HOW IMMIGRANTS
HONOR THEIR HERITAGE,
NAVIGATE SETBACKS,
AND CHART NEW PATHS FOR
THEIR CHILDREN

MASHA RUMER

BEACON PRESS   BOSTON

BEACON PRESS
Boston, Massachusetts
www.beacon.org

Beacon Press books
are published under the auspices of
the Unitarian Universalist Association of Congregations.

25 24 23 22   8 7 6 5 4 3 2 1

This book is printed on acid-free paper that meets the uncoated paper
ANSI/NISO specifications for permanence as revised in 1992.

Text design and composition by Kim Arney

Library of Congress Cataloging-in-Publication Data
Name: Rumer, Masha, author.
Title: Parenting with an accent : how immigrants honor their heritage,
navigate setbacks, and chart new paths for their children / Masha Rumer.
Description: Boston : Beacon Press, [2022] | Includes bibliographical references.
Identifiers: LCCN 2021032176 (print) | LCCN 2021032177 (ebook) |
ISBN 9780807021873 (hardcover ; alk. paper) | ISBN 9780807021941 (ebook)
Subjects: LCSH: Parenthood—United States—Cross-cultural studies. |
Children of immigrants—United States. | Immigrants—Family
relationships—United States. | Immigrant families—United States.
Classification: LCC HQ755.8 .R85 2022 (print) | LCC HQ755.8 (ebook) |
DDC 306.8740973—dc23
LC record available at https://lccn.loc.gov/2021032176
LC ebook record available at https://lccn.loc.gov/2021032177

To my family, here and there.

*Some names and identifying details have
been changed to protect the anonymity
of the individuals interviewed.*

CONTENTS

PREFACE

THIS BOOK is a portrait of the different ways immigrants are honoring their heritage while integrating their families into American life.

After becoming a parent, I searched for a nonfiction book about the contemporary immigrant child-rearing experience. I wanted something to relate to, commiserate with, and learn from, but found little written on the subject.

Yet the more I chatted with other foreign-born parents, the clearer it became that lots of people straddle multiple cultures and try to make sense of their fractured identities. I heard the same concerns over and over: "I feel guilty for not passing my language on to my kids" or "My mother rubbed my teething baby's gums with vodka, and when I confronted her, she just blew me off, saying I turned out okay."

The foreign-born population in America today stands at 44.8 million, the highest in the history of this country.[1] That's more than the populations of Florida, New Jersey, and Illinois together. In 2019, one out of four children in America, or 19 million, had at least one foreign-born parent.[2] And those numbers keep going up.

So I decided to write a book about it.

The objective of this book is threefold: to create a space for individuals and families to tell their stories, to provide factual information about the vastly diverse immigrant experience in America, and to share my own. I strove to be aware of my blind spots and educate myself along the way.

This book also shares the latest research and advice from experts in bilingualism, child development, and psychology. I am a writer, an immigrant, and a parent, but not a sociologist nor a psychologist, nor, might I add, a speech therapist, so I turned to a bunch of smart and accomplished folks in those fields, who generously shared their insights.

Allow me to mention what this book is not. It is not a "how-to" parenting manual. Though I do share my experiences on these pages, it's done in a "Hey, here's what happened to me" way, not in an "Everyone should do it like this" way. My vantage point is only one of many, and this book does not attempt to speak for all immigrants, because there is no one way to be either a parent or an immigrant. Anyone who says otherwise is probably trying to sell you something (or pass a dubious law).

The one bit of advice I do hope this book conveys is this: you do you. There is no formula for raising immigrant kids or for rebuilding a home from scratch in the new land. And if this book can make an immigrant feel just a tiny bit less alone and more at home, wherever that may be, then I will have achieved my goal.

All immigrants are different. Some fly in on a direct flight to their final point of destination, with a complimentary in-flight meal, hot napkin, and a movie selection. Others cross over with a coyote and contraceptives or languish in refugee camps in another nation. Some stay; some get detained; others get deported.

I came to America as a thirteen-year-old refugee, fleeing the tanking economy of the former Soviet Union and religious persecution. For generations, my ancestors were permitted to live in certain towns but not in others, often denied employment and schooling because of their beliefs and non-Slavic looks. From Belarus to Ukraine, my relatives have perished in the Holocaust and were targeted by pogroms well before then. After immigrating, I tasted culture shock and poverty.

At the same time, millions of others seeking refuge on America's shores have endured unspeakably more difficult circumstances. Many of my experiences were shaped by the color of my skin and by my documented status, as well as by US foreign policy, which at the time favored exiles from communist nations. This is a critical point to mention, because race and racialization affect immigrants and, subsequently, their languages, their parenting choices, and the ability to provide for their families.

While working on this manuscript, I learned a tremendous amount about the tapestry of cultures making up America today. I was moved by the relentless optimism and dreams every individual I spoke with had shared with me, as well as by the hardships many have endured.

I came away from my research with more humility and gratitude than ever before.

I made a few observations too. First, despite the unique challenges immigrants confront, our aspirations aren't all that different from those of our native-born peers. They are the essence of our shared humanity. We want to fit in, and we want our children to grow up safe, happy, and successful. We want to be treated as equals at work, at schools, and in our neighborhoods and not have to prove our worthiness every day. Okay, so maybe we also want our brood to speak a foreign language or two, eat lots of dumplings, celebrate all the festivals, and declare a practical college major. Yet, as these pages will show, things don't always pan out how we expect them to, especially when raising children.

Also, many adversities I heard about weren't necessarily rooted in immigration. They were the universal stuff of life: overbearing relatives, fertility challenges, broken engagements, dating horror stories, colicky babies. We are not an outlandish mob of aliens, after all.

The book is divided into fourteen chapters, including an introduction, with each subsequent chapter exploring a distinct stage of the parenting journey. I conducted nearly sixty interviews between 2017 and 2020, speaking to some individuals over a period of time. A little under half of the interviews were conducted in person, with the rest done by phone, video, and, in several cases, via email and online messaging platforms. I interviewed immigrants and their families living in fifteen different states. In doing so, I attempted to include residents of all major US regions and key language groups spoken in this country today. Despite my best efforts, it's impossible to capture every language and every truth, though I tried to be as representative as possible.

Given the US government rhetoric and policies that have demonized immigrants in recent years, I sought to dispel myths and treat each person's narrative with the sensitivity it deserves.[3] I am endlessly grateful to the many people who spoke with me for this project, including those who've opened up their homes, workplaces, and houses of worship and let me tag along during playground outings and piano lessons. Without them, this book would not have been possible.

San Francisco Bay Area, 2020

PARENTING
WITH AN
ACCENT

1. I AM THE GRINCH WHO STOLE CHRISTMAS

*What for will you need old feather beds? Don't you
know it's always summer in America? And in the new
golden country, where milk and honey flows free in the
streets, you'll have new golden dishes to cook in, and not
weigh yourself down with your old pots and pans.*

—ANZIA YEZIERSKA, Bread Givers[1]

WHEN CHRISTMAS ROLLS AROUND, just about every child around
me puts on an adorable fluffy dress or a sweater vest, sits on Santa's lap,
and sings carols from memory. Even my quiet California town, where
the speed limit is capped at twenty-five miles per hour, draws visitors
from all over to stroll through its Christmas Tree Lane, a spectacular
show of lights. By city hall, tap dancers dressed like Christmas trees
shimmy to "Santa Claus Is Comin' to Town" as the townsfolk cheer
them on.

Like the neighbors, I get misty when I hear "Silent Night" on the
radio. I dress my children in outfits of red and green and invite their
friends over for cookie-decorating parties. Holiday music plays on repeat in our home, and the scent of "yuletide" and "sparkling cranberry"
candles wafts through the living room.

Trouble is, I'm sort of an impostor. It's not really *my* holiday. My
holiday, technically, is Hanukkah, which I knew nothing about when
growing up. I come from a place where religion was considered the
opiate for the masses and Jewish people like myself often hid their heritage. Instead, I grew up with an atheist sort of Christmas in Leningrad,
Soviet Union. There, people ate caviar and fawned over Santa's blonde
granddaughter, Snegurochka the Snow Maiden, on New Year's Eve.

But with my two children and an American husband, who was brought up in a Christian household, we embrace the Christmas spirit. And the spirit of Hanukkah and New Year's Eve too, as evidenced by the Nativity scene wedged between the menorah and the Douglas fir.

"Look, Leah, the Russian Santa is just like the American Santa you met last week," I explain to my three-year-old daughter, coaxing her to go to a Russian holiday party, organized by a local language school. "Except the Russian Santa's got this granddaughter who looks like Elsa. You love Elsa, don't you?" (Elsa is the lead character in *Frozen*, my daughter's favorite Disney cartoon.) She agrees to go. We get in the car.

When we arrive at the community center rec room, Russian Santa pounds his silver staff against the floor. He jokes in a booming voice that he's already knocked back a few drinks in the morning and winks lasciviously at the Snow Maiden. The noise lulls my son to sleep in his baby carrier and he misses the whole thing. My daughter, on the other hand, is awake—and she's terrified. She yanks on my sleeve and demands that we leave.

On our drive back, I pop in a disc with an iconic Russian holiday song, "In the Forest, a Christmas Tree Was Born." As we roll down the suburban California road, the song's familiarity fills me with longing.

"What's that music?" Leah asks from the back seat.

I'm overjoyed at her question. Maybe now is that special moment to share the family holiday traditions with my kids. All the traditions, not just the ones sanctioned by upscale home furnishing catalogues. I can't wait to tell Leah about the sledding and the people in fur hats stocking up on smoked fish, about schoolgirls with bows in their hair caroling across eleven time zones. *We'll visit when you're older!* I want to promise to Leah. *You'll meet your cousins and go to the ballet and eat tons of pastries and see fountains made of gold!*

"Well, Leah," I start, "this is a *Russian holiday song*. Because you're a Russian girl, right?"

"No," Leah retorts. "I English girl. My daddy sings another 'Jingle Bells.' Can we listen to *that*?"[2]

Maybe when she's older. I turn the American radio station on.

And when she's older, maybe I'll also tell her about my last December in Russia. About how, instead of decorating the tree, my family secretly sold off most of our possessions: the books, the family china, my old doll in a fuzzy blue cardigan. The entire apartment of my child-hood, with the furniture and the wallpaper and the houseplants still in it, was gone in one fell swoop, days before our departure.

I'll tell her about the overnight train from St. Petersburg to Moscow taking my parents, brother, and me to a plane bound for America.

Boarding the train to Moscow, I wasn't thinking about the crumbling regime and poverty, where thieves yanked earrings out of women's earlobes and war veterans sold their medals on the sidewalk in order to buy bread. I didn't hear the swirling rumors about a pogrom being planned in my city and my parents' coworkers offering to hide us. I just helped push the suitcases into the train and clung to the window, clutching an envelope with photographs of all that was familiar, of all that was about to become the past.

Just before the clock struck midnight, a haunting classical melody blared from the station speakers. The train jerked and began to move. My grandparents, aunts, and uncles on the platform scurried after it. They waved and wept and said something about writing letters, their breaths swirling in the cold. They wafted in and out of the snow-streaked light. My grandfather Abram's walk resembled a march. An eye patch covered the place where his eye had once been, which he'd lost defending his city in battle. I had put drops in his remaining eye so many times to keep it healthy. But now he wasn't really seeing me. He just marched alongside our window, trying to keep pace. His chin was propped high; his teeth were clenched in an emotionless smile.

The train sped up. The people on the platform disappeared as the snow kept on falling.

■ ■ ■

I arrived in California in the early 1990s as the state was recovering from a recession. At the time, Governor Pete Wilson was campaigning against undocumented immigrants, blaming them for the state's ills and trying to deny them public education and medical care through an initiative known as Proposition 187. Television networks kept replaying footage of "the illegals" running across the border. California voters soon passed his ballot measure. Though this law was later found unconstitutional, Wilson's rhetoric divided people, regardless of their paperwork.[3]

Even in my high school.

"Welcome to California. Now Go Back Home" read a sign above the blackboard in my social studies classroom, designated for ESL students, or English language learners. It was a strange message to find in a public school with many teenagers from East Asia and Latin America. Yet there it was, the sign, in all its unwelcoming glory, and our history teacher Mr. Clark along with it.

"Do you even care about sports?" Mr. Clark mumbled when the announcements invited students to try out for the football team. "As if any of you care about theater," Mr. Clark would say flatly and look past us whenever the radio announced school play auditions. He even resembled Governor Pete Wilson a little: heavy jawed, with light-colored eyes and neatly combed gray hair. He was tall and projected the American confidence I'd seen in movies back home.

"All you do is speak Chinese and whatever else. Hey, English only, please," he'd rebuff the boys whispering in Mandarin in the back of the room and sigh.

I may have missed the meaning of some of his words, but the message was clear. Despite so many welcoming teachers, social workers, Jewish community leaders, and church ladies I'd met in the past few months, Mr. Clark didn't want us here. We weren't a desirable part of his history lesson. So I avoided Mr. Clark and never told him that I had actually auditioned for that school musical and got the part (because if you belt out "My Funny Valentine" very loudly, you can conceal your accent and the fact that you understand only about 30 percent of the lyrics). Nor did anyone bother to tell Mr. Clark that many kids in our class played sports, even if badminton was the name of the game.

A couple of times, a Russian classmate whose family had recently moved here for work gave me a ride home from school. Her mother was dressed according to the latest fashion back home. Their car was a foreign universe, despite our shared language. Inside, you immediately smelled leather and perfume. A set of tennis racquets leisurely rested against the passenger's seat. The sedan accelerated fast and smooth, zipping across the sprawling suburbia with its one-story houses, shopping plazas, and deserted sidewalks as Russian pop music blasted from the speakers. The seats were cool to the touch and the windows were sealed tight, in contrast to our old Buick with a nonworking air conditioner Anything that didn't belong here was shut out.

I'd ask them to pull over a few buildings away from mine and slither out into the heat of the late California spring. The car sped away with bass thumping in its wake as I walked over to my apartment building.

I'd open the creaky gate, careful to not shake the fence with baskets of drying vegetables on top of it, belonging to the Chinese immigrant family that lived downstairs. Upstairs, our building manager, Tracy, was arguing with her husband again. I'd pause by the cement staircase and listen, captivated by the unfamiliar vocabulary ("You pull that *English* on me again and I swear I'm gonna kick your *mother English* ass to the *mother English* curb!"). Tracy would then turn her attention to her teenage son, Ricky Jr., who'd talk right back to her. Ricky Jr. wore wife beaters and had recently gotten a mullet haircut like his dad. Despite our being a similar age, I didn't interact with Ricky Jr. much, other than hearing him bicker with his parents during the day and stumble home in the middle of the night. That, and the few times when he and his buddy, hanging out on the staircase with beers in hand, made whooping remarks about my body. Meanwhile, the argument upstairs usually culminated with a door slam. Tracy would then emerge outside with a cigarette, force a tired smile, and go handle repairs in the building units, as she did every day.

It's hard to stay mentally present in an unfamiliar world. Nostalgia tethers you to the past; worry pulls you into the future. Many immigrants who arrived as children often report fuzzy recollections of their early experiences, almost as if after a blackout. To make room for the new, you must let go of the old. But what if the old won't budge? What if the mind perceives memories as intensely as if they're still real, clinging to your skin, itching your throat? The overnight train rides to the Black Sea and the scent of sweet acacia and potatoes with dill. The strolls to the park with my grandfather, his hands folded behind his back. Sitting next to the birch trees I'd planted as a little girl and chattering with classmates over sunflower seeds. The ice over the Gulf of Finland glimmering beneath my kicksled in thousands of magical lights. How can these moments be gone if they'd just recently happened? In the mind of a child, how can they be pushed off the main stage and up to the nosebleed section of memory in exchange for bubble gum and neon-colored sneakers?

There's a story about a wise Zen master who once met with a professor seeking enlightenment. The Zen master, the story goes, offered the professor tea and kept pouring it until the cup overflowed. The mind is like that teacup, the Zen master explained: "How can I show you Zen unless you first empty your cup?"[4]

So, eventually, you make space for the present. You observe. You study. You learn English. You socialize, cautiously, for fear that the new people, too, might soon be gone.

Soon, I no longer wanted to speak Russian in public. I was embarrassed by my clothes, bought at a discount store or plucked from a donation bin, so different from what Kelly and Brenda wore on *Beverly Hills, 90210.*

Aside from being a fashion disaster, self-conscious teenagers generally dread three things: failing a test, romantic rejection, and nightmares of being trapped naked in a roomful of people.

For an immigrant, the list of public humiliation anxieties is even longer.

One is being unable to communicate. If you don't have the language, you don't have a voice. You'll be left out of all the important conversations in the girls' locker room about makeup, Sun-Ripened Raspberry moisturizer, and sex. And of most other conversations, actually. Even if you smile and nod. Even if you do their algebra homework (you're welcome, Britney). Even if you carry a paper dictionary in your backpack, it's of little use if you're piecing together the meaning of "Let's hook up and kick it" (seriously, don't even try) or "That dude is lame," which, as it turns out, does not mean "an inexperienced cowboy with a limp."

While learning English, you might speak in your native tongue with others from your country. But not everyone will approve. Like the girl in the lunch line who'll remark, "I hate when they do that. My parents worked hard to bring them to America, and they just don't wanna learn!"

With an eye roll, her girlfriend will agree: "*So* disrespectful."

You might develop a crush on a curly haired junior who plays guitar. He seems so poetically withdrawn that the language barrier isn't an issue. It doesn't even matter that he's often trailed by a girl in a hoodie who smokes by the creek and carries her JanSport backpack slung off one shoulder. You admire the boy silently, from afar, except for one glorious time when you end up walking upstairs to Algebra right behind him, an herbal fragrance trailing from his jacket.

"Yo, Jason," you overhear his buddy say. "So where do you see her, man?" (*His name is Jason! How Greek! How timeless! How Adonis-like!*)

"On my cock!" he responds.

The two chortle and high-five one another. Later, you consult various dictionaries to figure out what that word means, then spend the rest of the evening wishing you hadn't.

Another awkward immigrant teen situation is being watched by American peers from their windows as you deliver their newspapers with your family.

We would park our Buick next to the multicar driveways and get to work. I walked ahead with the bag, while my parents mapped out our route and sorted the American address system in Russian.

"This says Seven Forty Cherry Tree *Es Tee*, but we need Seven Forty Cherry Tree *Court*."

"Could *es tee* be short for *court*? *C* and *s* can sound the same in English."

"What I want to know is why name two adjacent streets in the same way? And how come half these houses don't even have an address marked on them? What, you bought yourself a Mercedes but couldn't afford a painter?"

"Maybe they don't want anyone to come over who doesn't know how to find them. You know, it's that thing about personal space in America."

"They want personal space? Then get a guard dog and don't sign up for newspaper delivery, is what I'd tell these nudniks."

I kept on depositing the newspapers on the doorsteps and praying for a mound of sand somewhere to bury my head in for a few years, or at least until my family and I could speak English without an accent and wear Gap clothes like everyone else.

My parents hustled and worked around the clock. They applied for jobs in bulk, reread their old Russian science textbooks in English, attended classes to learn the new language and new marketable skills, worked the night shift at an assembly line of a technology company.

Still, it wasn't enough. Which brings me to the awkward immigrant teen situation number three: the food bank.

There, at a local church, volunteers handed out free groceries: canned beans, bread, dehydrated potato flakes, powdered milk, jars labeled with "not for individual resale." The women looked at me with compassion and pity, smiling as they filled my paper bag.

On the walk back home that day, as I passed by a pink mansion, the bottom of the bag ripped open. Slowly and dramatically, out tumbled the beans, the bread, the containers labeled "not for individual resale." Some packages burst open, spilling across the sidewalk. I crouched down to try and salvage my family's weekly food supply.

That's when I saw my American classmate emerge from the pink house and head in my direction. She must have noticed me from the window. There's got to be a universal law somewhere that whenever you are caught in a compromising position, that's really the best time for an acquaintance to find you like this.

She handed me two new empty bags, her straight golden hair shimmering in the sun. I thanked her, avoiding eye contact, terrified she'd recognize me and figure out that I'd been living on handouts. That come tomorrow, she would snitch about it to everybody at our high school, sealing my reputation as a poor and clumsy "other," and Mr. Clark would be vindicated, and so would the "English-only" girls.

But she never did. She didn't say anything even after I'd learned English and bought my own clothes with babysitting money (more Hot Topic than The Gap), and we started running in the same social circles. By then the bag incident didn't matter anyway. My parents found work and, some years later, bought a home, taking out the largest mortgage they could and marking the address in large numbers to make it easy for the delivery folks to find. My next history teacher gave me an autobiography of Joan Baez, an American singer-songwriter from an immigrant family, which meant more than he'd realized.

As a young adult, I stopped hiding from my heritage. Instead, I began seeking out the old and familiar—the savory pies, the language, and the company of others who read the same poetry and reveled in the same songs.

It really hit when I first held my baby in my arms. Suddenly, Russian seemed like the most intuitive way to speak to her. It felt like home.

Whenever my daughter and I watched cartoons from my childhood together, my eyes welled up with tears. I wanted to dig up family recipes, to hum to her the lullabies my grandparents sang and their parents sang before them, to whisk her away into a familiar world, safe and secure, as seen through the eyes of a child. This nostalgia had nothing to do with politics. I'm not a supporter of Russia's human rights violations or foreign policy. If my relationship with the motherland were a social media status, it would probably be "It's complicated."

Sharing my culture with my children turned out to be a heavy lift for many reasons, not the least of which was because my home no longer existed. Leningrad was renamed St. Petersburg right before I left. My birth country, the Soviet Union, collapsed, taking the life as I knew it along with it. Returning to visit over a decade later, I was already a foreigner, whether while reconnecting with old classmates or conducting interviews in Russian for an American newspaper assignment.

And then there's that whole language thing. Raising bilingual kids turned out to be trickier than I thought.

I kept wondering: Is teaching a child about the ways of her ancestors un-American? Does bilingualism cause speech delays? (No, it doesn't.) We certainly didn't land here on a UFO, so why are we still called aliens? *You can't sit on two chairs with one ass*, goes a saying from my homeland. Admittedly, yes, it's uncomfortable, but does that rule apply to cultures? Few of us want to sever our roots, whether we trace them to the *Mayflower* or to Mumbai. So how do we hold on to the old and make room for the new, in our homes and in our communities?

New immigrants don't always get the red-carpet treatment. Arguments over who deserves to get in and whether foreigners can assimilate and benefit the economy—or drag it down—still loom large. This is the case now, and it certainly was the case a century ago.

Countless Americans today, as in years past, support immigrant causes, often dedicating their livelihoods to these issues. Yet others believe that America no longer needs immigrants. *Thanks, but we're all set now*, they say. Others wax poetic about the European wave of immigration in nineteenth and early twentieth centuries. They think immigrants used to be good back in the day, but the stock we're getting nowadays is bad. "It's not that I don't like immigrants or anything," they might say, "but . . ." and follow with a litany of grievances.

My ancestors came through Ellis Island the right way. So why can't these people now just bring their papers?, these critics wonder. *Why are they lazy and refuse to assimilate like everyone else? Oh, I don't mean you,* they might add. *I mean those other immigrants, the ones who don't speak English and take our jobs.*

Actually, that's pretty much all immigrants. We take jobs because that's how we survive. We're building the country's infrastructure, growing its food, and inventing the next supercomputer. Yes, we may butcher the English language after arriving and sometimes for our entire lives. But our kids will speak it just fine. And our grandkids will probably forget our native tongues altogether (more on that in chapter 6). Plus, "papers" wasn't a thing until a few generations ago. Passengers disembarking at Ellis Island during its busiest peak in the early twentieth century didn't need a visa or family here. For all intents and purposes, they were undocumented. Under current laws, many ancestors of American citizens today would not have qualified to enter the country.[5]

This book is not about policy. But knowing where we came from helps us understand where we are today, dispel myths, and find uncanny similarities between now and the past.

So here it is: a remarkably brief but necessary overview of American immigration history.

Since colonial times, both progressives and conservatives often greeted newcomers with suspicion. They worried about job security and spying. The feared new religions, strange languages, and different looks changing the way they went about things. New immigrants make easy targets. Individually, we have little power and we tend to stick out like a sore thumb. We can't help but be a little, well, fresh off the boat.

Historians Alejandro Portes and Rubén G. Rumbaut describe this experience as being "in America but not of it."[6] Immigrants fuel the economy, yet they are often viewed as different and threatening. "Although the words at the base of the Statue of Liberty speak of an open country welcoming the poor and wretched of the earth, realities on the ground have been very different,"[7] Portes and Rumbaut write. "This peculiar American waltz between labor demand and identity politics has repeated itself in every major period of immigration."[8]

There were few restrictions about who could immigrate when the Europeans started arriving in Colonial America.[9] (That said, a 1790 law stated that only free white persons could become citizens.)[10] A set of laws in the late nineteenth century barred criminals, polygamists, and those with contagious diseases, but for the most part, there were no major exclusions up until 1882, and no numerical caps on European immigrants until the 1920s.[11] Of the more than twelve million immigrants coming through Ellis Island between 1892 and 1954, only 2 percent was excluded.[12] That's not a whole lot.

So who were the people arriving? Based on the country's first census of 1790, most of the free population in the young colonies had English ancestry, as well as Scottish, Irish, German, French, Dutch, and Swedish. Despite the popular narrative, America was certainly not all European.[13] By 1790, the skyrocketing number of enslaved African people had reached one fifth of the counted population, or nearly seven hundred thousand (enslaved people made up 39 percent of Virginia's population, for example). Native Americans, ravaged by the colonial settlers and already in tragic decline, were not counted in that census at all.[14]

The Founding Fathers envisioned the new America as a place for asylum. George Washington and Thomas Jefferson, in particular, believed those fleeing tyranny should be able to find refuge here. George Washington proclaimed in a letter that "the bosom of America is open to receive not only the opulent and respectable stranger, but the oppressed and persecuted of all nations and religions, whom we shall welcome to a participation of all our rights and privileges, if by decency and propriety of conduct they appear to merit the enjoyment."[15]

Not all Founding Fathers viewed immigrants favorably. Benjamin Franklin, for example, wrote in a private letter in 1753, "Those who come hither are generally of the most ignorant Stupid Sort of their own Nation. . . . But now they come in droves."[16]

Much of Franklin's ire targeted the growing German population, chiefly artisans and farmers settling in large numbers in Pennsylvania.

"Why should Pennsylvania, founded by the English, become a Colony of *Aliens*," Franklin fumed, "who will shortly be so numerous as to Germanize us instead of our Anglifying them, and will never adopt our Language or Customs, any more than they can acquire our Complexion."[17] (Fast-forward more than two and a half centuries later to Donald Trump's speech: "When Mexico sends its people, they're not sending their best. . . . They're bringing drugs. They're bringing crime. They're rapists."[18])

The nineteenth century continued seeing major migration of Germans, as well as Irish Catholics, many fleeing the Potato Famine.[19] As the century drew to an end, Eastern and Southern Europeans, including those from Russia, Italy, and Poland, began arriving. They were escaping anti-Semitic pogroms, political unrest, and poverty; they sought economic opportunities. Many were illiterate and poor.

Becoming the backbone of the growing industrial and agricultural economy, immigrants forged steel, dug sewer and subway tunnels, built railroads, and served in the military.

In doing so, these men, women, and children laborers were perceived as a wage and job threat by skilled craftsmen and established labor organizations.[20] Competition for jobs incited nativist backlash. Sometimes it even led to violence.

In 1891, a mob in New Orleans brutally lynched eleven Italian Americans who were accused of murdering the city police chief. Most were acquitted. However, the lynch mob was not punished.[21] A *New York Times* editorial even praised the mob, calling the Italian victims "sneaking and cowardly Sicilians, the descendants of bandits and assassins, who have transported to this country the lawless passions, the cutthroat practices, and the oath-bound societies of their native country, . . . a pest without mitigations."[22]

Chinese immigrants, thousands of whom built the Transcontinental Railroad and toiled in the mines, were depicted as dirty and uncivilized in popular culture.[23] Employers saw them as an expendable workforce: they were willing to work for lower wages than their white counterparts. In 1860, the city of San Francisco forbade Chinese children from attending public schools, until the court repealed it over two decades later.[24] Anti-Chinese sentiment kept running high, driven by competition and racism. It culminated in the 1882 Chinese Exclusion Act, a law passed by Congress that outright banned the Chinese from immigrating to America. Still, in 1885, dozens of Chinese miners were massacred in Wyoming by their white miner coworkers, their homes set ablaze and hundreds driven out of town.[25]

The anti-Chinese immigration law would not be repealed until more than six decades after its passing.[26]

Bigotry showed up in government documents too. A US Army manual for World War I recruits cautioned that "the foreign born, and especially Jews, are more apt to malinger than the native-born."[27]

Besides competition, many disliked the idea of America's Protestant whiteness changing. So those wanting to restrict immigrant flow turned to pseudoscientific racism known as "eugenics." In the early twentieth century, eugenics societies sprung up across the country, claiming to make Americans a "better" race, urging birth control and sterilization, and keeping immigrants out.[28]

This wasn't just someone's crazy uncle who stockpiles ammo in his garage for the end days and spews out racist epithets after a few beers. Many of these nativists were progressives with public posts.

In the early twentieth century, the president of the American Sociological Society, Edward A. Ross, gave a piece of his mind to virtually every type of new arrival. Mediterranean people, he wrote in his 1914 book *The Old World in the New*, were "morally below the races of Northern Europe."[29] Immigrants from Southern Italy, such as Naples, had a "distressing frequency of low foreheads, open mouths, weak chins, . . . and backless heads," he wrote. Jews displayed a "monstrous and repulsive love of gain," Ross continued to observe in his book. And Slavic people, according to a doctor quoted by Ross, were "immune to certain kinds of dirt. They can stand what would kill a white man."[30]

His contemporary Madison Grant, a New York lawyer and one of the founders of the Bronx Zoo, in 1916 published a popular book about white supremacy called *The Passing of the Great Race*. He wanted America to return to the race of its founders, the Northern and Western Europeans: fair, tall, with blue eyes, and a narrow and straight nose.[31] If this reminds you of Hitler, that's no coincidence, because Hitler called Madison Grant's book his bible.[32]

Though little known today, in 1907 Congress even put together a special committee, known as the Dillingham Commission, to study immigration and figure out how to rein it in, writes Daniel Okrent, who researched the eugenics movement for his book *The Guarded Gate: Bigotry, Eugenics, and the Law That Kept Two Generations of Jews, Italians, and Other European Immigrants Out of America*. This commission published a gigantic forty-one-volume report of its findings, including a race dictionary, identifying—without a single citation—hundreds of racial and ethnic strains. The committee also measured the heads of eighteen thousand immigrants and their children, trying to link skull shape and size to race and determine if those features changed overtime (they actually did, the commission discovered).[33] Still, the Dillingham Commission concluded that Eastern and Southern European immigrants could not sufficiently assimilate. Allowing them into America would lead to disastrous consequences: the "detriment of the public health and the eugenic future of the race," they said.[34]

Congress listened. In 1917, it banned illiterate adults from coming to America, hoping to cut off Eastern and Southern Europeans. It also barred anyone "mentally or physically defective," prostitutes, alcoholics, and paupers, as well as people from most of Asia.[35]

Finally, the Immigration Act of 1924 reshaped American demographics for decades to come. It choked off immigration, limiting newcomers of each nationality to just 2 percent of its population in 1890.[36] Why 1890, you might be wondering? The law's architects thought that because America had all these pale Northern and Western Europeans, why not populate the country with more of them and less with others?

So, while in 1910, immigrants made up 14.7 percent of the American population, by 1970 that number plunged to 4.7 percent.[37]

Meanwhile, the industrial and agricultural economy kept growing. Mexican laborers were actively recruited by agencies, sometimes arriving in multiple trains weekly across the southern border.[38] By the way, when we talk about demographics, it's important to remember that a huge swath of the southwestern US was part of Mexico prior to the Mexican-American War. Technically, in 1848 it wasn't the Mexican people who crossed a border, but a border crossed them, writes historian David W. Haines.[39]

Many Mexican workers would return home after harvest or at the end of their contract. Often working in rural areas, they had lower visibility and faced less backlash than the city-based immigrants, who tended to dwell in poor and crammed urban neighborhoods.[40] Still, when America plunged into the Great Depression and grappled with unemployment, nearly half a million Mexican Americans, many of them citizens, were repatriated to Mexico.[41]

During World War II, the US needed working hands again. Tens of thousands of Mexican laborers were invited back to American farms as legal agricultural guest workers, under an agreement called the Bracero Program. Twenty-eight states received several million physical laborers, or braceros. After the program ended in the 1960s, the braceros, with established work patterns up north that their families depended on, lost legal protection, even though US farmers and ranchers continued hiring them.[42] At the same time, America began talking about the alien invasion crisis.[43]

The treatment of immigrants and their descendants is shaped by global events too. Following Japan's attack on Pearl Harbor, 120,000 people of Japanese ancestry were thrown into internment camps; most were US citizens. It is one of the most shameful chapters in US history.

And in 1939, nearly a thousand of mostly German Jewish refugees were denied entry into the US at a Florida port. Their ship, the *St. Louis*, had no choice but to sail back to Europe, where more than a quarter of the passengers perished in the Holocaust.[44] That same year, Congress also rejected a bill that would have let in twenty thousand Jewish children from Germany. "Twenty thousand charming children would all too soon grow up into twenty thousand ugly adults" is the line famously spoken by Laura Delano Houghteling, President Franklin D. Roosevelt's first cousin and the wife of the US immigration commissioner.[45] The fate of German Jews during that time is known all too well.

The tides turned after the devastation of World War II. In the decades following, America admitted hundreds of thousands of refugees and the foreign spouses of returning US military members. Eventually, admission of refugees, or those with a well-founded fear of persecution or physical harm due to national origin, religion, social group, or political opinion, was written into law.[46]

And in 1965, in front of the Statue of Liberty, President Lyndon B. Johnson tossed out the discriminatory quota law and signed the Immigration and Naturalization Act of 1965, prioritizing family reunification.[47] This new law was inspired by the civil rights movement and had been spearheaded by President John F. Kennedy until his death. Millions of migrants, previously denied, arrived in the following decades from all over the world.[48]

Today's immigration system remains complex. In recent years, it's been hard to ignore the increased demonization of immigrants.[49]

Meanwhile, thousands of young adults known as "Dreamers," who were brought to the US as children by parents without paperwork, are trying to shield themselves from deportation.[50]

Deportations have been on the rise since Barack Obama's presidency, although the Trump administration took it to another level by separating thousands of migrant children from their families.[51]

The grim reality of immigrant detention is something I saw for myself some years ago when I visited a facility in Queens, New York. It was housed in a brick, windowless warehouse with no sign.

On the other side of the glass in the visiting room of what was essentially a prison, a skinny, exhausted-looking man in a blue uniform told me he'd been detained there for four months. His name was Vardan. Back home in Armenia this thirtysomething tried to make ends meet by starting a business as his homeland reeled from economic turmoil while transitioning to a free economy, battling poverty and unemployment. But in doing so, he clashed with another entrepreneur and got muscled out. A group of men was now out to get him. Desperate, Vardan said good-bye to his wife and young son and paid someone $8,000 for a visa (whether he knew this was lawful or not, I do not know). At New York's John F. Kennedy airport, he was shackled for thirty hours and driven to this detention center housing two hundred asylum seekers.

Here, the detainees waited for a hearing for an average of six to eight months. The fluorescent lights were on day and night, so they slept with towels over their heads. There was no outdoor space, just a room covered by thick wire. While awaiting a hearing before an immigration judge, all Vardan did was sleep, eat, mop floors, and scrub toilets, earning a dollar a day. He used the money to call his family for 94 cents a minute, he explained. You can lose your mind like this, Vardan told me, in Russian, and tried to force a feeble smile. He thought immigrant detention was a waste of this country's taxpayer money. He'd given up. At this point, he just wanted to return home.[52]

Eventually he got deported.

That visit changed the way I viewed immigration and opportunity. Both Vardan and I had fled the former Soviet Union. Our people have endured genocides. There was one big difference, though: we were on the opposite sides of the glass.

I often wonder what happened to him and his family. What if he hadn't languished in prison for months and was turned away quicker? Or if he had been permitted to stay, would we be neighbors? Would our children attend the same school? Would he vote red or blue? What if I were the one without proper documentation?

I have no answers. All I know is that, in spite of challenges and inequities, people keep flocking to America's shores, working, learning, loving, and raising children here. And though immigrants are not the only part of this country's legacy, we are an integral one. Our voices deserve to be heard—even with an accent.

2. THE BEET TEST

I carried to my lips a spoonful of the tea in which I had let soften a bit of madeleine. But at the very instant when the mouthful of tea mixed with cake crumbs touched my palate, I quivered, attentive to the extraordinary thing that was happening inside me.

—MARCEL PROUST
("The Proust Phenomenon")[1]

ONE SATURDAY NIGHT IN DECEMBER, I invite the man I'd been dating to a Russian restaurant in New York. We'd been seeing each other only a short while, but given the spark that has yet to show signs of decay, it seems like the right time.

The Russian restaurant in midtown Manhattan, located over four thousand miles away from my birthplace, would be something different for us to try together, I figure. But novelty is just one of the reasons. It would also be a test, a conduit into the kind of vulnerability that comes with opening up one's home to a stranger.

The dining room is dim and abuzz with chatter. A pianist named Vladimir is playing torch songs on the grand piano. After we are seated, the waiter brings out vodkas infused with cranberry and ginger, to take the edge off.

The more my date and I talk, the more there is to say. The drink and the piano arpeggios are making my head spin in the most exhilarating way. I keep reassuring myself that if, for whatever reason, the date is a nonstarter, I'll have at least carb-loaded on comfort food that would do my grandmother proud.

"The appetizers should be coming out soon," I promise.

"Good!" he says. "Excited to finally try me some Russki food!"

"Yeah," I say feebly. "Good. Very good."

The server emerges with a magenta-colored pile of pickled herring topped with onions, potatoes, carrots, beets, and mayonnaise. He sets this national treat on the table between us.

"Herring under a fur coat," the waiter announces solemnly. "*Sel-yodka pod shuboy.*"

My heart skips a beat. Not because one of my favorite dishes in the world also happens to be the one with the least sex appeal. But because my date stares at the platter with panic.

"This looks interesting," he observes. "What is it?"

His question isn't surprising. Russian and Soviet-era cuisine can come across as peculiar. We've got potatoes, soups made out of dill pickles, eggs trapped inside the wiggly meat jelly, the Ashkenazi Jewish herring mush. A matter of acquired taste, this menu is rich and satisfying, but it's not exactly seductive. A boiled potato can only do so much to unleash one's erotic desires, and let me tell you: it isn't much.

After arriving in America, I turned up my nose at the fare of my ancestors. I couldn't get enough of the gigantic pizza slices with tiny circles of grease on the napkin and the perfectly round chicken nuggets, at once salty and sweet, served in the school cafeteria.

At the supermarket, I got dizzy marveling at the hundreds of types of cheeses and cereals lining the stocked shelves. After school, I'd binge on bologna sandwiches with presliced bread and chase them with off-brand soda from a large plastic bottle. Never before had I seen such abundance, such freedom when it came to eating. If ever there was a gastronomical paradise where a river of milk and honey doth flow, this was most certainly it.

There was also a local all-you-can-eat chain restaurant where staff continuously refilled dozens of trays beneath the fluorescent lights. A splurge like this cost around five dollars if you had a coupon, and even less for kids. But for a moment it left you feeling like royalty, even if it was suburban-mall kind of royalty with a stomachache, for you could indulge in Western delicacies like clam chowder and synthetic ice cream with utter abandon.

Still, it all had a strange aftertaste. Go ahead and try explaining the concept of an all-you-can-eat buffet to an immigrant from a country beset with food shortages, where the national saying was "Better for the belly to burst than let the goods go to waste." You want to try everything, even when there's no more room. You wonder if it's *really* all-inclusive. You're ashamed about leftovers but aren't permitted to take them home—someone is watching to make sure of that.

The American diners had a more cavalier attitude—I observed them as though they were specimens of the buffet menu. They'd pile an assortment of dishes onto the plate and smother it with several sauces, until the thing resembled a sludgy mountainous terrain. After nibbling on a couple of forkfuls, the diner would push the plate aside and get up for more. The employees—generally immigrants, people of color, or both—rushed to clear the patron's table, wipe it clean, and discard any evidence of leftovers, safeguarding the illusion of effortless abundance.

My embarrassment of Russian food—and culture—was just a phase. After moving out of my parents' house I began craving all the old and familiar dishes. So much, in fact, that they became a sort of a rite of passage for my dating prospects.

How was that going?, you might ask. Not well. At all.

I'd recently broken up with an American boyfriend who never drank tea and hated beets, both staples of Russian dining. I know, I know: who in their right mind would blame a failed relationship on a vegetable? Looking at the big picture, though, I'm convinced that beets did have something to do with that breakup. Another time, an Italian date rolled his eyes at the salad of boiled vegetables, peas, and bologna we were served at a Russian café. He then insisted that the peas were Sicilian capers. It was our last date. An Israeli ex-boyfriend was horrified by the fact that my relatives ate boiled unseasoned chicken "just like that."

Despite repeated failures, I keep hoping a significant other would understand—I'm not even saying *like* but *understand*—the cuisine of my birthplace. I want to sit across the table from someone who'd appreciate the honored space that food occupies in my tradition; someone who'd recognize its creativity with limited ingredients, its grit during long winters, its power to bring people together in small kitchens.

. . .

Russian speakers often have a complex relationship with their cuisine. For generations, we've had wars to reckon with, inefficient Soviet agriculture, oppressive leaders, and famines.[2] When I was growing up, butter and sugar were so difficult to get, they were rationed through a coupon system. My grandparents joked that guests could have only one indulgence at a time. "You washed your hands with soap?" they'd quip. "Ah, then you don't get sugar in your tea."

How do you explain that to a stranger when asked to tell him about yourself at happy hour? And, frankly, why? How do you talk about relatives surviving a siege on less than five ounces of bread a day or about your childhood errand of standing in line for flour before the store runs out again—all while remembering to "be yourself" and act friendly but not *too* friendly or high maintenance?

Now, in New York, as my date stares at the pink pile of fish and onions before him, things are looking bleak. Growing up at the tail end of the Cold War, he's read Dostoyevsky and watched anti-Soviet propaganda movies. He'd sent me videos of dancing bears and bad Russian drivers. And every May Day in college, he used to parade around campus with classmates and chant, "Ain't no party like the Communist Party, cause the Communist Party don't stop."

But this restaurant, this herring under a fur coat—is it too much? Will he order a burger and ask for the check?

My date picks up his fork, sighs, and takes a bite.

Seconds seem to turn into hours.

Maybe it was a mistake to bring him here so soon. Or ever. Maybe I should relegate herring under a fur coat to my list of secret pleasures. Do it in private, but don't expect balloons and flowers.

"You know," he finally says, "this kind of tastes like my mother's cooking." He impales another piece of herring with a fork.

I offer him the next dish that arrives.

And the one after that.

After dessert, I call the waiter over to take our picture.

It's this photo, with the kitschy paisley-upholstered seats and vodka bottles as the backdrop, that we use to announce our engagement three months later.

■ ■ ■

Turns out that the beet salad rite of passage is just the beginning of our cross-cultural education.

Exhibit one. I never watched *Sesame Street* growing up. Or most other American TV shows, for that matter. Pete, on the other hand, can quote films from the 1980s and early '90s in a heartbeat in the context of modern-day life. He reads the subtlest verbal and nonverbal cues, that invisible handshake that lets people know you're one of them. (On occasion, I still miss some of those cues, but I pick up on others from other Europeans, which he sometimes does not.) In his social circles, friendships can begin to blossom out of a simple knowledge of geography and sports. *Oh, yeah, you're from Pittsburgh? No kidding! Those Penguins sure crushed it yesterday, crushed it.*

It's not just the sports and the food. He speaks to his family infrequently while I talk to mine daily. He grew up knowing that if he wanted something reasonable, like shampoo or a winter coat, he could go out and buy it or ask his parents to. He's never had to conceal his religious background from peers or fear centuries-old blame for the nation's ills directed toward "his people." I experienced the opposite. Those memories are like an old, painless scab that hasn't healed.

Over the years I've heard a lot of things about Russians. About how we always speak bluntly and never smile in photos. About how all Russian women wear skimpy outfits, guzzle vodka, and dominate their sports-car-driving men. Apparently, I'm informed on more than one occasion, we even make excellent strippers and prostitutes.

"Look, I'm a citizen and everything, but I'll never be exactly like someone who's born in America," I say to Pete, before taking the plunge and introducing him to my parents. This isn't a point of embarrassment but a statement of fact. "I'll probably never lose my accent or drink soda or be good at crafts or understand the whole Ohio State and Michigan rivalry and church references."

Pete doesn't budge. He just politely points out that it's called pop, not soda.

An introduction to the family means commitment. It also means watching my parents conduct their "interview," which they've shortened over the years and perfected into an art form. My family quickly falls in love with Pete, claiming that his soul is more Russian than that of many Russians out there. I'm still not sure what that means.

■   ■   ■

Pat Benatar wasn't wrong when she said love is a battlefield. Immigrants are no exception. She didn't say that last part, but experience and even academic research show that multicultural relationships are just like any others, though often with an added level of complexity.[3]

And yet multicultural relationships are nothing new. "Intermarriage stirs the ethnic melting pot and blurs the color lines," points out a 2015 report on immigration authored by the National Academies of Sciences, Engineering, and Medicine.[4] And not only for the couple but for their families and networks too.

Roughly one out of seven marriages is an interracial or interethnic one, more than double what it was a generation ago, the report's authors point out. Also, between 2008 and 2012, more than half of the marriages involving immigrants were with a native-born partner, an increase from previous years. Still, the odds are significantly higher (thirty times higher, to be exact) that immigrants will marry other immigrants and native-born Americans will marry other native-born Americans.[5] Unfortunately, the study's authors observe, ethnicity and race continue to affect matrimony decisions.

For example, US-born white Americans are most likely to marry someone like themselves, research finds. Meanwhile, Black immigrant women are "far less likely than other immigrant women to cross racial/ethnic lines and integrate through marriage with non-Hispanic whites, despite high levels of education among [B]lack immigrants from Africa and the Caribbean," the report by the National Academies of Sciences, Engineering, and Medicine points out. And immigrant Asian men, of all immigrant groups, are most likely to marry a partner similar to them.[6]

Still, the authors of the study predict the rise in intermarriage is only going to continue.[7]

■   ■   ■

How do different cultures resolve conflict? Is there a script about who'll be the breadwinner and who'll mop the floors and get up with the crying baby at two in the morning? How accepting are those traditions of homosexuality and gender nonconformity?

The more I talk to immigrants about this, the more I see there is no singular answer.

A friend born in South Korea, now working as a hardware engineer in New York, says that at one point she swore off dating men from her home country. She felt they expected her to act agreeable and "like a princess": to be pretty and smart "but not as smart as the boys." She ended up marrying a white American man from west of the Mississippi.

Likewise, Irina, who came to the United States from Russia at eighteen as a student and now consults technology companies, had reservations about relationships with Russian men. "Russians to me are like my brothers," explains Irina, a tall blonde with hair cropped to her shoulders in a style that's at once casual and chic, as we have coffee in her kitchen in the San Francisco Bay Area. "It's a horrible thing to say. It would be a lot easier if I was with a Russian: just traveling to Russia together, speaking Russian at home. But I have no interest," she says and shrugs.

She gets along better with other foreigners, from South America, Asia, and Africa. "It was hard for me to date white Americans," Irina adds. "It's not that I had any sort of predisposition. It just didn't click for me at all, on any level."

Francis, a filmmaker who moved from Brazil with family when he was seven, doesn't seek out other immigrants to date. But be it first or second generation, they find each other anyway, he says, even in a crowded room.

"It's always like an aftereffect that I realize I'm dating another immigrant," Francis says. "We're talking and it suddenly comes up. Why are we so close? Our shared experiences have brought us together! That ends up creating this language that is super subconscious, just the way of talking to each other that transcends the bullshit. What team you like doesn't actually matter."

Francis has lived in Houston and Pittsburgh after immigrating, but didn't fully come into his own until moving to New York and finding himself surrounded with multicultural people like himself. ("The good thing about New York is no one gives a shit," he observes.)

He dislikes being othered because he's from somewhere else. As a child, he saw this happen to his own mother after they moved: she was talked down to by other adults because she didn't speak good English. It was infuriating.

Francis has been called a "Latin lover," including by women he doesn't even know, who'd assume he is on standby for sexual escapades because he is Brazilian. While flattering, it's a limited part of who he is, he explains. "Humans are incredibly tribal. We think we're so complicated, but in the end we're just these apes wearing jeans."

But it's a different story for Alejandro, a graphic designer who emigrated from Colombia as an adult. Although he's dated women from various parts of the world, he ultimately fell for a compatriot, a woman from Colombia's coffee region. "Blood finds its own," Alejandro explains to me. "That area produces great coffee and beautiful women. Meeting someone like her, with a similar culture, education level, with all her amazing qualities, made falling in love with her so easy." The two are now married and live in New Jersey. There's also Annie, my friend from high school. Back then, we talked about the pressing issues of the day, from grunge music and black nail polish to which classmate had a crush on whom and smoked what. But it takes more than two decades until we finally discuss the topics we didn't dare broach as immigrant teens: our free lunches, our small apartments in unglamorous parts of town, and our classmates who received new BMWs for their sixteenth birthdays.

Annie was born in a refugee camp in Hong Kong. Her parents, who lived on the border of Vietnam and China, were among the boat people in the aftermath of the Vietnam War; they fled to Hong Kong by water with her older siblings. Annie grew up in the projects in East San Jose, California, with her parents, siblings, cousins, and uncles crammed in a tiny apartment. Her father slept in a bathtub; they had no furniture and ate their meals on newspapers on the floor.

Annie's teenage lifestyle was also different from "the Americans," she says. "My parents were really strict. I just thought that's just the way it was." If a boy called, they'd assume she was going to get pregnant, she jokes. "I was only attracted to Asian guys for a very long time, all my life," Annie says. For a couple of years in college, she branched out with relationships due to "my own family dramas," she explains. "But then, after I got over my dramas, I realized, no, the values are very different, [that] actually I value a lot from my culture, like the community aspect, the way we take care of each other, versus American [mentality], is more independent, 'it's all for me.' It's not necessarily that I'm only attracted to [men from my] culture; it's any kind of cultural values that are community based, versus the Western approach."

. . .

Different communication styles can also take some getting used to. I learn early on that when an American-born person asks how you're doing—no matter how congenial the smile—he usually doesn't care about your speeding ticket or your root canal. You might think you're just sharing in an honest kind of way, but airing problems might brand you as a complainer, or worse, as *negative*, a social faux pas on par with stealing.

Where I come from, folks have a high tolerance for melancholy. I'm not saying it's a good thing. But live through a northern winter with barely any sun or fresh produce, and you'll understand why it's precisely here that *Anna Karenina* and *Crime and Punishment* were born.

One time, for instance, I went out with Russian-speaking friends after a long workweek. We dressed up, headed to a new bar downtown, and spent the evening exchanging stories about which of our relatives were murdered in the Holocaust, where, and how. We ordered drink refills and another basket of fries and kept going.

Communication style differences also crept up for Antonio and Ruth. Antonio came to the US from Mexico City to get his MBA, while Ruth was born in Washington, DC.

Antonio didn't experience culture shock, he says, because he studied at an American school in Mexico. "I feel like I can fit in pretty well. Everyone in my family speaks English," he says confidently. "There are lots of the cultural references I share, from music and movies and sports."

Meanwhile, Ruth grew up engaging in lively debates as part of everyday conversation with her family, she tells me.

"There have been times when you struggle to merge those worlds," Ruth says. "Antonio is from a more reserved, more quiet, and more private culture. Maybe I'll be speaking loudly and passionately about something and Antonio says, 'You're shouting.' I say, 'It's my normal talking voice. I'm not shouting.'"

Aside from communication styles, dating outside one's culture can also be a sticking point. For some diaspora communities, preserving an ethnic or religious heritage in a foreign land is, quite literally, a matter of life and death. Some would rather let their child marry an ex-convict with a drinking problem than an outsider who doesn't speak the same language or worship the same god.

The more conservative cultures often don't let their children, particularly girls, date or travel alone or go out past a certain hour. Western behavior, like sex before marriage, is taboo. Often, relatives themselves or a matchmaker will choose the suitable daughter-in-law or son-in-law.[8]

To shed light on immigrant dynamics when it comes to finding a spouse, I approach sociologist Nazli Kibria, associate dean of the faculty for the social sciences at Boston University. Kibria has devoted her research and teaching to the immigrant experience, families, and race. She's written extensively about these topics and authored books including *Race and Immigration* and *Becoming Asian American: Second-Generation Chinese and Korean American Identities.*

Immigrants are at a disadvantage if they are not fluent in English or familiar with the local norms, Kibria tells me. "There are particular stereotypes and prejudices that people associate with immigrants, especially if they perceive them to be nonwhite," Kibria says.[9]

All these factors can lead to mistrust. "People fear those who are sort of different," she says. When it comes to choosing a spouse, in particular, there are "a lot of very complicated stereotypes that shape what people see as attractive and beautiful."

But mistrust can go both ways. On the one hand, "people from immigrant communities may not be seen as all that favorable in terms of being marriage partners," she points out when we speak. At the same time immigrants may not be open to outsiders either.

"You have a tug of both things going on," she says. "There's both a lot of prejudice from the larger society and also the immigrant community and families trying to keep children within their community."

This makes sense to me. There are folks who make you feel you're at a United Nations meeting whenever they discuss their exes or swipe left on their phone. Others are determined to find a spouse who shares the same background. (An Indian-born acquaintance in her twenties tells me her parents are fine with her dating whomever she wants, as long as she marries an Indian engineer.)

Yet it's not uncommon for people raised in America to want nothing to do with their immigrant roots when it comes to romance. They bristle at the idea of a mate with similar origins because their brethren "are seen as culturally different," Kibria explains.

For example, arranged marriage is common among the Bangladeshi Muslim diaspora. Kibria conducted an in-depth study between 2001 and 2007 of their marriage patterns in the United States. The parents, she found, wanted a person from a "good family": pious, educated, and with a solid reputation. As was often the case, this didn't just mean a Bangladeshi American but someone harkening all the way back to the mother country.[10]

However, Kibria found that many young second-generation Bangladeshis were not interested in marriage partners with similar origins, often disappointing their families. "In fact," she wrote in her findings, "Bangladeshi identity could even be a point of disidentification—an affiliation from which young people tried to dissociate themselves due to its negative connotation, stemming in part from the images of poverty and corruption that surround the country."[11]

Anastasia arrived as a refugee from Uzbekistan, a predominantly Muslim nation in Central Asia and a former republic of the defunct Soviet Union. She is, however, a part of the Bukharian Jewish diaspora, many of whom have left Uzbekistan and settled in Queens, New York. With its own restaurants, synagogues, newspapers, and even a cemetery in Queens, this thriving community doesn't always look kindly upon marrying out. And sex before marriage is definitely taboo.

"Men like to be first" is the ode to virginity that Anastasia grew up hearing. "The only man is gonna be your husband." That, and the fact that she must marry young and find someone who is just like her. "That's how you're judged," Anastasia says. "You're Bukharian, so you should marry a Bukharian."

This was a tough pill to swallow for Anastasia, a career-minded attorney. She wanted to feel a connection with the matches she's been set up with by relatives, but just couldn't find enough in common. Also, most of the men she went on dates with did not have a graduate degree like she did, and sometimes gender expectations got in the way. "If you think about it, it allows only certain people to be with you," she says. "Here's your people. They all live in Queens. It essentially creates a vacuum. But you really don't know yourself well enough to say no to your family. That's why you always go."

Eventually, Anastasia decided to branch out and date outside of her community, but here she was thrown for a loop again. The men she'd met, including American-born New Yorkers, were new and exciting, but they expected to do the deed—or intimacy of some kind—by the third date. Or the fourth one at the latest. So for a while, whenever things got a little too frisky or the conversation veered toward the un- avoidable, it made Anastasia so uncomfortable that she'd end the rela- tionship. "I knew it was wrong, but I knew I couldn't do it," she admits. "You don't know how you're going to be judged or laughed at."

Often, things wouldn't even get to first base. Sometimes Anastasia found herself having to be the spokesperson for her culture, exoticized and misunderstood. One American date wanted to know if her family keeps donkeys to get to places, because he googled that donkeys were big in Central Asia. She joked back. "I said, 'Yeah, I have a weekday donkey and a weekend donkey.' He said, 'That's cool.'"

Another man told her on a date in Manhattan that he knew where Russia is. It's in Central America, he insisted. Without finishing her wine, Anastasia put a twenty dollar bill on table, said, "Get a map," and left.

■ ■ ■

In a groundbreaking study, sociologist Philip Kasinitz and his col- leagues interviewed nearly thirty-five hundred young New Yorkers who are children of immigrants, known as second generation immi- grants, and those who came to the country before the age of twelve and grew up here, known as generation 1.5.[12]

I decide to speak to Kasinitz about immigrant marriage patterns and his findings, which he copublished with colleagues in an award-winning book, *Inheriting the City: The Children of Immigrants Come of Age*. I visit him in his office in Manhattan, just a block away from the Empire State Building, at the Graduate Center, City University of New York, where he is a Presidential Professor of Sociology.[13]

Kasinitz's office is lined with multiple bookcases. A poster of New York neighborhoods hangs on the wall behind his desk. The high-rise buildings—one of which is decorated with a giant American flag—peek into the office window to the sound of the bustling city and the honking cabs outside.

I ask him about the unique challenges immigrants might face when starting families of their own.

Intergenerational issues are certainly a part of it.

"Every teenager in the history of the planet, at one point or another, told their parents: 'You don't know what I'm going through, your advice is completely wrong, you have absolutely no understanding of my world'" Kasinitz tells me. "I think this was originally written in hieroglyphics," he jokes. "Problem is, for the second generation of immigrants, it's actually true.[14] If they tell you on the Disney Channel, follow your bliss and be the best *you* you can be and your parents will eventually come around because they love you, but your parents believe in arranged marriage . . . there's gonna be some issues."

Immigrant families are constantly negotiating and making compromises, he says. Sometimes they fall back on their cultural resources for answers. Other times they turn to the American norms. And "sometimes they're making it up altogether because neither of those exactly works for them. And that notion that they have to create a new path is quite empowering," says Kasinitz, who has chaired the university's doctoral program in sociology and directed its International Migration Studies program.

His study of immigrants to New York found, much like Nazli Kibria observed, that a spouse's demographics are a big deal for many immigrant parents. This often showed up as race bias and colorism. For example, Kasinitz and his colleagues found that the partner's race was a factor for Chinese parents. Likewise, most Hispanic immigrant parents preferred a "lighter-skinned partner,"[15] their children reported. Russian Jewish parents usually insisted on nice Jewish boys or girls, but only those who weren't too religious and who came from only specific parts of the former Soviet Union.[16] (Oy vey!)

Defying the wishes of the elders, many young people in the study said it's important to be open to relationships with those from other cultures. Yet when the time came to settle down, the vast majority were partnered with others who shared a similar linguistic or racial background.[17] "There was a kind of conservatism that took over as relationships became more serious," Kasinitz explains. "'I could fall in love with anyone,'" he recalls the respondents saying. "'but boy, if I brought home a person of X group would my parents freak out,'" the researchers were often told. Frequently, the pool of partners was also limited by segregation at schools, work, and neighborhoods and by the stereotyping they were subjected to.[18]

The good news? Experience, mine included, and studies like this suggest that parents eventually come around. As time passes and their bundle of joy is still flying solo, families tend to ease up on expectations, even if they'd once threatened to disown their progeny for marrying an outsider.

"It was told to us by numerous respondents, this was sort of waiting out parental objections," Kasinitz tells me, "which is to say, 'When I was twenty-one, I had to marry a white guy. At thirty-one, they just wanted me to marry a guy. And by forty, anybody would do. A gay marriage with adopted kids would be alright—we're just looking to get some grandchildren out of this.'"

But once parental expectations are tempered, are immigrant relationships more challenging?

It really depends on the individuals, Kasinitz says. Being with someone from a similar culture means there's less to explain. The couple might be more in agreement when raising children. On the other hand, an outsider might not care as much about adhering to customs to a tee, so there's less to fight about.

Gender roles and misogyny factor in as well. Although America's got a long way to go in terms of gender equality, in many parts of the globe, my birth country included, a "no" often means a "yes," with few repercussions for violence against women. Many countries practice child marriages, lack protections against sexual harassment, and don't invest in education for girls: they'll soon be married off anyway, tending to the children and the domestic duties, so why bother, the thinking goes.

"The countries that have more egalitarian gender norms than we do don't tend to send us a lot of immigrants," Kasinitz points out. "There are not a lot of Dutch or Swedish immigrants coming here. [Among US immigrants,] the traditional woman from the 'right' ethnic group is from a family that left that place, and she has grown up in this country, and . . . may even have less patience [with tradition.] An American wife might say, 'Well, that's his culture, and I have to learn to adjust to it.' But somebody from the same culture might not put up with that," he observes. "Very often, traditional gender norms are a better deal for men than they are for women. He's getting more nostalgic for the traditional culture, where men run the household. And she's not buying it."

. . .

Immigrant families are everywhere around me. Heck, I'm a part of one. I need to step out of my everyday experience and see if maybe I'm taking some things for granted. Perhaps others have different sticking points and beet tests that they don't discuss at family barbecues. How do they navigate cultural quirks? What makes their relationships work?

I decide to chat with my neighbor Paola, a biologist who came here from Brazil on a student visa. Paola grew up in a devout Catholic family: her parents go to mass every day. "My parents are super protective," says Paola, a soft-spoken brunette. "They never wanted me to be away from them: I had to go to college in the city [where] I was born." Her father even plays guitar in a church band, she says, emphasizing his piousness.

Paola's parents did let her study English in America for a few months. On one condition: she'd be living with her uncle, who'd keep a close eye on Paola. Which he did to the best of his ability.

A few months later, they got a call from their daughter. She'd met a man, a Muslim immigrant from Syria, and she was going to marry him.

Upon hearing the news, Paola's mother took to her bed for two weeks in a bout of depression. Her brother stopped speaking to her for two years.

It was a classic immigrant love story. They saw each other in a community college hallway as she walked to her English class. "I was like, 'Oh my God, he's so handsome!'" Paola says. She approached Oscar and asked him for directions to her classroom in broken English.

At first, she hesitated because Oscar was too outgoing for her taste. "He sounded like a player. He'd always make jokes—'Oh, I'm Muslim and I can have four wives,'" she says. "My type of guy was the quiet, shy one." But Paola soon realized it was just for show, especially when she saw the doting way Oscar took care of his parents and younger siblings.

Despite differences in languages and faith, their new life unfolded organically, Paola explains as we walk through a park on a sunny afternoon, her toddler riding a balance bike next to us.

Their wedding was officiated by an imam in California, and her family flew in to attend too. Paola decided to wear a hijab whenever she'd see her mother-in-law. This was her own choice, she emphasizes, as a way to show respect.

Paola and Oscar speak English, Portuguese, and Arabic with their little girl and eat Brazilian and Middle Eastern meals that Oscar prepares. He never expected her to cook. "That's why he's skinny!" she tells me. She takes their daughter to church and Oscar, a software engineer, occasionally brings her to the mosque, though neither attends regularly.

"But is it hard to manage three cultures in one household?" I ask. I throw in specific examples, like division of labor and language barriers.

Paola considers it as for a few seconds, as if that question hasn't even crossed her mind before. "No," she says. "Not really."

Both are worried about Oscar's relatives in war-torn Syria. Sometimes they both mispronounce English words in the same way. There's also that time Oscar taught her a special Arabic greeting to make a good first impression on his family, which she practiced diligently. When she finally said it, everyone burst into laughter. Turns out she told them that her father is bald.

There is one sticking point, she admits as we walk into their house. Paola's Brazilian parents keep hoping that one day their daughter will finally come to her senses and get married in a Catholic church, then baptize their granddaughter.

"I just want her to be a good person and be happy," says Paola while quickly throwing an art smock on the girl, who's just popped open a couple of paint jars and is charging across the room toward her easel.

"We're a team. We have to be firm with them. I'm not gonna let them get to my head and say 'Oh, if we don't baptize her, we're gonna get divorced.' Because if you are in a relationship, you know there are differences," she adds. "And if you don't accept that, it's not gonna work."

. . .

I'm starting to pay more attention to this delicate cultural dance everywhere around me. Next, I decide to visit Natasha, who emigrated from the former Soviet Union with her family when she was twenty and now works for the local government. The resources of her virtual Rolodex range from where to find a babysitter who'll also make soup and teach your kid the Cyrillic alphabet to where to buy honey cake like in the old country. (That baker lives nearly an hour away, but once I take her advice, I realize it's worth it.)

Natasha's own relationship came to her as a surprise. Not only because she and her now husband, Trevor, were colleagues (she was his boss), but also because she was used to dating Russian-speaking men, who had seen the same movies and chuckled at the same jokes. Plus, family expected her to marry someone Jewish, like herself.

But Trevor is neither Russian nor Jewish but Chinese American, born soon after his parents immigrated to San Francisco.

As their romance blossomed, the lack of a shared heritage didn't faze them.

"It was completely uncharted territory," Natasha says. "You didn't have to finish each other's sentences, but it was so much more fun because everything was just so new. And he has a really good sense of humor," she says, winking and lightly elbowing Trevor, sitting next to her on the couch. "He would make me hysterically laugh at things."

Trevor nods.

When things got serious, Trevor decided to take a trip to visit her parents and introduce himself.

The family patriarch opened the door. Trevor, the story goes, surprised him by exclaiming, "Shalom!"

The future in-laws invited him in and offered him tea and pastries.

"I didn't want to, but I read you can't refuse," explains Trevor. He'd already been reading up on Natasha's traditions and knew that when a Russian person invites you to the table, saying no is a sacrilege on par with kicking a puppy. After that, he was welcomed into the family.

Trevor's parents, who owned a Chinese restaurant, wanted him to marry a woman who was Asian, like him. And he did, once. But after that marriage went awry, his mother declared it didn't matter where his next wife was from, as long as she was a nice person.

Trevor and Natasha had "the talk" about expectations early on. And it turned out they shared a vision of the future: vacations, good food, community, a minivan with kids who would master English, Russian, and Cantonese and attend a plethora of extracurricular activities.

They also found crossover in their cultures, from honoring family to the importance of a practical education and a stable job, Trevor explains.

I look around their apartment with a view of the San Francisco Bay from the window. The common area is stocked with Russian- and English-language books and multiple bins with crafts and toys, labeled and organized by type. There is Chinese takeout on the table and a pressure cooker in the kitchen. Family photos line the walls. And instead of seeing three disparate cultures, I just see a family.

The more I talk to people about their coupling and uncoupling decisions, the more I notice a trend. Multicultural relationships have their share of quandaries, but it's a crapshoot either way. It also depends on how adapted the partners are to local ways and how long they've lived here.

It's nice to think that love always wins, but it's not that simple. One can be in love and still disparage the partner's heritage. The society's treatment of interracial and multicultural unions is often laden with prejudice. Need I bring up the landmark 1967 *Loving v. Virginia* US Supreme Court case, prior to which interracial marriage was outright illegal in multiple states? As future chapters will show, many couples still struggle with colorism and racism in their communities and even in their families.

What does matter, I'm noticing, is acceptance of differences and respect for the other person's origins. They aren't forcing one another to convert or cook stew just like Mom does. Much of the time, they don't even speak each other's native languages. A shared country of origin can mean shared values about dinner, diapers, and debt. But it isn't always the culture. It's how you use it.

Pete and I tie the knot soon after that Russian restaurant visit. We welcome a baby, and then another one, into the world, shoring up new routines and questions.

3. THEN COMES BABY IN A BABY CARRIAGE

A multicultural child is born in the United States, and beneath all the warm smiles and congratulations, a gladiator arena unfolds itself within which the wider world will watch the epic blood sport of identity play out.

—DANIEL JOSÉ OLDER[1]

NAMING OUR FIRST BABY goes without a hitch. I'd known what I'd call my future daughter since I was a teenager. The name Leah was short and lyrical, with a certain gravitas to it. It was also international, not bound to any one culture, leaving its bearer free to choose her own adventure. Things get complicated, however, when time comes to pick out a name for my second child.

After Pete and I find out we're having a boy, we get the obvious duds out of the way. It's pretty standard to not name your baby after an ex-boyfriend or ex-girlfriend, or after that beach fling in college, even if it technically "didn't count." Or after literary villains. And if *The Simpsons* taught us anything, it's to check how the whole kit and caboodle sound together, so you don't end up with progeny called Hugh Jass or Anita Bath.

More important, I want to parcel my son's triple heritage into a perfect first and middle name. My Ashkenazi Jewish tradition says the name must honor a nonliving relative. Meanwhile, Pete's family looks to Christian saints and forebears, many of whom harken back to the British Isles.

It would also be nice if he could "pass" in both cultures, kicking it in the sandbox with American buddies as, say, *Nick*, then eating borscht with his grandmother as *Nikolai*; all of it, conveniently, as the same person.

We also look to the Old Testament for inspiration. Growing up, the only people I knew with names from the holy book of Torah were old or deceased, gazing from black and white photographs. Many Soviet Jews changed their names to conceal their heritage with the rise in anti-Semitism and Joseph Stalin's purges. They feared getting passed over for a college acceptance or job promotion, public insults, and violence. That fear never fully went away. When the economy crashed before my family immigrated, Jews became the unwitting scapegoats again. On some days we'd see a Russian grandmother consoling her grandchild at the empty-shelved grocery store with "There's no more bread, sweetheart: the kikes ate it all." On other days we'd find our car tires punctured at a parking lot after a Jewish-themed event or a brick thrown through the apartment window. Jewish names were a liability long before my birth. *Baruch* turned into *Boris*; *Moses* went by *Michael*; *Esther* became *Irina*. To me, these names are filled with awe and also with foreignness.

The door of our refrigerator is plastered with the picks of the week, and debates drag on for months. *"Can you say* Ezekiel *between vodka shots?"* *"Jim's fine, I guess, but isn't it where people work out?"*

A name isn't a pair of new shoes you take back to the store if they cut off circulation in your toes. It's not a bad haircut that will grow out. It's a lifelong commitment, a unique identifier, a link to the past and a harbinger of the future. No pressure, though!

My son arrives into the world nameless. He doesn't have a name the next day either. Or the day after that. We just call him "baby."

Nearly a week later—after the annoyed lady from the birth certificate office calls again—we finally settle on what to call the child, launching him forth into this world as a distinct person, sanctioned in the eyes of the law.[2]

But the name isn't perfect, we soon realize. Two courthouse visits and several hundred dollars later, Pete and I officially change it. Nobody keeps those birth announcements anyway. Hopefully.

■ ■ ■

The naming conundrum is just one of many I suddenly face as a new parent. I thought it would be easy. We'd pull together Pete's baseball and my ballet and get symmetrically bicultural humans, a sum of two unchanging parents. (I also thought I'd never feed my children dinosaur-shaped, microwaved chicken nuggets for dinner or pacify them with screen time. The joke's on me.)

But when you hold that tiny creature for the first time, the past can sneak up out of nowhere. Traditions clash and entwine with the arrival of a new baby—and even in the months preceding it.

And so I must report that I am, quite unexpectedly, turning into my mother.

My children are always cold. Cold and starving. Or so I think, as I overpack their lunches and regularly feed them hot soup, the mainstay of a Russian diet, as a first course. They are bundled in at least one extra layer of clothing compared to their peers, even during the summer months. They own multiple pairs of indoor slippers in case one gets lost. I'd rather do away with the excessive cooking and dishwashing and freaking out about inclement weather. Judge all you want. I can't help it.

Sociologists, too, observe this pattern once a baby's in the picture. When the younger immigrant generations have children of their own, they often reevaluate their criticism of their parents, sociologist Nancy Foner observes in her book *Across Generations: Immigrant Families in America*. The once-reproachful daughters seek their mothers' advice and support. "They may end up acting more like their own parents than they would ever have imagined and sharing many of their parents' attitudes toward child-rearing," Foner writes.[3]

I first got a taste of this heritage flashback in my early twenties, at a party I hosted with a roommate in Brooklyn. One of the guests came out on the balcony, proudly showing off his infant, who was dozing off in his pastel-colored onesie. Suddenly, several women, all of them Russian, lunged at the new dad. "Are you out of your mind?" they shouted, some with accents, shooing him back inside. "In *this weather*? God forbid the baby will catch a cold! Where is his hat? Where is his blanket?" The dad ran back indoors, clutching his bundle of joy to his chest. He was afraid to come back out for the rest of the night.

These women probably didn't realize that in America, generally speaking, doling out parenting advice to strangers is typically done by people in medical scrubs or when someone specifically asks, "Hey, can you give me parenting advice?"

But I can understand how those women, not even mothers at the time, reenacted the dynamics they'd grown up with years ago and an ocean away. It's also how they showed affection. The past is hard to shake.

■   ■   ■

But what, exactly, is American parenting? There are numerous approaches out there, from helicopter parenting to attachment parenting. There's even snowplow parenting.[4] Different as they may be, these philosophies have something in common. No, it's not giving kids cash for teeth and fixing them separate dinners. It's the hyper vigilance over our children's success and the anxiety that accompanies it. (Some are taking exception to this vigilance with a less-supervised approach, known as free-range parenting, though it isn't without controversy.)[5]

Christine Gross-Loh writes in her book *Parenting Without Borders*, "There is a distinctive American script about what constitutes 'good parenting,' especially for a typical middle-class or affluent family whose kids are college bound, . . . the protectiveness, the degree and type of involvement and intensive cultivation. . . . Despite the considerable and unprecedented amounts of parental investment we commit to our kids, we worry we are simply not doing enough."[6]

Claire Cain Miller makes a similar observation in her popular *New York Times* article "The Relentlessness of Modern Parenting." "Over just a couple of generations, parents have greatly increased the amount of time, attention and money they put into raising children," she writes. "Mothers who juggle jobs outside the home spend just as much time tending their children as stay-at-home mothers did in the 1970s."[7]

Parental involvement, much like educational opportunity, is all too often at the mercy of socioeconomic status. Children in households with an annual income of $75,000 or higher are much more likely to do sports and be enrolled in a dance, music, or art class, compared to households with lower incomes. When you work two jobs to put food on the table, toddler swim classes on Wednesday mornings take the back seat. For other families, safety overshadows extracurriculars. At least half of parents with household incomes less than $30,000 are concerned about their child being kidnapped, beat up, or attacked.[8] Racial disparities also affect access to opportunity. The Pew Research Center found that four in ten Black parents worry about their children getting shot at some point, almost twice as many as white parents.

Despite inequities, hands-on child-rearing is still seen as the best approach by many Americans across social divides, even when they lack the means to do it, argues Cain Miller.[9]

． ． ．

Perhaps in line with these findings, I find myself agonizing over the most minute decisions as a new parent. I'm eager to do the right thing. Trouble is, it isn't always clear what that thing should be. Which baby food is better: chunks of organic vegetables, store-bought purees, or rice cereal—or is it going to poison my baby with arsenic like that news article said? Huggies and Pampers that will stink up the landfill and decompose over hundreds of years or the pricey compostable-diaper delivery services? Feed the baby on schedule or on demand? Teach her to self-soothe or pick her up the moment she cries? Will toys in the crib stimulate her development or turn her into an addicted zombie?

The more conflicting reviews and articles I read, the more I'm paralyzed with guilt and indecision about what stuff my baby needs, what stuff will kill us, and what will maybe kill us but not necessarily right away, according to experts.

My upbringing didn't prepare me for this. As I spend hours gazing at the towering store displays of pinks and blues and clicking across multiple browser tabs on my computer, I can almost see my teachers from the old country shaking their heads. "Look how the American bourgeoisie have corrupted her. Drop and give us fifty! Go peel some potatoes!"

I'm starting to think that shopping for baby products is not unlike being psychologically interrogated by a hostile nation. It would probably go something like this:

"Tell us which baby high chair you want." [Switches on the bright light.]

"I don't know! There are so many to choose from, and all these expert recommendations!"

"Who are you working with? 'Fess up, or we will torture you with sleep deprivation."

"Ha, ha, too late, I'm immune to that by now! And I'm alone in this, I swear. That's the problem. You'd think a high chair is just a place to sit and eat Cheerios on, but is it BPA-free and phthalate free? Bet you didn't think of that, tough guy! Research says flame retardants cause cancer, but I also read that flame retardants are important in case of a fire. Oh, God, a FIRE? Also, can the chair recline? Does it have a three-point harness, a five-point harness, or no harness? Is it padded? Is that pad washable?"

"Why, now that you mention it . . ."

"Did the manufacturer use sustainable production and fair labor practices? I feel like a terrible person for not buying American and stimulating our econ-omy, but come on, I'm not paying half my rent for some artisanal baby chair."

"Well, yes, the economy must be stimulated . . ."

"Ooh, look at this adorable pink Minnie Mouse chair! But did you read that article about how pink can wreck girls' passion for engineering and technology?"

"That's awful."

"These online reviews are so good, they must be fake. Here, check this one out!"

"Actually, we are releasing you at once. Unshackle her!"

"But wait, I can tell you more!"

"No, no, please, just go. Really."

[Interrogation light switches off, interrogator swears in a foreign language, then bends down to light a cigarette.]

The answers to parenting decisions don't always come naturally. If they did, then how come something as basic as picking a kid's name or a teething toy can throw some people into a frenzy? If this were easy, then why do I keep hearing folks from all over the world grapple with the same questions?

* * *

Mitali, who lives in Seattle, thought she had it all figured out as a new bride. She met her husband in her home of Delhi, India; after the wedding, she joined him in the United States, where he'd earned his graduate degree earlier. She did not expect immigration to affect her parenting choices. But it did.

For one, the couple kept putting off having children.

"I always thought that after you're married, you're supposed to have kids," Mitali, a product manager for a technology company, tells me. "But years went by and we were thinking, are we ready? You just don't know what to predict about yourself. I just couldn't even think of starting a family."

Mitali figured the long work hours had to do with it (she admits she can be a bit of a workaholic). Also, the couple would move every few months for work. But many people move and work overtime.

It wasn't culture shock either. Mitali had always marched to the beat of her own drum. Back in India, she had no problem stealthily going to temple while on her period, even though this is frowned upon. ("You should be able to go to a place to worship at any time," she declares.) After moving to the United States, she stopped celebrating traditional festivals, though she dutifully kept on with daily prayers. She even refused to fast for Karwa Chauth, an annual festival when Northern Indian women fast for their husbands' long life and their return in the next seven lifetimes.[10]

"Indian girls who were born in America still do it for their husbands," says Mitali. But "you can't live one lifetime with this guy, and you want to commit to seven lifetimes?" she jokes.

She eventually softened up about fasting, on one condition. "I told my husband: if you're keeping it for me, then I'll keep it for you, to make your mother happy."

Now they both fast for each other on the day of Karwa Chauth. Especially, she adds, when the in-laws are visiting.

And with a slight modification. "We eat salad in the afternoon."

Mitali's ambivalence about kids soon became clear: she needed to have family near. In Delhi, she grew up with fifteen people and three generations under one roof. If she couldn't rebuild a familiar enclave in a foreign land, her children would miss out on what she cherished about her upbringing the most.

"You don't go to your friends' houses that way," she says, sighing.

Then the couple moved again, this time settling near her sibling's family. Mitali finally felt ready. They now have two young children.

She's embraced the festivals again. "Now I'm very, very consciously trying to tell them about the Indian culture. I just want them to feel connected. But at the same time I want them to question everything," she says. "We should do it, but if we don't do it, it's also okay."

Indian cooking is another way for her to capture this connection. Recently, she pondered meal prep after a long workweek. "I could have said, I won't have time, so I'll just buy some croissants and make an English breakfast," Mitali says. "But I had some time and decided, let me make a traditional breakfast!"

. . .

Chinese-born Lilian also discovered a number of surprises as a new mother in America. She wanted to replicate her modest upbringing, but it wasn't easy.

She and her husband, also from China, try to stick to a few rules: they don't let their kids, four and one years old, eat junk food; they limit toys and don't allow videos on the iPad. But it's a struggle, Lilian admits, especially when her son wants the latest superhero toys like the ones his friends play with, in their mostly upper-middle-class Bay Area neighborhood.

. . .

So how do people like us keep our legacies and chart new paths for our families at the same time?

To weigh in on the matter, I turn to a therapist in one of the most iconic American immigration gateways: New York City.[11] Jaime Cár-camo is a licensed clinical psychologist who's spent over two decades working and volunteering with immigrants and their families, including those who have experienced trauma and face deportations.

By the time he turned twelve, he'd witnessed more violence than any person, let alone a child, should see. His homeland, El Salvador, was on the brink of a civil war. He fled the country with his mother and siblings and settled in New York, but he never forgot where he came from. He became determined to help other immigrants, eventually earning his doctorate in clinical psychology. Cárcamo has since taught at Columbia University and Icahn School of Medicine at Mount Sinai in New York and traveled to Venezuela as a visiting professor.

Cárcamo's two-story clinic is situated at the bottom of a brick building in a largely Hispanic neighborhood in Queens, not far from a bodega, a law office, and a bakery where you can pick up a scrumptious pastry for $1.50.

I stop by the clinic on a Saturday morning, entering under a burgundy awning with his and the clinic's name: The Psychological & Stress Management, PC. The waiting room is brightly lit. Relaxing piano music is playing on the TV monitor on the wall, painted with a fresh coat of light gray paint. Two bilingual receptionists are answering calls. Several people await their therapy appointments.

Cárcamo is a familiar face to many nonimmigrant New Yorkers too. One of his TV appearances was on September 12, 2001, in a segment with then-senator Hillary Clinton, where he shared coping tips in the wake of the World Trade Center terrorist attacks. He counseled first responders, survivors, and victims' families and trained therapists in post-traumatic stress treatment. Many who sought Cárcamo's help at the Columbia University clinic, where he worked at the time of the attacks, were undocumented Spanish-speaking immigrants suffering from PTSD (and later, from other health problems).[12] They were cleaning up the devastation at the Ground Zero site and are among the unsung heroes of the recovery efforts.

He also treated New Yorkers affected by mental health issues related to the COVID-19 pandemic, especially since the virus and its economic fallout has disproportionally hurt the Latino community in addition to the Black community.

"There's a dearth of research in trauma treatment for Spanish-speaking populations, especially because of acculturation," Cárcamo says. Treatment manuals often don't take important cultural issues into consideration. "It's not just translating an English treatment manual to Spanish that has been written mainly for, let's say, middle-class Americans or Anglo-Saxons."

"What are some common challenges immigrant parents experience in their day-to-day lives?" I ask. "And what are some ways to overcome them?"

Cárcamo's first recommendation is fairly straightforward: Be open-minded about different cultural norms and expectations. Don't pretend they don't exist or brush them aside.

"Listen and learn is the best they can do," Cárcamo says. "This is easier said than done, as many parents want to hold on to their traditions and values. This is why it is important for them to be educated about accepting differences while preserving their own values. They are not mutually exclusive."

Understanding individual differences goes a long way. "I've seen couples where, let's say, the Hispanic husband is not as fluent in English, and he's married to a US-born white person," he says. "And they can still get along well because they can understand the differences and they can work through them."

Another point Cárcamo makes is immigrants aren't all the same. Even if our homes are adjacent on the map. Even if we share a language. This may sound obvious, but all too often foreigners are lumped into one nebulous category.

Take a couple where one partner is from the Dominican Republic and another one is from Mexico. "Even though they speak the same language, they have large differences in the way they perceive the world. And so, that could be conflicting," he tells me.

Differences can show up in a number of ways. Cárcamo brings up *familismo*, or intense loyalty to the family and interconnectedness among relatives, common in many Latin American communities. *Familismo*, however, can clash with the individualistic American mentality,[13] where the progeny is traditionally expected to flee the nest at eighteen, then check in by phone once in a while and visit for Christmas.[14]

Many other traditional cultures also rely on family as the cornerstone of identity and support, often superseding individual needs. To them, independence isn't a Western pinnacle of achievement and the triumph of the will. It's an affliction. A person who didn't grow up with this *familismo* mindset may struggle to understand a partner who did, says Cárcamo.

I get it. Middle-class white American friends often find it strange that I didn't have my own room until sixteen and didn't live in the dorms during college. But this isn't uncommon among immigrant families. It's what we can afford. It's what we know. Even if it isn't always what we enjoy.

Another common cultural difference is discipline. In many nations across the globe, the adage of "a child must be seen and not heard" and corporal punishment are business as usual.

A Chinese friend, whose children, now young adults, grew up in the United States, explains the key distinction between the two parenting philosophies in this way: "Being a parent in America, I can't beat them up," she tells me. "Here, I have to treat them as my best friend, but in China, I can just order them. That's the difference. I am more American now," she adds hastily.

Sociologist Nancy Foner observes this conflict too. Children in many immigrant households are expected to show a greater level of respect for elders than in American ones. In turn, parents often discipline children in ways the American system might find abusive, she writes.[15]

Discipline comes up for Cárcamo's multicultural clients as well. "In the Hispanic culture, they have traditional ways of spanking, sometimes even screaming. Treating kids that way could create a conflict in the family," he tells me.

It's true that "spare the rod, spoil the child" is also practiced in many American households, but not necessarily to the same degree. (I'm floored to learn that hitting a child is legal in all fifty states, though states differ in what they deem acceptable;[16] harsh physical discipline has been shown to be ineffective in modifying behavior and is associated with aggression, anxiety, and depression.[17])

Acceptance of mental health as health is another challenge within immigrant families, Cárcamo notes. It's a documented fact that many of us are taught to view mental health as something different from, say, a common cold or a stomach ulcer. Instead of getting treated, mental health issues often get stigmatized or swept under the rug.[18] Therapy can be prohibitively expensive at a time when many foreign-born folk are trying to keep their heads above water. In some close-knit communities, prioritizing one's psychological well-being can even get pegged as shameful or indulgent.[19] That's why many immigrants don't look for outside help for mental health until after they've exhausted all other resources, Cárcamo says. They may turn to the family, religion, or folk healers. "Some individuals would benefit from mental health services, but they avoid seeking professional help because they rely on the family so much for dealing with mental health issues."

Men in many traditional cultures are expected to project certain ideals of virility and stoic masculinity, says Cárcamo. These deeply ingrained beliefs make it harder to seek assistance when needed.

Another multicultural therapist in Southern California I speak to swears by the power of an ongoing dialogue, especially when two people of different origins start a family.

Ruth and Antonio, who live in Washington, DC, did have a conversation like this. When Ruth was pregnant, they made a deal: their son would grow up speaking Spanish.

"I don't really care about religion," says Antonio, a project manager from Mexico, whose Catholic relatives still live primarily back home. "But I told her, I want my son to be Mexican. To me, that doesn't mean dressing in a traditional way or eating specific foods or celebrating specific holidays," he says. "To me, that means two things: being able to talk like people in Mexico and being able to socialize in Mexico."

That's exactly what ended up happening.

Ruth, who works for the government, knew a decent amount of Spanish when they met, but she's since mastered it to such an extent that they interact primarily in Spanish, at least when their toddler is awake. It's no surprise that the little boy speaks the language exclusively.

As if on cue, their son protests the cereal he's been given. Ruth quickly goes to pour a different cereal into his bowl and kisses him, adding a tender "*un besito*." "It means 'a kiss,'" she translates for me. The boy goes back to enjoying his snack and a Spanish-language cartoon about trucks.

Ruth's family made America home a couple of generations ago, but she had an equally important legacy to carry out. Her son had to be raised Jewish. She's made a promise to her grandparents, who fled the anti-Semitism of Eastern Europe. This promise to raise Jewish children continues to guide her parenting decisions. "It's my motivation through my fertility struggles to have another child," she tells me.

Nurturing a Jewish identity takes time and effort. "The pervasive culture is Santa Claus," says Ruth. For every Jewish event they attend, she tries ensure that her son plays with his Spanish-speaking friends too.

Then there are the day-to-day routines. The couple's American friends keep a strict schedule for baby naps and meals, and the location of the nap is often inflexible. Meanwhile, Ruth and Antonio's son doesn't go to bed until nine or ten o'clock (his American peers are typically snoozing by eight). He stays up for family celebrations, influenced in part by Antonio's upbringing.

"I think Americans are 'Let's get together from four to six,'" Antonio says. "People from where I come from, they arrive an hour later and it's very open-ended."

This throws a wrench in their social plans. "Half of the people are going to arrive at the time it starts and half of the people are gonna arrive an hour and a half late," Ruth says, exasperated. "When do you have the cake?"

. . .

The contrast between parenting approaches also became apparent to Hannah, an American, after she met her now husband, who is French. Hannah cherishes the fact that her mother always played with her growing up. "We were kind of the center of her world," Hannah reminisces about her childhood. "As an American parent, you always see moms as very involved."

When visiting her in-laws in France, Hannah did the same: she'd jump in the yard with her husband's nieces and nephews and frolic with them in the garden. Soon, though, she noticed that while she was out playing, the French mothers "were inside and watching from the sidelines because they knew the kids were okay."

Now, as a mother, Hannah has been influenced by that French parenting philosophy, especially when she's out with her toddler son.

"Now that I have been around that culture so long, there are times where I'm at the playground, there are times at playdates and stuff, I just let him go," Hannah tells me. "He's okay, I can see him. [I say,] 'Go play in the sand over there!' as opposed to being hands-on. Sometimes I feel other moms are checking that out."

. . .

It's common to believe our own parenting approach is the best one. But in this world of almost eight billion people, it's not necessarily the case. For example, many American families practice "crying it out," a sleep-training technique that involves letting the baby cry until she learns to fall asleep by herself, in her own room (the parents usually cry too, parked on the floor on the other side of the nursery door).[20]

Co-sleeping, where the mother shares her bed with the baby, is discouraged in many Western nations and by the American Academy of Pediatrics, citing the risk of accidental falls and suffocation. But in much of the world, from Japan to Nigeria, it's common for infants to share a bed with the mother.[21]

Co-sleeping is common in India too.

"Children are allowed to sleep with their parents until children decide they don't want to sleep with their parents anymore," says Lakshmi, a writer and business analyst originally from the south of India. She now lives with her Indian husband and three daughters in Pennsylvania.

The couple couldn't comfortably fit their twins in their queen-sized bed after adopting them at ten months of age. The babies ended up having separate sleeping arrangements. But Lakshmi couldn't let them cry it out. She'd run to her babies any time one cried at night, only to return five minutes later when the other twin woke up.

After giving birth to her youngest daughter a few years later, Lakshmi realized she couldn't do without sleep anymore. So she tweaked her approach to be "kind of in the middle," she explains. "My five-year-old will still sneak in to sleep with me, even now. I'm not worried about it. She'll do transition when she's ready."

I also speak to Denis, who came to the United States from Cameroon as a young adult to study, then stayed on to work in information technology.

I can tell by the mathematical references sprinkled throughout our conversation that he's got a technical background: "Thirty percent of my entire life has been in Yaoundé [the capital city of Cameroon]," Denis says when we talk.

Denis met his wife, an American, while playing soccer on Sundays in Washington, DC.

Now the two have a baby. This makes him reminisce about the communal child-rearing of his homeland. Large families and households are common in Cameroon, and relatives help take care of the new mother and baby, a living testament to the phrase "It takes a village to raise a child."

"If your wife gives birth, there's a probability that you will have at least five, six people permanently there in your house taking care of the child," Denis says. The house had more than twenty people living there—and we were talking about it—eleven, twelve women that were living there. There were certain times that [my mother] needed to carry me because the women, they were fighting to carry me!"

Neighbors were an indispensable part of the community too, says Denis. "My mother reminded me that when I was growing up . . . my neighbors would take care of me."

.   .   .

Like psychologists suggest, understanding differences and working through them is key for multicultural families.

Miguel, an immigrant from Mexico, has quite a bit in common with his wife, Christine, an American. Both are Mormons (they fell in love after meeting at church in Salt Lake City, Utah). Both speak Spanish, which Christine started learning on a mission trip before they met. Both work demanding jobs that serve the community: he is a registered nurse at a local hospital and she is a Spanish immersion teacher at a public school. More important, they are the loving parents of a four-year-old girl.

But they didn't have the same level of security and comfort growing up, they learned.

Miguel doesn't let friends and close neighbors babysit his daughter, particularly overnight, which can be a challenge when he has to work the night shift and his wife has to travel out of town for church work.

Back in Mexico City, Miguel had to be street savvy due to high crime levels in his hometown. He avoided sharing personal information about himself and his family. He often made up fictitious names at medical clinics and when applying to rent apartments. This vigilance has followed him all the way to Utah, where he's lived for ten years now. In fact, he's amazed by what he considers to be carelessness here in the United States.

"You see people walking on the road and they don't even look, you know, to the side," he observes. "In Mexico, you always have to be attentive of the cars. Or of the strangers, or even your neighbors. You see in the news or [from] friends that something happens. I have that fear."

In the beginning Christine was confused by his guarded behavior. "Why are you giving a fake name?" she'd want to know. "Give them your name. What do you think they're gonna do?"

She soon recognized that Miguel's cautiousness was shaped by his formative experiences, and they were fundamentally different from hers. "I definitely grew up with a lot of privilege and I can trust in the system of government and the justice system," says Christine. "I don't have things working against me. I have a lot of good faith in everybody."

At the same time, the couple is making an effort to pass their traditions to their daughter. They listen to Spanish-language music in the house and read children's books with Latino characters, like *Maya's Blanket* and *My Papi Has a Motorcycle*. The other day, their daughter asked their Alexa device to play a Mexican band, the Los Ángeles Azules. Her favorite doll, which she excitedly shows me, has dark brown skin.

Still, Christine tells me, the girl self-identifies as white, like most of the people in the neighborhood and like her mom. "Why are you brown, Dada?" she recently asked Miguel.

Their exposure to the Latin American community is limited ever since they stopped attending Spanish-language church services (there was no nursery available). Both parents work full time and often don't have the time to socialize with other multicultural families as much as they would like.

"I see things that they do, like teaching them how to cook the typical foods or do a lot of traditional things," Christine observes. "I'm like, oh, I should be doing things like that or reading to her more in Spanish."

Miguel takes care of their daughter on days when he's working the night shift at the hospital. He cherishes those afternoons. They go to gymnastics or the trampoline park with the family dogs, then to a neighborhood Chinese restaurant for their favorites: egg drop soup and orange chicken.

Watching his daughter become more English dominant as she grows in America, Miguel sometimes feels his heritage is slipping away.

"I have my accent," Miguel says. "I worry that I'm not gonna be able to talk to her friends like I should. Or that she's gonna be—what do you call . . . ?" He turns to Christine and quietly says the Spanish word, which she translates for him. "*Embarrassed* of me," he tells me and looks away.

4. VODKA RUBS AND OTHER FAMILY ADVICE

They are people who have spent the whole of their lives crossing borders that were, often, unfriendly and unwilling to welcome them. They could not, I imagine, tolerate inhospitable borders within their own family, so they loved us in a wild, irrepressible, boundless way. They taught us to love that way in return, and so we do.

—ROXANNE GAY[1]

WHEREVER YOU COME FROM, whatever language you speak, there's one thing you can count on for certain: baby advice from relatives. They have opinions, and they want to share them. *Don't praise your child—it will make her lazy. If you paint your son's toenails, he'll grow up gay. Is nursing a child this old even legal?*

Even the all-American grandma and grandpa haven't necessarily kept up with the changes in baby care since they were in the parenting trenches a few decades earlier, back when car seats were optional and formula was king. In one recent study, almost half of participating grandparents thought a baby ice bath was a good way to bring a very high fever down (it isn't). And many didn't realize infants should only sleep on their backs,[2] not on their stomachs or sides, to reduce the risk of SIDS (sudden infant death syndrome), something pediatricians have been staunchly advocating since the 1990s.[3]

But parents in America are far from having it all figured out. We tend to tune out family advice and seek expert opinions and the latest studies on ways to avoid indulging, depriving, understimulating, and overstimulating our children.

Jennifer Senior, author of the bestselling *All Joy and No Fun: The Paradox of Modern Parenthood*, says in an interview with TED Ideas that the mothers she spoke to for her research turned to websites, books, and friends for parenting advice. Nobody named her own mother.[4]

If we don't trust family elders in America, all the more troubling is the fact that we don't really trust ourselves either. Inundated with information, American parents are often at a loss of what good parenting is supposed to look like. When sociologist Caitlyn Collins asked middle-class American mothers what it means to be a good mom, many deferred to experts from podcasts, blogs, and so on. They rarely had a personal definition, writes Collins in her *Atlantic* article.[5]

What about immigrants? Who do we listen to when caring for our brood? What informs our decisions?

There is no one recipe.

After my postdelivery haze wears off, the questions of what to do with the baby now and whose advice to listen to become very real. (I do skip the old home remedy of rubbing a baby's skin with vodka to bring a fever down, since it can lead to alcohol poisoning.)

More than ever, I recognize the sacrifices my parents have made by uprooting themselves to provide their children with a better future. This gratitude is just one of the reasons many conventions follow me from my northern birthplace to the California maternity ward, then slip into our second-floor apartment. Like the earthy smell of buckwheat, the familiar routines settle by the crib and the multilingual bookshelf with a tea-themed wall calendar nearby, above a plate of cut-up fruit.

I marvel at the ingenious ways households stretched their hard-earned ruble when I was growing up. Adults whipped up feasts out of canned sprats and repurposed hand-me-downs into magnificent outfits for their children. Benevolent strangers would bring a child lost on the street or on the city bus back to safety. When ill, I'd receive packages of sweets and get-well letters from classmates, a custom for all sick students the teachers had organized. Those are the rituals I cherish.

Communal child-rearing does mean that your business is the community's business. So you better believe that others will notice if you or your children have deviated from the norm and brought minor or sizable shame, known as *pozor*, upon themselves or your family, and that you will be informed about this in no uncertain terms. This is seen as a gesture of goodwill. For me, though, it doesn't translate well.

．　．　．

The families of Natasha, born in the Soviet Union, and Trevor, who is second-generation Chinese American, are convinced the couple spoil their children.

"*Spoil* is probably the wrong word," Natasha says. "My parents think that we're whipped by our children. We choose battles we can win. And for Russian parents, the priorities are eat, stay inside, do what we tell you, my way and not your way."

Whenever the family visits their in-laws, Trevor says, they close the windows even if it's hot outside, to protect the grandchildren from drafts. "They want to keep it warm. Or the wind will blow on [the kids]," Trevor explains. "You know?"

"Sure," I nod, not sure who I'm actually relating to more: to Trevor's incredulousness about his in-laws or to his in-laws' anxiety about air. I catch myself trying to remember whether I'd put an extra sweater on my kid at preschool drop-off and asked the teacher to please not remove it.

The grandparents also disagreed with the couple's approach to feeding. Trevor and Natasha used the baby-led weaning method, a popular practice of letting an older infant feed herself with finger foods and regulate her intake, rather than adults spoon-feeding her purees. "Both of them said, you're trying to kill your babies, because they should be eating purees until they are two," Natasha says.

The couple's heritage cultures overlap in many ways, making it easier to reach consensus. Their parents instilled in them a respect for education as a survival tactic. Both grew up in communities that tend to take an authoritarian and, sometimes, a shame-based approach to childrearing.[6] Filial piety, or honoring the elders, is a critical part of the Chinese culture. Similarly, children who grew up in the Soviet Union had to obey the parents and the party.

Now the couple is choosing to do many things differently. They don't give ultimatums. They don't force their littles to eat when they say they're not hungry. If their preschooler insists on wearing the same pink ballerina dress for several days in a row, they let her, despite pro-testations from the grandparents.

"We don't rule with an iron fist. We try to explain and make them rational," Trevor tells me.

As we wrap up the conversation, Trevor adds one more point. They agree on most things. But not on all.

"Natasha told me I try to be the good cop," he notes.

"No," Natasha counters. "You try to be a popular dad." When their son wanted to quit his kung fu lessons, Natasha wouldn't budge. Quit-ting was not an option. "I said, you gotta go and finish till you get the green belt. You committed to something. You can't just jump from one to another activity. You have to have an accomplishment."

So her son stuck it out through the academic year and got his green belt. He broke a board with his foot, Natasha says proudly. She shares a video of the test and his magnificent kick.

■ ■ ■

Christine from Utah didn't understand why her mother-in-law, who lives in Mexico, insisted she cover her pregnant belly with red fabric and keep an open pair of scissors and a safety pin near her during a lunar eclipse. (The ancient Aztec superstition is the eclipse could harm the developing baby.)[7] So Christine didn't do it.

After the baby's birth, her mother-in-law arrived from Mexico City to stay with her and Miguel. For one, they didn't see eye to eye about *la cuarentena*, a forty-day postnatal period when the new mother re-cuperates, bonds with the newborn, and gets looked after by female relatives, commonly practiced in many Spanish-speaking countries[8] (a 2010 cross-cultural study found this postnatal period of roughly forty days to be almost universal[9]). Christine's mother-in-law wanted her to take special herbal baths with sage and other plants she had gathered and to drink *atole*, a warm cornmeal beverage said to boost milk supply. Christine was reluctant, though she did let her mother-in-law draw a bath once and she did drink some *atole*.

Miguel's mother worried about the baby being cold and getting sick, so she'd bundle her up in multiple blankets, which alarmed Chris-tine. She'd read that babies shouldn't get too warm and mustn't sleep in a hat, to avoid overheating and the risk of SIDS. She also grew up with the comfort of central heating, unlike her husband's family.

Christine meant no disrespect. She just wasn't raised that way. During some of the more vulnerable and exhausting moments of her life, Christine, like many of her American peers, turned to experts and doctors for guidance. "I was always checking what was the American [Academy of Pediatrics] saying?" she says, skittishly. Sometimes those recommendations would change right before her eyes. "They said I have to do it this way now, and I would be really nervous about it," she explains, looking back. "As a new mom, you feel like [you] have to do this the right way or, you know, something could happen and you're a lot more scared of things. You need to be using the right materials, the right bottles, the right diapers, the right car seat. It's more about consumerism . . . After a while, I just realized, you know, it's not that big of a deal."

Miguel tried to referee the tension between two of the most important women in his life.

He admits, though, that he finds some local baby-wrangling customs odd. He wonders why the communal doting over the new mom and baby is lacking in America. He was petrified whenever he'd see a grown-up strolling through the park with a newborn in tow. In Mexico, he says, you don't see newborns outside. They're warm and snug at home, as Grandma bustles around to take care of the household and the new mother, cooking meals and binding her postpartum belly. People here are different, he says. "They want to be by themselves."

Miguel knows that privacy is a big deal in the United States: he's seen this firsthand in the hospital where he works. "Whenever there's a Caucasian person, it's weird when they have visitors. It's a really private time for that person, to be healing and stuff. But if there's a Latin family, there's like twenty people in the room and two people stay at night."

■ ■ ■

Sometimes, the rites of passage and elders' advice are the cherished lifeline, especially when the new family wonders what the heck to do with the screaming bundle of joy they'd just brought home.

Americans might be baffled by some foreign postbirthing customs. Go to a Western discussion board online and you'll likely find mothers voting garlic out of their menus because babies dislike its odor in the milk.[10] And although swaddling, or snugly wrapping newborns for that baby burrito look, has been practiced for millennia around the world, it didn't become popular in the United States until the last couple of decades. (It's come under fire in recent years.)[11]

For many Indian mothers, these customs are the golden rule, dutifully passed from one generation to the next.

Priya, who was born in India and lived in the United States for a decade, followed her mother's advice after the birth of her two children, now six and one years old. (Her family currently resides in Singapore.) Priya tightly bound her belly with her mother's old cotton saris, like a corset, to support the abdominal muscles. Her mother encouraged her to eat garlic to prevent bloating and fenugreek seeds and leaves to boost milk supply. She also consumed copious amounts of clarified butter, ghee, thought to be healing. And she gave her babies daily massages with special oils.

Priya, a writer and a former human resources specialist, feels lucky that her mother came to stay when her children were born.

"I'm really happy I listened to her advice," she tells me. "The same traditions were followed when she had me and my sister, so this was her passing on these traditions to me."

The belly binding helped her posture and made her feel stronger. And though she was skeptical about the baby sari swaddle, she found that her newborn napped better that way.

Priya did do some sleuthing to make sure her mom's recommendations checked out. She googled them. "I guess I did doubt them a bit after all," she admits. But with the second baby, she heeded her mother's counsel without reservation.

■　■　■

When I speak to Lakshmi, the Indian American mother of three in Pennsylvania, she tells me she yearned for the birthing rites of passage of her ancestors. It was a dream she cherished as she tried to get pregnant. She craved the joyous baby shower, *valaikappu*, when guests adorn the expectant mother's wrists with bangles ("By the end of the function, you literally have bangles that go from your wrist to your elbow," she says). It's the only time in a woman's life when she wears a black sari.

She also longed for *seemantham*, an elaborate religious ceremony with a fire offering, where a priest prays for the health of the unborn child and the mother-to-be.

"When I was going through infertility, I had this hope of someday wearing a black sari," Lakshmi tells me. "That's the only thing I asked of my mother: when you come, I want you to get me a black sari."

After Lakshmi adopted her twin babies, her mother flew in from India and brought a silk sari. But to Lakshmi's disappointment, the sari wasn't black. It was red, with a black border.

Several years later, Lakshmi got pregnant. Her mother brought a different sari this time. It was black, but not completely. "She got me a black sari with a red bottom," Lakshmi notes.

.   .   .

American-born Shoshana, whose husband is from the Czech Republic, turned to her Czech mother-in-law for potty training advice, which is how she learned about the elimination communication approach. It involves reading cues from the baby when nature calls and is often done in combination with cloth diapers. Common in many parts of the world, it encourages a toddler to be independent before the age of two and cuts down on disposable diapers. It's also cheaper. In comparison, American tots are typically potty trained later, around three years of age and older.[12]

As a result, Shoshana's son was the first of his peers to go diaper-free during the day.

.   .   .

Ultimately, family advice comes down to keeping what works and discarding what doesn't. Amira, a refugee who left Iraq when she was one year old, calls this process "cafeteria style."

Amira's family escaped from Baghdad shortly after Saddam Hussein took power: her parents were educators and her father was politically active before the dictatorship's stronghold. Amira's family is Chaldean Catholic, a persecuted Iraqi Christian minority.

One ritual Amira adopted from her upbringing was swaddling, similar to the Indian way.

At the time, it was just becoming the norm it the West; her American friends weren't swaddling yet. But her people have been doing this for hundreds of years. She'd take thin muslin cloth and cut it in a large triangle to wrap the baby in. "It simulates the experience of being in the womb," she explains. "They are less likely to be startled or to cry or to fuss."

And similar to many Latin American cultures, Amira also stayed home for forty days, leaving only for pediatrician checkups. Her mother and mother-in-law rotated in caring for her around the clock: doing laundry, cooking, cleaning, and washing baby bottles.

"I remember nursing my baby and my mom would be putting food in my mouth," she says.

Amira's mother fed her lots of sweets, to boost milk production and make it thicker, is how she explained it. So in the early days of parenthood, one of Amira's go-to treats was baklava, a decadent Middle Eastern dessert made with layers of filo dough, chopped nuts, and syrupy honey. There was lots of baklava. Baklava from her mother. Baklava from relatives that came to visit.

"I don't know if there is any scientific data behind it: it was an excuse to eat very delicious dessert," Amira tells me. "I had an ungodly amount of milk. I had bags and bags in the freezer."

Amira didn't mind the doting relatives and the lack of privacy in her Michigan home. She knew it was temporary. "The reality is there are so few days of rest that follow that, when family no longer visits to support you and you are alone." It's a modern act of self-care, she says, caring for yourself so you can better provide for the baby.

Her mother also shielded her from anything startling or upsetting, to avoid passing that energy to the baby through milk and even in utero, while pregnant. "My mother would say, don't watch scary movies or don't do anything to upset yourself because that would affect the baby."

This strikes a chord, reminding me of the counsel I heard in my own family, on the other side of the world.

In retrospect, I should have listened to my relatives' wisdom and practiced some of that tender loving care when expecting and recovering from labor. To be fair, I did try prenatal yoga, once per child. I'd even bought a pregnancy journal with glossy pages and prompts about the sacred power of the womb.

But those meditations would be cut short in crowded trains on the way to the office, by pregnancy complications, by work deliverables. Like many, I worked until the day I gave birth. Even after arriving at the hospital in labor, I rebuffed the nurses' offer to sit in a wheelchair they'd brought out for me. For reasons unknown, I plopped my bag on the wheelchair and marched alongside it straight into the delivery room, poring over outstanding client deadlines and planning meals in my head.

I wish all expectant and new mothers would ditch the guilt and have the audacity to advocate for themselves, feeling a wall of support from their communities. Unfortunately, in our busy world, where women still earn eighty-two cents on every dollar men make, endure workplace discrimination, and lack adequate prenatal and postnatal care, this support is not a given.

■   ■   ■

As far as traditions are concerned, it didn't all go smoothly for Amira either. In the Iraqi culture, people want to congratulate the new family immediately. But Amira, a physician, cocooned in the Western way and limited visitors in the first few weeks to avoid germ exposure before the newborn vaccinations.

"Your uncles want to come visit, your cousins, sisters-in-law, brothers-in-law. And they're almost offended if you say no," she tells me.

Breastfeeding became another point of contention. Her mother-in-law felt it was inappropriate for Amira to nurse in public, even when covered, particularly in front of her father-in-law. "I was upset by that because, obviously, it is not a sexual act, feeding your child," Amira shares. "If it makes him uncomfortable, he needs to look away."

■   ■   ■

Figuring out baby care routines can be particularly challenging for LGBTQ immigrant families. As they navigate prejudice and the logistical terrain of building a family, heteronormative roles are of little use.

A friend introduces me to Edwin and Aleksey, a couple raising their two-year-old daughter in Maryland.

Aleksey, a former ballroom dancer, came to the US from Ukraine with family when he was fifteen. Edwin fled El Salvador during the bloody civil war. Most of Edwin's relatives, including his mother, escaped when he was just eight years old. He was raised by his grandmother until he got his paperwork and rejoined them three years later in Washington, DC.

The couple met in the nation's capital through a shared passion: flamenco. Edwin is a renowned flamenco artist: he's directed and performed in productions as far as Spain and Nicaragua; he is also a teacher and flamenco festival coordinator in Washington, DC, having earned the Cross of the Order of Civil Merit from the king of Spain.

They have been together for nearly twenty years, married for six of those. Shortly after their wedding, they decided to codirect and choreograph a flamenco production.

"It was really the first baby that we had," explains Aleksey, who leads a team of product managers at a technology company. "We thought, either that's going to make us or break us. So that seemed to work out."

Their daughter, Sofia, used to fall asleep to the rhythmic sound of the rehearsals coming from Edwin's studio downstairs.

The two are reinventing many conventions as they raise a daughter in a country where neither of them grew up.

"Being a gay couple, even without kids, having come from very traditional backgrounds, we've had to challenge many of our own traditions," says Aleksey. In college, he was enrolled in a medical program, but then switched to liberal arts, surprising his immigrant parents. "I was not really sure which one was the biggest tragedy for them: me coming out as gay or me dropping out of the medical program," Aleksey tells me. (He later went on to earn his MBA.)

"It's not like there's a book on how exactly gay relationships need to work. In a gay couple, who brings whom flowers?" says Aleksey. "There's a little bit of a blueprint we'd like to follow to the degree that it's useful, but ever so often, you run into a wall with that because it's not useful to us or to our child."

After Sofia was born, Edwin's cousin called up the new parents and teased, "So who's in *cuarentena* and who's eating the chocolate?" (In the Salvadoran tradition, chocolate is said to help new mothers with milk production.)

"I'm more of a chocolate guy," says Aleksey.

"I'm drinking the wine," Edwin quips.

It's been a negotiation since.

Edwin comes from a large Central American family: he's got forty cousins in the Washington, DC, area alone (they don't all get together at the same time, though; at family celebrations, it's only about twenty-five to thirty cousins and their kids, Edwin clarifies).

He is no novice to child-rearing. His mom needed to work, so he raised his baby brother when he was just seventeen, until the little boy was two years old.

"I always go back to what the women in the family do," says Edwin. "Now, sometimes that seems a bit too cultural and too severe, so then I pull back a little bit and read a little bit about behaviors." When it comes to handling tantrums, for example, the usual [family] advice is "just ignore him or just smack him on the butt, and he'll get over it," he explains. In cases like these, Edwin consults a book for a solution instead.

The girl's Salvadoran and Ukrainian families insist that the child must eat meals prepared from scratch. Edwin recalls a recent discussion with the grandparents. "'She needs to eat fresh fish,' they said. I said, 'It was freshly frozen!'"

Aleksey, meanwhile, sings Russian and Ukrainian folk songs to their daughter. His parents got her a *sarafan*, a traditional floor-length dress. "She's still a half Central American girl, wearing the Russian attire. It was so cute and funny and also sort of warmed my heart."

But there are some cultural aspects that Aleksey is glad to part with. Besides rampant homophobia, some books and jokes of his Soviet-era upbringing were sexist and derogatory to people of color. This worldview was so ingrained in the popular mindset that it often lacked ill intent: it was just there. When reading the beloved childhood books to Sofia, he sometimes edits.

"There would be some image there that's sort of like, you know, I'm not really sure I feel comfortable making a jest that way," he says. "Okay, we're gonna skip this poem . . ."

■   ■   ■

As immigrant parents decide whose advice to listen to, one thing is clear. Everyone I talk to is holding on to some vestige of their upbringing or wish they were doing so more. The old and familiar lends an unmistakable stronghold in the new world.

It may seem counterintuitive. Aren't we the trailblazers who set off in search of a new life (or were toted along as kids)? Why, then, this urge to look back?

Sociologist Philip Kasinitz brings up this paradox during our interview in New York.

"As conservative as they might seem to their kids, they're all people who got up and did something else," Kasinitz tells me. "Immigrants are the people who say 'Fuck it, I'm out of here. I can change my fate . . . I can come up with something that isn't in the playbook, which is exit.'"

The messages from the parents are often contradictory, such as "'I don't want you to become an American,'" Kasinitz says, "but then everything they actually do pushes the kid in the other way. So they're often saying one thing: 'Keep with our customs and our traditions, our best ways of doing things. But we're moving out of the ethnic neighborhood and into a nice suburb because schools are better and there's a little higher status. And I want to make sure that you marry a person from the old country who's got our good values. But on the other hand, I want you to be on the school team to get along with people.'"

Yeah. It's confusing. And it makes total sense.

■ ■ ■

Denis, who came to the United States from Cameroon as a young adult, thinks about legacy ever since he became a father four months ago. Teaching his languages to his son is a must. He's fluent in French, English, and Ewondo, a language of Cameroon, and his American wife also knows Japanese. Sometimes, when Denis sits down to watch soccer on TV in Spanish, he'll have his infant next to him so that he can hear Spanish words too.

He also wants to teach his son about family heritage and paying respect to those who have passed, just as he did in Cameroon. "The most important thing is my ancestors," Denis says. "Probably start with my parents, my father, my grandparents, and the history of the family, where they come from."

At the same time, he hopes to be a more lenient parent than what he'd seen growing up, he tells me. "Where I come from, it's a very rigid society. For example, when you serve food, you shouldn't serve yourself before your father and your uncle. And the belief is that if you don't do that for them, misfortune is going to happen."

"I want to learn about who he is and try to guide him according to who he is," adds Denis. "I just don't want to be in a situation where I have to tell him, okay, this is how your life is supposed to be. I want to be more like a friend."

Sorting through the cultural baby-rearing wisdom and the counsel of modern experts, sometimes it feels like I'm groping my way through the dark. But aren't we all?

Maybe there's no singular "right way" to raise a child of immigrants. Perhaps there's no authority figure to say, wait, wait, you're doing multicultural parenting all wrong. Here, let me show how to do it right!

This uncharted path is a little bit terrifying. But at the same time, it's incredibly liberating.

5. THE POLYGLOT BOARDINGHOUSE

Like everybody, I am the sum of my languages.

—EVA HOFFMAN[1]

THE LOCAL PLAYGROUND is bustling with kids, mothers, nannies, and an occasional dad. The sandbox is popping. The line for the swings is out of control. Squealing tots zip down the brightly colored slides, as caregivers check their phones and chase the littles to reapply sunscreen.

"Look, Harper, what's this toy called?" one woman asks her toddler.

"Ball!" The boy jumps for the ball in delight.

"That's right. Ball!" The woman beams. "Do you want more snack, Harper?"

"More, more!" shouts Harper as he climbs out of the sandbox.

"Now what's the magic word, Harper?"

"Harper!"

"Hmm, no," the mom says. "What do we say when we want something?"

"Peeease?"

"Good job, Harper!" The woman hands him a plastic cup with puffy rice stars. Another mom nearby smiles at the heartwarming scene. The two women chat.

In that code-free conversation, a cat is a cat, not sometimes *gato*. Their children are probably growing up secure in the fact that dogs in America say *woof-woof*, and not *hau-hau* or *bow-bow*. Unlike in some existential riddle, the dog's bark does not depend on who is listening.

These moments may be commonplace, but to me, they're fascinating. Part of the reason is they're unlike my own reality. From the moment Leah is born, I speak, sing, and read to her exclusively in Russian.

It's not a conscious decision. It just happens. The language becomes a portal into a different universe, authentic and safe, stashed in an old suitcase from years ago. Oddly, I find myself addressing pets and other people's babies in Russian too.

Baby Leah and I attend sing-alongs at the neighborhood library and socialize with American friends, but it's Russian the rest of the time. Even when Leah waddles over with her favorite English-language book, *Goodnight Moon*, I try to translate it on the spot for her, wrecking the book's poetic value. Or I ask Pete to read it instead, keeping our division of languages consistent. It feels alienating. It's busywork. But I don't budge. If my daughter is exposed to a language from birth, I assume, it will stay with her forever, sort of like acquiring a taste for blue cheese or learning to ride a bicycle.

As I soon learn, we're in for a wild ride.

■　■　■

Having come of age in the San Francisco Bay Area and in New York, both with dense immigrant populations and tourists, I've always taken it for granted that at any given moment, in any given bakery or bus, I might hear foreign speech. To be sure, I'm still the language minority in a crowd of people named Katie and Josh. But I'm far from alone. Not too far there is a Korean supermarket across from a building with a large solemn sign: Russian School of Mathematics. At our local parks, there are women in hijabs telling their toddlers in Arabic to slow down on their tricycles, and men shouting "*Gooool!*" as they kick a soccer ball with the kids.

Still, as soon as I venture outside my bubble to different neighborhoods and parts of the country, my assumptions about the way people in America talk go out the window.

Being a nonnative English speaker can feel like an anomaly, especially when you're constantly asked to repeat yourself and spell your name, until you've had enough and almost want to say, *Screw it, just call me JC.*

Then there's the question of which language to use with the kids in public. Will the others understand? *Should* they understand? Is that shopper at the supermarket staring because our cart is blocking the dairy aisle, or is he wondering if I'd hacked the presidential election or got hitched for a visa? Does speaking a strange language in public drive a wedge of mistrust between people?

Actually, more than half of the world is bilingual.[2] There are more than seven thousand languages spoken today, with the most common ones being English and Mandarin Chinese, followed by Hindi, Spanish, French, Arabic, Bengali, and Russian, according to *Ethnologue*, a catalogue of living world languages.[3] Globally, bilingualism is the norm rather than the exception.

What makes someone bilingual, though? Is it the ability to read the menu? To understand the grandparents? To ace a standardized school test? What if the language has no writing system? And who gets the authority to define what bilingualism means, anyway?[4]

As soon as I start to pay attention to the way people around me talk to their kids—and to notice how I talk—I realize that attitudes about bilingualism can be strangely complicated.

For much of the twentieth century, a person's language ability used to be judged by their fluency. American linguist Leonard Bloomfield, for example, defined it in 1933 as native-like control of two languages.[5]

Several decades later, a diplomatic interpreter, Christophe Thiery, proposed a similarly arduous definition. To him, a "true bilingual" was someone who is accepted by each language community as one of their own, has learned the languages before the age of fourteen, has no accent in either, and doesn't let one get in the way of the other when interacting with monolingual people.[6]

Even reading this description might make some people flinch, because honestly, how many of us can speak all of our languages without an accent, write without an error, and "pass" in either culture as one of its sons or daughters? After returning to visit St. Petersburg as an adult, cabbies and museum ticket sellers charged me up to fourfold compared to the locals whenever they heard me speak.

In recent decades, researchers have steered away from defining bilinguals as those with impeccable fluency and grammar and began looking at how they communicate with others.[7] A perfectly balanced bilingual, or two monolinguals rolled into one, is a myth. "The majority of bilinguals simply do not resemble these rare individuals," writes influential contemporary psycholinguist François Grosjean in his book *Bilingual: Life and Reality*.[8]

Many people still fall into the trap of perfection, though. When it comes to assessing our own language skills and those of our children, we can get a little bit judgey.

"Bilinguals themselves rarely evaluate their language competencies as adequate," Grosjean writes. "They complain that they don't speak one of their languages well, that they have an accent, that they mix their languages. . . . Some even hide their knowledge of their weaker language. All this is unfortunate," he concludes. Instead, Grosjean defines bilingual people as "those who use two or more languages (or dialects) in their everyday lives."[9]

It's hard to talk about bilingualism without also briefly looking at its history in the United States, which I'll get to in a moment. That's because language does not exist in a vacuum. It is a living thing, influenced by culture, politics, and attitudes.

"Language is political!" declares one linguist that I speak to as I start my research. I am beginning to see why.

. . .

The United States, many people are surprised to find out, does not have an official language. But it isn't for lack of lawmakers trying to establish it, even though the majority of Americans speak only English.[10]

In colonial times and into the early twentieth century, schools were frequently bilingual, from Dutch and German to Spanish and Polish.[11] Linguistic diversity was often the norm, with a range of newspapers and religious services in different languages serving the multilingual population.[12] There were stark exceptions, of course. Native American children were forced to speak English at boarding schools and punished for using their indigenous languages;[13] enslaved African people, too, were forced to give up their languages and speak only English.[14]

Then, during World War I, anti-German sentiment swept across America, shaking up attitudes about bilingualism. As many as twenty-three states banned foreign language education in American schools.[15]

Iowa governor William L. Harding took it a step further and outlawed all public use of all foreign languages in Iowa, in what's known as the Babel Proclamation. Only English would now be legal in schools, in public conversations, on trains, on the phone, and during religious services, he decreed in 1918.[16] German language instructors were fired and textbooks burned; German newspapers disappeared.[17]

Former president Theodore Roosevelt supported this sentiment. "We have room for but one language here, and that is the English language; for we intend to see that the crucible turns our people out as Americans, and not as dwellers in a polyglot boarding-house," Roosevelt wrote.[18] To him, dual language meant divided loyalties. "There is no place here for the hyphenated American," he remarked in a speech in 1915, "and the sooner he returns to the country of his allegiance, the better."[19]

With World War I raging, anti-German bias snuck into fermented foods too. Sauerkraut consumption in America plunged by 75 percent, and vegetable dealers suggested renaming it "liberty cabbage" (not unlike french fries turning into "freedom fries" in the United States when France refused to support the 2003 Iraq invasion).[20]

This was, understandably, a rough time for bilingualism. Some called it a "social plague."[21] An influential educational researcher even suggested in 1926 that speaking a foreign language at home caused "mental retardation as measured by intelligence tests."[22] These attitudes went hand in hand with the anti-immigrant sentiment touched on in the beginning of this book.

Researchers kept conjecturing that bilingual children had a language handicap. Their study methodologies, however, were a mess.[23]

Finally, in 1962, Canadian researchers published a groundbreaking study of French- and English-speaking children, showing their superior mental flexibility and verbal intelligence on tests. "Bilingual education would not create a social or cognitive Frankenstein," is how linguists would later describe this discovery.[24]

Other researchers began to see these benefits too.

Does this mean bilingualism is finally considered normal? Nope, not really.

Knowing a foreign language is widely accepted as a symbol of worldliness and erudition. "My father spoke five languages!" some people reminisce. Or "I'm sending my child to a Mandarin immersion preschool to give her a leg up in the global economy." Or "It's wonderful that you are teaching your children a foreign tongue. I wish I could read Don Quixote the way it was *meant* to be read."

At the end of the day, though, these views depend on which language someone knows and how that person came about learning it. Many foreign language speakers often find themselves marginalized, particularly if they are immigrants or nonwhite or both.

In the United States, monolingualism is usually seen as the norm and bilingualism as an unstable condition, even a problem, unlike in many Asian and African countries and smaller European nations with multiple official languages.[25]

That stigma can come from politicians and from everyday folk too.[26] Three in ten Americans say it bugs them to hear foreign languages in public, a 2019 Pew Research Center survey found.[27] (I'm fairly certain, though, that some of those beleaguered respondents were also foreign born; they just had a bone to pick with other immigrant groups.)

The way we talk is one of the most obvious markers of identity. It's easy to pathologize. Bilingual education keeps stirring up controversy, and our news feeds are abuzz with stories like the one about a New York lawyer threatening to report restaurant workers to ICE for speaking Spanish.[28]

But foreign languages are intimately tied to the identity of this country. Today, one in four children in America has at least one foreign-born parent, a 50 percent increase from just a couple of decades earlier.[29] One out of five people in America now speaks a language other than English at home.[30]

So yes, multilingual families are on the rise, and so are our living, breathing languages.

■   ■   ■

As I chat with other families, scroll through social media and, heck, talk to the people inside my own home, one thing is clear: passing down a heritage language takes work. Like an Olympic sport type of work, but with no formal competition or gold at the end; just moody little athletes slogging through the mud, and whining, "Ugh, do we *have* to?"

Amandine, who moved from France to the United States with two small children and an English-speaking husband, also fought the good fight.

She spoke French with her children when they were little. But then her daughter headed to an American daycare. "She quickly realized everybody around her was speaking English just like Daddy, and Mommy is speaking English with Daddy, so why should she be speaking French?" Amandine reflects. "She started to ask my husband to read to her in the evening rather than me, because she didn't want to hear it in French."

For a while, her daughter did study French as an elective. But only until middle school. Then she switched to Spanish, "just because she was contradictory," explains Amandine, and because she was self-conscious about her American accent.

So why, I occasionally ask myself, do we even bother?

There's an extraordinary number of reasons. Knowing another language helps us see the world beyond the immediate field of vision.

It can be a perk in the job market.

Bilingualism makes people better communicators. Even mere exposure to a multilingual environment can boost social communication skills and teach children to see things from a different perspective.[31] In one study from the University of Chicago, children were asked to move objects like toy cars to different locations, taking into account the point of view of the adult in the room. The bilingual kids and kids from multilingual environments moved the correct cars more than 75 percent of the time, while monolingual ones got it right only half the time.[32]

Bilinguals constantly monitor for clues in social situations to figure out what language to use with others. This makes them more socially aware, research suggests.[33]

Speakers of two or more languages are said to be more creative thinkers.[34] Studies have also shown that bilingual children have better-developed metalinguistic awareness (the ability to think about words and language as abstract things). This may help them learn to read earlier.[35] Plus, being bilingual in childhood makes picking up another language easier.[36]

And let's admit it, it is also a nifty invisibility cloak in public once in a while. "Sometimes we speak the other language intentionally, so that they don't know what we're saying!" jokes Christine from Utah about speaking Spanish with her husband, Miguel.

Yet a huge advantage of bilingualism is cognitive. It's a workout for the brain, helping with focusing and multitasking.

I decide to speak to Professor Ellen Bialystok, a renowned cognitive neuroscientist at York University in Toronto.[37]

Bialystok has spent over forty years researching bilingualism, earning the title of the Officer of the Order of Canada, one of the nation's highest honors, for her discoveries. She first got involved in the field in late 1970s, at a time when the cognitive benefits of bilingualism were already known but the specifics weren't clear. It was an exciting new area of research. Psychologists and parents were wondering what it meant for children and whether those benefits persisted into adulthood. Bialystok arrived at a few groundbreaking conclusions.

One is that bilingualism can delay the symptoms and diagnosis of dementia, such as Alzheimer's disease, in older bilingual adults by four to five years.[38] Switching between languages stimulates the brain and builds up cognitive reserve. Although bilingualism doesn't stop Alzheimer's in its tracks, it empowers the brain with better coping skills and gives the attention networks more resiliency, protecting against neurodegeneration.

In another famous study, Bialystok and her colleagues showed that bilingual children are better at focusing, multitasking, and weeding out unnecessary information, skills collectively known as executive function[39] (although some have debated these findings[40]). These cognitive processes "are the most energy-expensive processes we have," says Bialystok. In this study, children were asked to say whether certain sentences were grammatically correct or not. But there was a twist. Those sentences were illogical, like "Apples grow on noses."

"We said, just tell us if this sentence is said the right way or the wrong way. That's all we want to know," says Bialystok. "We don't care if the sentence is silly—it's fun to be silly."

All kids thought the sentences were hilarious. Their answers differed, though. The monolingual youngsters stated that the sentence was said the wrong way. But the bilingual ones said the sentence was said the right way. They all understood grammar equally, but their ability to focus on the task and tune out the irrelevant information wasn't the same.

"What we realized is that the bilingual kids could do that, and the monolingual kids could not," Bialystok tells me. "That's now been demonstrated many times. But we introduced distraction that they had to ignore. You have to ignore this silly meaning. And in order to ignore something that salient and really hitting you in the face, you need executive functioning."

In the bilingual brain, both languages are active at the same time, forcing the speaker to constantly control which one to use and which one to suppress.

"That's a crazy way to build a brain. A smart thing would be to put in a switch, so you flip it. But that's not how the bilingual brain is organized," Bialystok explains. "Bilinguals are always having to solve a problem of attending to the language they need to be using right now and not getting distracted by that other language, which is, unfortunately, also active," she says.[41]

Bialystok's team went on to test children on other tasks and kept concluding that bilinguals had better executive function.

Her more recent study, conducted with colleagues and published in 2019, revealed benefits even among tiny participants: babies as young as six months of age. Infants were shown pictures in different parts of the screen above their cribs and their eye movements were tracked. If the babies could learn to predict where the image would appear next, they'd be "rewarded."

"A silly dancing star is going to appear on the left side—they like it a lot, so they want to see this silly dancing star," Bialystok tells me.

Turns out the infants who heard two languages at home were better at learning these rules. They had better attentional control than babies from monolingual households.[42]

"What bilingualism is really doing is it's shaping up the attention system to be more selective, more responsive, and to be better at picking up important information in the first year of life," Bialystok explains.

These executive function skills predict long-term academic success and well-being, she adds. "There's just nothing more important in terms of how this person is going to do in life."

Bialystok does caution that bilingualism is not a magic bullet. "The kinds of outrageous claims I've read, you know, bilinguals are taller, prettier, nicer, kinder—come on, it's all rubbish," Bialystok says. "They're none of those things. They just have better executive functioning."

Besides, people don't study languages to be smarter.

"You learn a foreign language because it's going to make you more knowledgeable, it's going to give you a better perspective," she says. "People who speak more than one language can see things in more than one way. It's going to make you a more sympathetic person, because if you learn a language, you learn about other people who speak that language."

. . .

Those are all excellent reasons to teach a child a foreign language. But for immigrants, they don't tell the whole story. Sometimes, those reasons are immeasurable.

"It melts my heart when my son speaks my language with me," a friend says.

For Paula, a Colombian-born writer and a mother of an eight-year-old girl, Spanish is a link to family. "I just couldn't imagine my child going [to Colombia] and not being able to communicate with my relatives," says Paula, who lives in Houston. "I never thought of cognitive advantages or, you know, advantages in the workforce."

Paula and her friend Monika, born in Puerto Rico, even cofounded a popular podcast about raising bilingual kids, called *Entre Dos*, which they host together.[43] Both women have proudly kept the Spanish pronunciation of their names, not anglicizing them. Monika pronounces hers as MOH-nee-kah and Paula is PAH-oo-lah, with rounded vowels.

To Monika, Spanish is like a warm *croqueta*. (Aptly, this is also the title of one of their first podcast episodes.)[44]

"I feel very emotional when I think about the possibility that I might not be successful in passing on my language," Monika tells me. She doesn't want her young daughter to sense this worry, "because, oh my God, what a burden! You wonder if that's right or wrong, but immediately, you feel protective, like you want to build a little bubble where you can keep them there."

. . .

Teaching the family language to my kids is a link to something bigger than words. It isn't a sweater one can just peel off on a warm day.

Its cadence is in our DNA and the conversations waiting to happen, the words of affection and the untranslatable humor. It's in my grandmother's wrinkled fingers, mincing onions to the tune of a folk song like they have a thousand times before. It's the muscle memory forming the familiar vowels, like in that dream where you soar above a city and recognize every brick, every clothesline, so vivid you can swoop down and almost touch them. Almost.

6. BILINGUALISM: AN UPHILL BATTLE, SOMETIMES

If you talk to a man in a language he understands, that goes to his head. If you talk to him in his language, that goes to his heart.

—NELSON MANDELA[1]

MY FRIEND MITALI came to the United States as a young adult after getting married in India. Ever since her kids were little, she's been lamenting the difficulty of getting them to speak Hindi.

In their Seattle home, the family listens to music in Hindi and watches movies in Hindi. She and her husband interact in English when discussing work, then switch to Hindi for topics like the household. After Mitali's maternity leave ended, she enrolled her son in an American daycare. Later, the younger one was entrusted to the care of an American nanny. English has been the name of the game for her children ever since, she says.

Back then, as a brand-new parent, I had a hard time wrapping my mind around this issue. I figured that since (a) Mitali's Indian, (b) Mitali's husband is Indian, and (c) their children live right there, in the same house, wouldn't they talk in Hindi by default? It's just math, right?

Wrong.

"Have you maybe tried *asking* them to speak it?" I offered, naively and gratuitously, as we were crossing a busy street in the Nob Hill neighborhood of San Francisco after work. Mitali, a fierce go-getter who's won professional accolades, stalled in the middle of the intersection. "Um, yeah," she mumbled, then promptly changed the subject. I got the point and didn't bring it up again.

A couple of years later, bilingualism comes up when we talk. Hindi is still an uphill battle in Mitali's household.

"My older son was not talking for a long time, and people said, try introducing just one language at one time. And he just never picked it up," Mitali shares on the phone disappointedly, as she drives to pick up her youngest child from preschool. "We let it go, and now I feel bad about it. We still try, and he is still so reluctant." (The idea of children being confused by multiple languages is a common but unfortunate myth, discussed in chapter 10 in more detail.)

Their conversation style is all too familiar. The parents address the kids in their mother tongue. The kids respond in theirs: English.

But Mitali will take whatever wins she can get. The other day, for example, she and her husband were discussing the boss in Hindi. "And then my son said, 'But why are you talking about him like that?' We think they're not understanding something, but they understand everything!" she tells me with hope in her voice.

. . .

Like in Mitali's case, many children of immigrants aren't as fluent in their heritage language as their parents had assumed they'd be. Or it may roll along smoothly for a while, with the little ones stringing together adorably authentic sentences to the effect of "May I please have another crêpe, Mommy?" But with time, it may become "But *Mom*! I want another *PANCAKE*!" in English. Le sigh.

The grownups are having all sorts of feelings about this, from surprise to frustration to guilt, as if parents need more things to feel guilty about. And I get it, because I'm finding myself in a similar situation.

After I enroll Leah in an American daycare and go back to work full time, her Russian starts to dissipate. I try bribes, from sweets to TV, but to no avail. My toddler won't speak it.

"*Okno*," I say cheerfully and point to her nursery window.

"Window," she says back.

"*Okno*. See, right there!" I point again, trying to muster the exuberance of someone who'd just seen a flock of winged unicorns fly by. Maybe Leah just didn't notice the window the first time. "The thing with the curtains. You are such a smart girl—you know what window's called in Russian."

Leah considers this.

"Window."

"That's right! In English, it *is* window!" I press on with an enthusiastic smile. "But what is window in Russian?"

"Window."

Fine. Window it is.

We sit down to read, and Leah hands me *Goldilocks and the Three Bears* in Russian. "Can you read me a bear book?" she says.

"You mean, *mishka* book?" I coax.

"Bear," she says.

"It's *mishka* in Russian, remember? *Meee-shkaaaah*." I try to roar like a bear, which takes her by surprise.

"Bear."

"*Mishka*. I'll give you candy."

"Bear. Daddy say bear."

For a moment, I almost forget I'm reasoning with a pigtailed toddler, my own flesh and blood, and not a parking citation judge.

"Please, sweetie, why won't you say *mishka*?" I implore. "And we'll read it, like, a hundred times!"

"*Mishka*," she finally says, quietly.

I can barely fight back tears. These interactions feel inauthentic, even cruel. Being away from home eleven, sometimes twelve, hours a day, I miss her so much when I'm at work. I begin to question the value of cramming language education into the minutes we have together during the workday.

. . .

How did something as basic as a discourse between a parent and a child get so thorny? You'd think maintaining a sourdough bread starter or using artificial intelligence to irrigate crops would be more complicated. But, turns out, passing down one's native language is not far behind. Talk to just about any immigrant family, and you'll hear gut-wrenching stories about somebody's grandpa, the war hero or the master craftsman of his village, who now sits alone in an armchair at family holidays, unable to communicate with his grandchildren.

As I read about immigrant languages, I stumble on a cautionary tale about a boy named Kai-fong whose Chinese family moved to the San

Francisco Bay Area in 1989, when he was five years old. Kai-fong, the story goes, got teased by classmates for his funny haircut and home-made clothes, such as pants with a floral pattern. Later, he made friends, with whom he spoke in English, and began spending less time at home, writes linguist Lily Wong Fillmore in her influential article "Loss of Family Languages: Should Educators Be Concerned?" He started wearing jeans and T-shirts and calling himself Ken. He also stopped speaking Cantonese. The more Kai-fong's family scolded him for be-ing withdrawn, the more withdrawn he became. Eventually, Kai-fong could no longer communicate with his monolingual grandmother, who used to cut his hair and sew his clothes.[2]

I also come across a case study about a boy who got whisked off to India by his parents in the 1950s and started talking like the lo-cals. Robbins Burling, an anthropologist, describes how quickly his sixteen-month-old son picked up the Garo language. By three, the boy was bilingual with the help of his Garo nanny; he even spoke Garo in his sleep. Sounds easy peasy, right? But no, there's no happy ending to this tale. Just months after the family returned to the United States and the boy no longer heard Garo around him, he began forgetting the language, even such basics as names for body parts.[3]

■ ■ ■

These stories hit home. The more I learn about language acquisition, the more I realize that immigrant tongues are remarkably fragile. So fragile, in fact, that a famous linguist, Einar Haugen, described Amer-ica as "a modern Babel, but a Babel in reverse."[4]

It takes just two generations for the native language to disappear. First-generation immigrants, the ones born abroad, speak it fluently. Their children are generally bilingual and use that language at home. Their grandchildren, for the most part, don't speak it at all.[5]

Today's immigrants are picking up English as quickly or faster than the Europeans arriving in the early twentieth century. They are also losing their mother tongues at the same rate as their predecessors, shows a study by the National Academies of Sciences, Engineering, and Medicine.[6]

Erika Hoff, a developmental psychologist and professor at Florida Atlantic University, says children can lose the heritage language even if they live in areas with large immigrant communities, such as in South Florida.

"On average, the children's English skills are stronger than their Spanish skills, even if they hear both languages in equal amounts at home. The older they get, the closer their English skills come to their Spanish skills, and Spanish skills tend to drop off," says Hoff, who directs the university's Language Development Lab and is an associate editor of *The Journal of Experimental Child Psychology*.[7] She's written and edited multiple books about bilingualism.

Hoff has observed this trend even with toddlers from bilingual households. Many are "English dominant from as early as I've tested them, which is twenty-two months," she tells me. "It is certainly true that English skills develop faster than Spanish skills, given equal input at home."

This isn't an outcome one might expect. It flies in the face of the narrative about the language of Shakespeare teetering on the brink of extinction.

"This is very surprising to monolingual speakers," Hoff points out. "But actually, the children's Spanish skills are the skills that are really at risk."

Then why do I keep hearing all those other languages in public?, skeptics might wonder. Foreign speech doesn't mean the speakers are immigrants; that's why. They could be born here and using the family language to communicate with relatives.

"Their accent may sound great, but they do not have the language skills of an adult native Spanish speaker," says Hoff, referencing her study of second-generation immigrants raised in bilingual homes.[8]

My friend Irina, a technology consultant in the San Francisco Bay Area, did everything in her power to teach Russian to her six-year-old daughter Simone. She knew that if she didn't, nobody else would. All her relatives are back in Russia. The girl's father, an immigrant from Nigeria, speaks Ebu.

"It's weird for me to speak English to her," says Irina, even though she's lived in this country for over twenty years. "I convey my emotions better and feel more comfortable speaking Russian."

I recognize the nesting-doll magnets on the fridge; on a shelf above the doorway is a decorative *samovar* for boiling water for tea. She shows me Simone's "About Me" collage she'd put together for school. It's got Nigerian and Russian flags and drawings of a beach and an onion-domed church. Photos of her Nigerian grandmother and the European family are affixed to the poster board, side by side.

From the get-go, Irina spoke with Simone in her native language and hired a Russian-speaking nanny. "They were constantly talking, like nonstop," Irina tells me as we chat at her kitchen table.

Then the Guatemalan nanny replaced the Russian-speaking nanny, and Simone headed off to kindergarten. Irina decided to put heritage-language reading on hold to help Simone fortify her English literacy.

"In kindergarten, it's important to be successful. I felt it's important to build that confidence," she says. Simone was soon reading English chapter books by herself.

But to her dismay, Irina discovered that the girl responded in Russian less and less.

"I saw how the environment affects the language. In a month, I'm like, oh my God, she's not talking! She never rebelled, like *Mama, I don't want to speak Russian anymore*. I think it just happened naturally, because it is my fault. I started pushing reading," Irina says with regret and glances at her daughter, who is studiously practicing "Jingle Bells" with a Russian piano teacher in the living room. "You don't want to nag, right?"

There aren't many babysitters from her homeland in the area. "I have to work; I need to have a babysitter. I tried, I tried, and then I gave up." But when Irina's home, they're back to reading in Russian together. "We sit down and look at the picture, and I say, tell me in Russian what you see, even if it's two or three sentences."

From the living room, I hear Simone playing the festive *Nutcracker* melody. "Good!" her music teacher exclaims. "*Molodez!*"

. . .

Native language retention is also a concern for cognitive neuroscientist Ellen Bialystok. "In the US, the primary imperative of immigrants is to become American," she tells me during our interview. "They drop their heritage language, and when that happens, you drop your culture. Children can't speak to their grandparents; people lose interest in where they came from. . . . I think this notion of turning people as quickly as possible into monolingual speakers of English does a great disservice to immigrants," says Bialystok.

.   .   .

The possibility of our languages disappearing can be uncomfortable, even tragic. Sometimes even first generation immigrants also feel like their native tongue is slipping away. If you don't use it regularly and then stall when looking for the right word or get frustrated about your less-than-sophisticated vocabulary, you're not alone, research suggests.

Even the prolific bilingual novelist and translator Vladimir Nabokov fretted about this. In the afterword to his English-language novel *Lolita*, he lamented, "I had to abandon my natural idiom, my untrammeled, rich, and infinitely docile Russian tongue for a second-rate brand of English."[9]

Yet, translating *Lolita* into Russian a few years later, Nabokov felt that it was his native tongue that's gotten rusty. "The story of this translation is a story of disappointment," he wrote. He'd expected to find Russian waiting for him, "blossoming like a faithful spring," and yet, "there was nothing beyond those gates but smoldering stumps."[10] (His readers would surely beg to differ.)

There is, however, good news about forgetting the mother tongue, known as attrition. It can generally be reversed if the person spoke it fluently until puberty, or roughly the age of twelve, according to Monika Schmid, linguistics professor at the University of Essex in England and a leading researcher in native language loss. There isn't a lot of information available about how it long it takes to get the language chops back, but probably "a few weeks at most," when immersed in a native environment, Schmid tells me.[11]

It's different for kids. "Children can forget it entirely if they no longer use it, and then later on have little advantage over people who try to learn that language with no prior experience," says Schmid.[12]

Why does language attrition affect children and adults differently? There are two theories. "One possible explanation is that longer experience with a language leads to stronger 'entrenchment' of the skill, and that after a certain point, it makes it stable," Schmid explains. There's also a theory of a "critical period" in language learning, where "the language knowledge 'crystallizes' in the brain around puberty," Schmid says.

Emotional trauma can make people forget their mother tongue too. Schmid studied the German skills of older Jewish wartime refugees from Germany in the UK and the US.[13] Their age upon leaving and the length of time spent abroad weren't the deciding factors. Emotional trauma was. Those who left Germany in the early days of the Nazi regime generally spoke better German, but those who had fled after the violent Kristallnacht pogrom of 1938 spoke it with difficulty or not at all.

■　■　■

Language loss makes me think about my own ancestors, who once spoke Yiddish. For generations, the Russian Empire segregated its Jewish population to only specific areas. Many dwelled in poverty as a result of restrictions in education, trade, and residence. Then, as German troops advanced during World War I, the Jewish residents fled to Russia's interior, and in 1917, Russia's provisional government struck down the segregationist laws altogether. In the years following, many moved to Russia's major cities and adopted its tongue. My ancestors had witnessed the outlawing of Yiddish schools, the Holocaust, and Stalin's purges. In the end, most were left with but a handful of choice Yiddish expressions. The rest had been forgotten.[14]

■　■　■

For some people I talk to, native language is tied to divergent politics and painful memories.

After Amira immigrated to the Detroit area from Iraq as a young child, English at home wasn't just discouraged. It was forbidden.

"If my father would ask us a question in Arabic, the expectation would be that we would respond in Arabic," she says. It wasn't always easy on her and her siblings. They just wanted to practice their English and share what they learned in school. But whenever they'd let the outside language slip into conversation, their father made them repeat it in Arabic, even though he knew English well.

"When you step out of these doors, you will speak English with your friends, and you will speak English at school, and your career will be based in English. Who's going to speak Arabic to you, if you don't learn it here at home?" her father chastised them. "Here, in this home, you'll speak Arabic."

Looking back, Amira is grateful. "In hindsight, I praise him," she says, "because that's why I speak Arabic as well as I do; it's why I speak Chaldean as well as do."

Things turned out differently with Amira's own children. When the time came to return to work, she had a decision to make. Have the grandparents watch the kids, exposing them to the language and the beliefs, or enroll them in an American preschool?

"I try to embrace the good qualities of my culture—the emphasis on family, the importance of community, the importance of elders," Amira points out. But some values rubbed her the wrong way.

Growing up, Amira was not permitted to date, use makeup, and talk to boys. Going away to college was out of the question. Those rules didn't apply to the young men around her in the same way. "Parents say boys are not allowed to date, but it wouldn't upset them if they did," she says, yet "it is perceived as disrespectful and almost tarnishing of the family's name and image if the girl dates too many people."

She also disliked having separate seating arrangements for men and women during social occasions, and the gender-based order of partaking in meals.

"There are lots of practices in the Middle Eastern culture, like men eat first in households. You always allow the elder men to dine together, then all the men, then women," says Amira. "Had I not endured some of the double standards, I wouldn't be as progressive and forward-thinking that I am as a woman. I promised myself that if I had daughters, then I would raise them very differently."

So when Amira rejoined the workforce, she chose the American preschool.

Now Amira gets to teach her daughters the values she holds dear. "I say, you might see these practices, but it's not something that's acceptable in our home, and I don't want you to be alarmed. I want you to respect the difference, but it's not something I would want [you] to adopt."

The girls visit with the grandparents often. The whole family cherishes those moments. They play cards and backgammon and cook together, like traditional hand pies and homemade cheese with chives and garlic.

But the American preschool came at a cost. Yes, they picked up the Western norms, but also the language. As time went on, her father's no-English rule was hard to enforce in her own busy household.

Now Amira's children can understand the family languages but do not speak them fluently. "That's something I'll always regret," she admits.

Not all is lost, though. Multiple studies show that even if a child has passive knowledge of a language (if she understands and maybe reads it), these passive reserves can become active again. It just takes some major ramping up of the exposure to this language and the necessity to speak it.[15]

In pursuing bilingualism, sometimes, the parents burn out. Other times, the children burn out. In any case, many households alternate between phases of high interventionism and laissez-faire, then let the language chips fall where they may.

"I have friends that are 'Russian at any cost,'" says my friend Natasha, a mother of two, who immigrated to California as a young adult. "And I feel resentful and maybe acknowledge my personal failure, but I realized I didn't want to do that."

"You have to go certain lengths," weighs in her husband, Trevor, whose immigrant parents speak Cantonese. The couple's friends send their kids to Russia for three months in the summer, he says, and this helps their fluency. "I believe immersion really does do that. When I went to Hong Kong, my Chinese got better."

"That's three months of a childhood gone!" Natasha adds, not buying it. "We do not see being away from them more than ten days."

Their son's Russian tapered off after their contract with a Russian-speaking nanny ended and he started attending an American preschool, Trevor says. So they enrolled the boy in weekend language classes in a nearby town. "He kept saying, 'I don't like it, I don't understand what they're saying," Trevor recalls. "I said, I don't want to push him."

The boy recently became interested in the language and the books again, says Natasha. "He's looking at the pictures and saying, 'I want to know what's going on.'"

The couple is also trying to fit Cantonese in. The grandparents have been teaching the kids the Cantonese version of rock, paper, scissors. I hear giggling from the dining room. Their children must have overheard us, because they're emphatically calling out Cantonese words and making hand gestures.

"See?" Natasha tells me. "They're playing it now."

The earlier immigrant generations, in particular, weren't always keen on passing their mother tongue on to their progeny for fear of being seen as "low brow" or unassimilable. Many choose a clean slate in the new land—not just for themselves but also for the next generation.

Jasmine, a daughter of immigrants who left Iran after the 1979 revolution, didn't learn to speak Persian fluently at home, she tells me. "I think it was a combination of my parents' strained relationship and the fact that my dad always wanted us to assimilate to US culture fully," she speculates. She sees it as a missed opportunity. Jasmine is now trying to teach the language to her child, but it's hard to teach what she doesn't know.

. . .

There's also Julie, a second-generation Korean American, who was raised by a single mother. An immigrant from Korea, her mom was too overwhelmed with the day-to-day responsibilities to worry about language preservation. Instead, she spoke to her kids in English and tried to get better at it. They would correct her English mistakes sometimes.

As an adult, Julie, a nurse practitioner, has visited South Korea and is close to her cousins there. "But," she says, "there have been other times when I've felt excluded and been seen as a white person. It's complicated."

Now, as a mother of two, Julie is teaching her children basic vocabulary. She signed them up for tae kwon do and enrolled her kindergartner in an online Korean class, which morphed into an exciting epiphany. Turned out she remembered more Korean than she'd realized. "He didn't get into it," she tells me, "but I did."

. . .

Similarly, Casey, a technology consultant and personal coach, was born in the United States soon after her parents arrived from the Philippines.

She understands Tagalog, Bisaya, and Surigaonon, the languages of the Philippines, but cannot speak any of them. "I would never be able to insert myself in the conversation. It's almost like being mute," she says, with disappointment. "I wish I'd learned, definitely, 100 percent."

It started like this. One day, while playing with her cousin, little Casey strung together a sentence blending all three native languages into one. Her parents were mortified. They didn't want their daughter to be confused and began addressing Casey in English from then on. They also wanted to ensure she didn't have a foreign accent, like they did.

After becoming a mom, Casey asked her family to talk to her two sons in Tagalog or Surigaonon. They do it briefly, then switch to English.

Resolved to become fluent in the language of her ancestors, she downloaded a Tagalog phone app prior to a recent trip to the Philippines. Dutifully, she spent twenty minutes a day, every day, studying and doing vocabulary drills. But upon arrival, she felt awkward about her proficiency. "I just reverted right back to English," she remembers.

At least, Casey jokes, "I know when they're talking crap about me," like at a recent family event. "I was like, oh, they're talking about [my cousin and me]."

"What were they saying about you?" I ask.

"They were saying something about our politics." She rolls her eyes. "How they disagree."

Can we talk about English for a moment here? English isn't just dominant in America but globally, with well over a billion speakers, though most are nonnative ones.[16] On top of being a colonizing language, English has taken over as the tongue of the internet and mass media. It's taught in schools all over the world, used as a lingua franca in business, science, and diplomacy, and romanticized as the golden ticket to success.[17] It's clear that English is practical.

Anindita, an environmental health scientist, came to Chicago from India as a postdoctoral scholar with her husband and baby daughter. Native Bengali is not a huge priority for her.

"Instead of imposing a particular language on her just because it's our mother language or just because she's born to us, we would want her to be free to choose," says Anindita about her five-year-old.

Like a trusted friend, English has been there for Anindita most of her life. She and her husband have studied, worked, and attended conferences around the world, from China and Dubai to West Africa and Brazil, and operated in English through all of these experiences.

When she was growing up in India, Anindita's parents enrolled her in an English-language school to empower her with communication tools, there and abroad, says Anindita, who also knows Hindi. "They had faced problems because they got educated in institutions which taught them in their vernacular, Bengali. They didn't want us to face the same difficulties." Her parents have never been outside India themselves.

Anindita's daughter has been hearing English at home and in daycare since she was little, and the couple is fine with it. It feels natural. "To me and my husband, language is just a medium to communicate," says Anindita. "She is growing up in a country where almost everyone around her is speaking in English. Let her grow up as a free soul and embrace the language, the culture she wants to embrace."

■   ■   ■

Meanwhile, my two-year-old keeps resisting saying Russian words. I try to be serious and I try to be fun, deploying games and snacks. I even get her a toy pony, who, I assure her, understands only Russian, but to no avail.

Eventually, with a heavy heart, I abandon these efforts. I'd rather cut the losses than watch her grow up resenting the language.

I decide to meet her where she's at, because the opposite would mean not meeting her at all. "I love you no matter what language you speak," I assure Leah. Aren't I just trying to stave off the inevitable, anyway?

The ambient noise of the language keeps on humming in the background, at home and socially. But I no longer ask her to say what she doesn't want to say. She chooses the language of her books, entertainment, and conversations. I follow along, trying not to hover or emote about her choices.

Besides, I've got an inkling it's not over yet.

7. STANDING WATCH

*All day her decks had been colorful, a matrix of
the vivid costumes of other lands, the speckled
green-and-yellow aprons, the flowered kerchief,
embroidered homespun, the silver-braided sheepskin
vest, the gaudy scarfs, yellow boots, fur caps, caftans,
dull gabardines.*

—HENRY ROTH[1]

FROM THE PORCH of a white multistory building with golden domes, I hear the sound of chanting and the rhythmic clapping inside. There are two flags at the base of the stairs: American and Ethiopian. I cover my hair, remove my shoes, and open the door.

I'm inside an Ethiopian Orthodox Tewahedo church just outside New York City. I'm not here for Sunday services but to observe an Amharic language class for the children of the local Ethiopian diaspora.

Ever since setting out on my bilingualism journey, I keep being confronted by a stark reality: a living language is more than words and sentences strung together. It is intimately tied to what its speakers believe, how they worship, how they're treated. And now, walking down the church corridor past the full sanctuary, I remember that language is also intertwined with what people eat. The aroma of Ethiopian *berbere*—a heady blend of paprika, cardamom, ginger, fenugreek, and other spices, both sweet and hot, fills the hallway. The ebullient fragrance gets stronger as I walk downstairs, practicing Amharic greetings in my head and looking for my contact, Zewditu.

The church's dining hall, bedecked with balloons, feels a world apart from the wintry New York suburb just outside these walls. Women scuttle around the room setting up hot food trays for the churchgoers who are about to come downstairs after services. There are the traditional Doro Wat chicken stew, homemade cheese, sautéed greens, fresh salad, and more next to the towering platter of spongy flatbread, *injera*. The women's hair is covered with delicate white scarves, the embroidery matching their festive dresses. Nearly everyone is speaking Amharic, an ancient Semitic language.

The parishioners and their young trickle in for lunch, greeting one another with three kisses on the cheek and firm handshakes. The long tables at the dining hall are abuzz with conversation.

I finally spot Zewditu. I'm overjoyed to finally meet her in person after communicating for months by phone and email. She insists I sit down and join her for lunch before we head to class.

Zewditu, who has five children and four grandchildren of her own, emigrated from Ethiopia in 1991 toward the end of its violent communist regime. Soon after, she noticed that her kids started losing their Amharic skills. Getting them to speak it was a pain, she tells me as she scoops up the fragrant stew on her plate with pieces of *injera*. So she joined a local church and connected with the community there. She also started teaching Amharic to children and adults and writing her own Amharic instruction books.

"You can't separate culture and language. You must come in and start learning, otherwise it's just daycare," states Zewditu, who takes a holistic approach to language instruction: it's got to be accompanied by reading, writing, and, most important, cultural literacy. She wants the younger generations to know their roots and take pride in them.

"The living standard matters for teaching language; otherwise, you don't understand," she says. Her voice is assured and calm, with a soothing cadence. "Back home, mostly, the people don't have a bathroom. There is no hot water, the way we cook day to day [is] with wood. The kids here, they don't know . . . But if they know the language, then they know the country and how people live there. For those who know their ABCs—it's easy to teach them."

Zewditu also organizes trips to Ethiopia for families. "Egyptians have pyramids, [but we] have so many different structures!" she says. On these trips, she ushers families across Addis Ababa with its historic churches and to the ancient city of Aksum. They see the domesticated hyenas living in the walled city of Harar (the fourth holiest city in Islam). They visit Lalibela, known as the Second Jerusalem by Ethiopia's Christians, with eleven medieval churches carved out of rock.

After lunch, Zewditu and I head to the upstairs floor with classrooms, past the dozens of parishioners engaged in jubilant conversation.

The students in the classroom get up from their desks to greet Zewditu as she walks in, a traditional show of respect. The teacher, whom the kids call Teacher Tadesse, is instructing in Amharic.

He writes a sentence on the whiteboard and asks for a volunteer to fill in a missing word, holding out a marker.

"Who's going first?" queries one girl.

"Not me," her neighbor objects.

"Not me—*you're* going first!"

"She! Her!" the girl points at another classmate.

Someone finally answers, but in English. The teacher asks her to repeat it in Amharic.

"Oh!" she corrects herself.

There's murmuring in the room.

Zewditu speaks up. "Don't talk to another student," she admonishes with the authority of a seasoned instructor. "Focus and follow his direction." She then delivers the same message in Amharic, I presume, because the room is now still and the students are staring down at their notebooks.

"Make a sentence," teacher Tadesse says. "Make a complete sentence." A student walks up to the whiteboard, consults the alphabet poster on the wall, and tentatively writes a phrase with curlicued characters.

"*Govez!*" the teacher Tadesse exclaims, pleased. [This means "smart" or "good job" in Amharic.]

Sometimes the students are reluctant to learn, teacher Tadesse explains to me after class. We're Americans, they say. Why do we need this? His response is always the same: you must know where you came from.

"Plus, the more languages you speak, you have more advantage, to meet your family, your relatives, to go somewhere to visit," he says. "One day you'll need it, so I explain to them. All immigrants know their languages. I advise all kids and the parents: start from their language because they'll have more attachment with their origins. That's the reason."

Most kids in these classes are American born, attending local public schools.

Teacher Tadesse arrived from Ethiopia in the 1990s. After settling in America, he returned and married the girl he'd known since childhood, from his old neighborhood. The couple now has three kids. He drives a cab in New York City during the week and volunteers at the church every Sunday.

A few years ago, the old language instructor at the church moved away, leaving a teaching void. Teacher Tadesse decided to take matters into his own hands. "One time I went to a Coptic Egyptian Orthodox church—I saw them, how they handle the kids. So I was jealous, like I wish for our kids the same thing," teacher Tadesse says wistfully. At the next church board meeting he recommended reinstating an official language program. The church elders agreed. Now he and two other instructors lead Sunday classes, organized by age and level.

He points to a group of children chatting in the hallway. "Those two are my kids. Yonas, come here!" he calls one of the boys, who is twelve. "This is the oldest one. He is a deacon," he says, proudly. "He serves in the church."

"And that's the second one—Amari!" he motions to the younger boy.

"Did you always speak Amharic well?" I ask Yonas.

"At the beginning, not really," Yonas says, shyly. "I struggled sometimes." But it's gotten easier, especially since he comes every Sunday with his dad, he explains.

"Wherever they go, they use English," adds teacher Tadesse. "Nobody speak. If nobody speak, they lose their interest!"

Not all families make it every weekend, he remarks with displeasure. Some have different priorities; others go back to Ethiopia. "But if the parents bring them here, the kids, they learn. Sometimes I even can't believe—they learn fast!"

A couple of preschoolers on the stairs are tinkering with a cellphone. Even while surrounded by Amharic-speaking adults in the packed church building, they're speaking English to each other. This must be generation two. When they have children of their own, the third generation, I reflect with a pang of sadness, will the mother tongue disappear?

After class, I'm invited to stay longer, to observe a raffle of a Last Supper carving in the dining hall (the carving is said to hail all the way from Jerusalem).

Then, just as unexpectedly, the church dining hall transforms into a postbaptism celebration. A man and his wife, dressed in traditional white garb and holding their infant, stand next to a giant baby-blue cake with a cross designed out of frosting. The congregation around them bursts into song, smiling, ululating, and clapping in unison.

Next comes another cake, for two church members' birthdays. There's more singing and clapping. The room fills with a joyous melody and the congregants huddle together, swaying to the rhythm.

I thank Zewditu in broken Amharic and try to excuse myself, not wanting to impose on these intimate community celebrations. But she and another church lady take hold of my arms and shake their heads disapprovingly. "In my culture, it is forbidden," one of the women says. "You have to eat!"

I know this language.

I stay for the cake.

.   .   .

Everywhere I see heritage language learning taking place, I find more than grammar books. Instead, it's a multidimensional, performative human experience, sustained through relationships, food, and art, through collective trauma and prayer.

Maybe that's why so many flock to language classes housed in arts organizations, places of worship, and ethnic heritage centers all over the country, I reflect on my train ride from the Ethiopian church back to New York City.

Meanwhile, on the other side of the United States, the Arab Cultural and Community Center teaches kids in California to speak Arabic.

Housed in a white brick building in a residential neighborhood, this nonprofit, founded in 1973, draws people from just about every Arab country, from Egypt to Syria and Lebanon, says Tayeb, the center's go-to man and ex officio on the board of directors.[2]

Every Saturday morning, the center opens its doors to Arabic classes for kids as young as three years. Many are children and grandchildren of immigrants. The young learners focus on one letter each week and play games. Sometimes they venture out to a local zoo and the market, where they practice naming animals and vegetables. They learn how to say "cheese and tomato," "big and small," "dark and light," explains Tayeb, who is Palestinian, was born in Syria, and grew up in Saudi Arabia.[3]

One of his proudest moments was seeing an eight-year-old girl read an entire story by herself in class. "Not many adults could read as good as her. It made me so happy that we are succeeding!"

Tayeb himself doesn't teach. "I'm not allowed to be an instructor because I spoil kids," he chuckles, referring to them as "his kids."

But the center offers more than just language classes to the approximately 185,000-person-strong Bay Area Arab community.[4] It has social and cultural events, from networking and the Eid al-Fitr festival marking the end of Ramadan for the Muslims, to tabla drum lessons, domestic violence case management, and culturally sensitive therapy. They are open to all faiths, Tayeb emphasizes.

"I have one parent who was so religious, and he didn't want his daughter to attend our Christmas party, and I had a big issue with him. I said, I'm not going to have to cancel. I'm going to be open to everybody and welcoming everyone."

The Arab Cultural and Community Center also works to combat discrimination and educate the public, including the local high schools that often reach out for advice.

After the World Trade Center attacks, many Arab and Muslim students struggled with bullying. "We have kids who came crying, who didn't want to go to school," Tayeb says. One child begged his parents to change his name because his name was Osama. "Can you imagine [being] a kid named Osama and going to junior high? Imagine what happens with these kids," he says. Some community members continue to face discrimination, like the time a child was "called so many times a Muslim terrorist—and the other kids didn't even pay attention to the fact that he's a Christian," says Tayeb.

The center also helps students, including immigrants, navigate situations where traditions clash, such as when a school cafeteria serves ham sandwiches for lunch or when a young Muslim woman in a hijab wants to take a swim class. They educate the local Arab population about diversity and inclusion too. "We had a girl—she's Arab and she's Black. I said, she's an Arab, like you," Tayeb told the other children.

"My culture is not falafel or hummus or hookah," he says. "My culture has language, has calligraphy, has music, and so many things. I want my kids to be proud of the culture, so when someone asks, where are you from, I want them to proudly say, 'I'm an Arab.'"

. . .

Back in my home, things are still language agnostic. It's been this way ever since I stopped coaxing Leah to speak Russian.

I know it's the right decision for her, even though it feels to me as if something incredibly significant has been lost. I don't discuss it with others much. What good would it do? Some would call me permissive. Others would doubt this approach would result in any substantive language skills beyond ordering a meal at a restaurant.

A few months go by. Then Leah becomes transfixed by a YouTube video series from the old country. In the video, a mom and daughter duo set up a play medical practice for toys. The woman and her miniature assistant, with a missing front tooth and a lab coat, administer pretend flu shots to Minnie Mouse. They diagnose a teddy bear with a broken arm and give him soup as medicine (in my culture, soup is said to cure just about any ailment).

"Next patient, please," the doctor calls out.

"Help! I ate too much candy and my tummy hurts!" whimpers the stuffed puppy.

"You know too much candy is bad for you, Mr. Dog. Well, step into our office. Our nurse will check your ears," the TV doctor says.

One day, I find all of Leah's stuffed animals lined up on the floor. She is wearing an apron and a toy stethoscope and tending to each of her make-believe patients, talking to them in Russian, just like in the video. She then turns to me and speaks in—you guessed it—Russian.

And with that, I realize, her veto is no more. It's showtime, baby.

8. THE EXPERTS WEIGH IN

In every job that must be done there is an element of
fun. You find the fun and—snap—the job's a game!

—MARY POPPINS[1]

SO WHAT DOES IT TAKE to raise a bilingual child?

"Make them speak it—end of story!" I sometimes hear from well-wishing folks. They share accounts of someone's neighbor's cousin whose *amerikansky* son became trilingual practically overnight with a simple technique—so simple, it's a wonder more people haven't done it. "Send them to live with Grandma for the summer!" others advise. "Relax, they'll just naturally pick it up," as if it were just like picking up a twenty dollar bill on the sidewalk or pinkeye at preschool.

Well, I'm here to tell you that after trying out some of these popular recommendations, I'm not really sold. When I talk to other families about it, many report a similar experience.

To get answers, I pick up books about language development and speak with professionals working with bilingual populations: academic researchers, speech language pathologists, and other parents.

Pretty soon I discover something I've been suspecting for a while: there is no foolproof formula for raising bilingual kids. There's no magic pill. Everybody's family, abilities, and circumstances are unique.

A FEW EXPERT TACTICS TO
ENCOURAGE BILINGUALISM AT HOME

I do, however, come across a few recurring suggestions. Those eight things—need, exposure, positive associations, keeping it fun, being realistic with expectations (and then even more realistic), making a plan, and not going it alone—end up making all the difference.

Need

I head over to Teachers College, Columbia University in New York City, to visit Erika Levy, a trilingual speech-language pathologist and an associate professor in the Communication Sciences and Disorders program.[2] On top of teaching at this graduate school and running its Speech Production and Perception Lab, Levy's also got pop culture cred: she coached Elmo and Big Bird of *Sesame Street* on their pronunciation.

"The child must need to use a particular language in order to speak it," Levy says as we chat in her tenth-floor office overlooking the Morningside Heights neighborhood in Manhattan. "Kids might be able to learn some grammar in school, but they'll learn it best when they need to use it." Passive listening to audio programs and videos has benefits, she says, "but it doesn't work at all as effectively as communicating, because speech is there for communication. That's how the children will be motivated."

By the age of two, bilingual kids can already tell which language to use with whom and in what situation.[3] If they know we're fluent in English, they'll be more likely to address us in English, even if we pretend to not understand.[4]

Exposure

Children need lots of input in the target language, and the more varied, the better. That's because speaking it at home is essential but not enough, experts say. Caregivers, extended family members, and friends can all help get that exposure.[5]

Levy recommends spending time with monolingual speakers of the language, such as with a grandparent, or enrolling the child in an organized activity in that language, like a camp. But "it can't be something unbearable for them," she adds. "English will come, but it's that other language that needs a lot of nurturing, and the earlier and the more continuously you do it, the better."

When it comes to the tiniest learners, parents can repeat what their baby says, then expand and add to it, as Levy describes in her book

Baby's First Words in French. For example, if the child says "doggie," the adult might respond with "Yes, doggie. Nice doggie," showing her how to construct phrases and, later, sentences, writes Levy.[6]

And don't be shy about using the playful "parentese"—with elongated vowels, slower tempo, and an exaggerated tone of voice (it's not the same as baby talk). This type of speech engages babies socially and boosts their language development, studies have shown.[7]

Another frequent piece of advice is to visit the homeland and become immersed in its way of talking. Trips like that can be prohibitively expensive for many families or impossible because of visa issues and political instability.

Still, those who can make the journey, often do.

Monika, a cohost of *Entre Dos*, a podcast about bilingualism, visits her native Puerto Rico regularly with her family. As a result, she says, her daughter has formed an emotional bond to Spanish. "I wanted her to, at the very core, abstract level, feel the way that I feel about it, and that has been the one thing that really made it happen," Monika says.

It's not just exposure to a language that's important, but actually using it too. It needs to be spoken and not only heard, points out Erika Hoff, a professor of psychology at Florida Atlantic University and a leading bilingualism expert.[8] The more a bilingual child speaks a target language, Hoff and her colleagues found, the more rapidly its vocabulary will develop.

Positive Associations

Since the start of our family's bilingual journey, I keep noticing how delicate immigrant languages are. Even if the parent keeps up religiously with bilingualism at home, outside factors play a huge role too. Having many speakers living close together makes a difference; so does the availability of schooling, media, and stable jobs in the heritage language, research shows.[9] Strong ethnic identity and easy travel to the homeland also help languages survive. Basically, picture living in a place where your nieces are your babysitters, your TV plays local programming in the mother tongue, and you catch up on local gossip with your countryman the baker and kvetch about the weather in Celsius.

On the flip side, the mother tongue won't fare too well if there's only a small number of speakers scattered over a wide area with limited educational and cultural opportunities. Discrimination and nativism also put its survival at risk.[10] Kids and teenagers are sensitive to messages from society, and they might look down at their family's way of talking if they sense that it lacks prestige—in other words, if they think it's kind of uncool.[11]

I'm surprised to learn that even our attitudes can endanger a heritage language, such as low emphasis on family and community in favor of individual achievement.[12]

That's why parents should try to create as many positive associations with the target language as possible. "Surround them with happy things in that other language," says Levy during our interview. She gives an example of a croissant-baking class for French learners, where children might ramp up their vocabulary while noshing on the buttery pastry.

Levy shares a quote by a bilingualism researcher and author Colin Baker, which resonates so much that I jot it down on a sticky note later and hang it above my desk. "Language growth in children requires the minimum of pruning—these are tender, young plants. Correcting language continuously, getting the child to repeat sentences, is the kind of pruning that research shows to have almost no effect, even a negative effect on language growth. The role of the language gardener is to provide a stimulating soil."[13]

In these words, I recognize my own mindset from a while back, as a brand-new parent. Grudgingly, I picture myself as a gardener with giant pruning shears, laughing maniacally and trampling a flower patch. It's exactly what I try to not do anymore.

Keeping It Fun

Language learning should strike a balance between serious and playful, advocates Adam Beck, a teacher, bilingual parent, and author. "It's vital to maintain a strong sense of humor and playfulness," he writes in his book *Maximize Your Child's Bilingual Ability*, "particularly through the younger years—so that your children will come to feel positively toward the minority language and be willing, even eager, to make this long journey with you."[14]

Some tools in his bilingual toolbox include telling stories with cliff-hanger endings and leaving funny notes around the house (yes, even in the bathroom) for the kids to find. Beck recommends lots of daily conversation and interactive reading in the target language, suited to the child's interests.[15]

Based in Japan, Beck reads to his children at breakfast every morning and has been giving them daily English homework since they were three years old.[16] These small efforts and routines, he assures, will add up.

Being Realistic with Expectations

Our own mindset matters too. Parents should have reasonable expectations, says Erika Hoff, at Florida Atlantic University, when we speak by phone. "There is nothing magical in the child's brain that allows them to learn any language they hear without lots of environmental support. Parents who want to raise their children to be bilingual are swimming upstream because the environment in the US is not supportive."

After all, kids are not sponges who absorb everything they hear. "You're not going to have a child who is two monolinguals in one," Hoff tells me.[17] "It's hard to engineer the kinds of experiences that support really strong bilingualism. . . . My most important message I try to communicate is it takes longer to learn two languages than one. And chances are it's never going to be exactly the same, as you don't use the same languages in exactly the same amount."

Bilingual kids have a smaller vocabulary in each of their respective languages than monolingual peers.[18] This is true even for households with a high socioeconomic status. The big picture, however, suggests that the total vocabulary of bilingual kids is similar to that of monolingual peers.[19] As these children get older, the English vocabulary gap shrinks yet becomes more pronounced in Spanish, Hoff found. And if they keep up with their Spanish, their total vocabulary knowledge even surpasses that of monolinguals, she tells me.[20]

For cognitive neuroscientist Ellen Bialystok, all that superior executive function can compensate for vocabulary differences.[21] Yes, bilingual children do "have a smaller vocabulary in each language," Bialystok says during our interview. "That doesn't mean they don't know a lot of words. It's just spread over two languages." Their vocabulary size is not a disadvantage.

Being Even More Realistic

As I study and implement some of these tips, I hear the familiar little voice of parental guilt in the back of my head. *You're not doing enough to cultivate bilingualism*, it cackles.

In our busy monolingual-normative society, heritage language retention is tough business. And not just because of language fragility but also because life happens. We've got jobs, sometimes more than one. We have work commutes and other relatives to tend to. And laundry. We prime our kids for success and emotional intelligence through crafts, chaperoned playdates, academic and play-based activities, and homework that starts trickling in as early as kindergarten. Yes, one might carve out thirty minutes a day to practice the ABCs in a foreign tongue, but then who'll make dinner and fill out preschool permission slips?

But slow results aren't the same as failure. Stay the course and your efforts will pay off, writes Adam Beck: "The only way to really fail at raising a bilingual child is to give up entirely."[22]

Making a Plan and Starting Early (If You Can)

Having a family means planning ahead, from where to spend Thanksgiving to the most optimal time to conceive. Many households also plan how they'll be using their languages.[23] Experts recommend taking stock of the family's circumstances and bilingualism goals, then mapping out ways to achieve them, leaving wiggle room as needed. Ideally, this should be done early on in the child's life. The language experiences with neighbors, friends, and childcare providers are especially important before the age of three, researchers note.[24]

A few words on timing. Babies are tiny language wizards, born with an awe-inspiring capacity to differentiate between all the sounds of all the world languages, or roughly eight hundred sounds.[25] In the latter half of their first year, babies begin to tune in to the language they hear most around them, opening the door to its sounds and fantastical possibilities.[26] At the same time, they start to lose the ability to differentiate between the sounds of other languages. (Babies from bilingual households stay open to other language sounds longer.) So to make the most of the child's language development, it's best to expose her to it as early as possible.[27]

This isn't to say that people can't become fluent in another language at any age. They definitely can.

Some scholars argue there are biological advantages to learning a second language before puberty. Others say older learners can pick it up quicker and more efficiently, albeit often with an accent.[28] (And by the way, an accent for a bilingual is actually the norm and not the exception.)[29]

Still, early childhood and elementary and secondary school are thought to be the most advantageous periods to learn a language, notes bilingualism researcher and author Colin Baker. This isn't a matter of potential but of motivation and opportunity. And, Baker writes, rather reassuringly, "Adults can learn to a native-like level of competence in a second language."[30]

Not Going It Alone

It takes a village to raise a child—and a bilingual child is no exception. Some families team up for activities in a target language. Paula, from Colombia, has put together a Spanish-language story-time playgroup with friends in Houston. "When you're here, we're functioning in Spanish" is their modus operandi. The kids are usually itching to revert to English. But if the organizer sets the expectation right off the bat, "they'll do it," says Paula.

These grassroots events aren't like your tutor or a weekend class. At the end of the day, there's only so much desk sitting a kid can take. "I want it to be just being a kid in Spanish," explains Paula.

Paula's friend Monika raves about her child's Spanish-language art space in Miami, with crafts and theater activities. "The point is to just play in the target language and have fun," says Monika. "It's not direct teaching."

After Leah becomes a toddler, I also participate in events with the local families. We attend language-centric get-togethers and host sing-alongs and baking parties. There, Leah and Greg's peers don matching mini aprons and play with squishy dough (and binge on sugar and sprinkles when no one's looking). Even though language often ends up taking a back seat, these get-togethers normalize our traditions and build relationships, not to mention result in delicious treats. And, I'd like to think, they develop a reserve of sounds and vocabulary.

DIVIDING AND CONQUERING: HOW FAMILIES USE LANGUAGES

So when it comes to implementing these tactics, how do families decide who should speak which language, how much, and when? There are a few ways households can go about it.

One Person, One Language

When the parents want to teach the child multiple languages simultaneously, one popular method is one person, one language. It even has its own acronym: OPOL. It's exactly what it sounds like: one parent—or person—speaks language A with the child and the other one speaks language B, exclusively.

OPOL is considered to be highly successful in cultivating bilingualism. Successful, but not perfect. A Belgian study of nearly two thousand Dutch-speaking families found that a quarter of the children growing up in an OPOL household did not become bilingual.[31] Then again, the other three quarters did.

Edwin and Aleksey, the couple from Washington, DC, tell me they speak Spanish and Russian, respectively, with their almost two-year-old daughter, Sofia.

"We've always been very consistent about that," Aleksey says. "If overall it seems to be working, then the little moments where things get difficult, they're just moments in time. And they will pass or we just have to laugh them off and, you know, move on."

For Edwin, language is the most critical thing to pass down to Sofia from his heritage. Specifically, the Spanish spoken in El Salvador.

"The way I speak to her is not a neutral Spanish," Edwin explains. "It's very important for her to learn that. If you spoke Spanish, you would not understand what I'm saying."

Their friends, many of whom are conversant in different varieties of Spanish, have taken notice. Even Edwin's mother has. "Oh my God!" she said to him. "You're teaching her the hardcore roots of Salvadoran slang!"

"When you drop something," explains Edwin, "a lot people would go, *Oops, you dropped something!* She goes, *VAYA!*" (It loosely translates to "there it goes.") He demonstrates with a dropped jaw and a throaty, dramatic utterance.

Sofia is already figuring out who speaks what.

Sometimes she asks Edwin for a cookie in Russian.

"*Pechenye?*" she says.

Edwin doesn't budge. "I don't understand you," he answers, telling her to say it in Spanish.

"*Pechenye?*"

"I don't understand," the dad repeats, in Spanish. "*No entiendo.*"

The tot gets impatient. "*PEH-CHEN-NYE!*"

And then it clicks. She exclaims, "*Galleta!*"

"*¿Quieres una galleta?*" Edwin says, and Sofia, delighted, immediately gets her cookie.

Aleksey responds similarly when Sofia comes to him looking for a *galleta*.

Back when the couple met, Edwin's arsenal of Russian words was fairly utilitarian: he knew only *hello, thank you, good-bye,* and *red wine.* His vocabulary has expanded since, but not enough to follow conversations with the grandparents. Meanwhile, Aleksey is fluent in Spanish.

They realize that English will eventually become dominant in their daughter's life. That's why they're sticking with the OPOL method for now. "My Spanish is starting to decrease, and I didn't think that could ever be possible, but it can happen," says Edwin, who immigrated when he was eleven. "I will continue to go as far as I can with her in Spanish, but it's going to be difficult."

Aleksey, who left Ukraine at fifteen, has had a similar experience with his mother tongue. "If at some point I start needing to put in English words, I mean, that's what it's going to be."

When the dads speak English with each other, Sofia feels left out. She often interrupts them, Edwin says. "She goes, '*Bla bla bla! Pechenye?*'"

. . .

A word on trilingualism. Trilingual language input doesn't guarantee that the kid will grow up equally proficient in all three, studies suggest.[32] However, if both parents speak only their target languages in the home and not the majority one, the likelihood of getting a polyglot kid out of it is higher.[33] Plus, continuous and early exposure means they might speak without a foreign accent in them all.[34]

. . .

The OPOL approach isn't without problems. It can be a bit of a mental workout, especially when the adults come home from work tired, with little energy to switch from English and cajole the children to do the same.

Paula, from Colombia, spoke to her daughter consistently in Spanish for the first few years. Her American-born husband addressed their daughter in English. But with time, it got to be too much. "When we're sitting at the dinner table or just in general, the three of us, a lot of things happen in English now, whereas before, I might say it in Spanish, and then I might turn to him and say it in English," admits Paula.

Others feel uncomfortable about leaving family members out of the conversation. Or their partners aren't on board.

"I know families where the dad gets upset when the dad doesn't understand his own child," an immigrant friend in California tells me. "They feel excluded and they think the child won't learn English at all."

There's only so much we can control. Just go ahead and try to tune out the influence of school, friends, videos, and social media. Besides, one adult is usually home more than the other one, so there's rarely a balance of language experiences.[35]

Take a classic example of a girl named Hildegard, whose linguist dad published four whole books about her speech development. The father, who emigrated from Germany in 1925, spoke to Hildegard in German and the mother spoke to her in English. When the little girl visited Germany, she was more German dominant. But back in the United States, Hildegard's English got stronger, showing the tremendous role the environment plays in the way we talk.[36]

Some researchers also criticize the one-person, one-language method for being inflexible. In reality, they say, we use all our linguistic resources when interacting with our world.[37] For others, OPOL is associated with middle- and upper-class families who may have more resources to make careful choices about their child's language development, but not as often by immigrants and working-class households.[38]

Heritage Language at Home

Another method is to use the target language at home and the community language outside the home. This approach has quite a bit of variation.[39]

Fernanda from Brazil speaks Portuguese with her three-and-a-half-year-old daughter at home, while her husband speaks in his native German. But in the company of others, Fernanda often reverts to English. "When I want to tell her, *Don't throw sand in people's eyes,* I'll say it in English because people around can participate and understand, 'cause I don't want her to feel excluded," she explains. "My husband just speaks German all the time. He doesn't care. But I'm really concerned about her not feeling singled out," Fernanda adds, pushing her daughter in the swing, as the delighted preschooler squeals and asks to go higher.

"At this age, [children] are not mean to each other," Fernanda tells me, but "sometimes I'm afraid of the time when they will say: 'What did you say?'" she adds, with concern in her voice.

Some criticize this approach for sending the wrong message to the kid. If the grownups quit speaking their language when company's present, does it mean it's something to be ashamed of, rather than proud of?[40]

Still, many households choose it as the best-fitting option for them.

A twist to this tactic is using the target language for specific occasions or times of day.[41]

"Just keep speaking Russian as much as possible," urges the pediatrician at Leah's fifteen-month checkup. "Even if you've got to make rules for it. Like 'Taco Tuesdays.'"

Mix It Up

A third method is not as structured but very common: mixing languages.[42] Like a good cocktail, it's got a bit of everything, but it does the job.

This is now the style of talking in my household. With its alternating speech patterns, it's more manageable than my earlier attempt at one-person, one-language. In our case, it feels less forced and more helpful.

Even though language mixing isn't regimented like the other two methods, it can teach a child to effectively communicate in the target language, especially as she figures out that each one has a different purpose, experts say. Kids will likely imitate this conversation style around other bilinguals, but not with the monolingual folks.[43]

Remember that study of two thousand bilingual Belgian families from earlier? When both parents mixed two languages at home, their children were 79 percent likely to be bilingual. However, when only one parent mixed languages and the other parent spoke only the majority language, this yielded a paltry 36 percent success rate.[44] Yikes.

Don't throw in the towel just yet, however, writes Annick De Houwer, the study's author. Yes, parents play a critical role in passing the mother tongue down to the next generation, but outside factors influence it too. Plus, she says, the study only looked at language use, not at how well the children spoke it.[45]

Actually, it's common for bilinguals to mix languages with each other—sometimes even in a single sentence. This is known as *code-switching*.[46] We do this when there's a better term to capture our thoughts and feelings in another language, or to show allegiance, or to, ahem, spy on someone's conversation like a fly on the wall.

Not everyone looks favorably upon code-switching. Some think it's lazy and careless. Others claim it's disloyal to the purity of a language. However, those assumptions aren't correct: people code-switch for deliberate reasons. It doesn't mean they're not proficient.[47] Linguist Shana Poplack insists that it's not a defect but actually a skill that requires language competence, she writes in her article with a perfect title: "Sometimes I'll Start a Sentence in Spanish y Termino en Español."[48]

The stigma remains, though. When a scholar, Ilan Stavans, translated a part of *Don Quixote* into Spanglish and published a Spanglish dictionary in 2003, he received angry messages and even death threats from around the world. Critics claimed that mixing languages is barbaric and broken. His response? "Baloney," Stavans writes. "Languages are never in a state of purity. Instead, they are always changing."[49]

English Later

A fourth approach is for both parents to speak the target language at home, exclusively, building a foundation from the very beginning.[50]

What are the odds of a kid growing up bilingual in a household like that?, you might wonder. It's 97 percent, according to that Belgian study of bilingual families.[51] Not too shabby.

It's not an option, of course, if your partner doesn't know your language (and isn't planning to learn anytime soon, despite saying he would back when you were dating). Writer Amy Chua weighs in on this with some pessimism in her book *Battle Hymn of the Tiger Mother*: "A tiny part of me regrets that I didn't marry another Chinese person and worries that I am letting down four thousand years of civilization," she writes.[52]

• • •

The "English later" approach works well for Ruth, an American, and Antonio, who is from Mexico. It's all Spanish, all the time for their toddler, whom they are raising in Washington, DC. This isn't without challenges. Ruth's American father has had a harder time building a relationship with his grandson. But those are "the choices we made and they are super positive," says Ruth.

"In a very few years it will be a struggle to get him to speak Spanish," observes Antonio. "I'm very thankful to Ruth, because she made a huge effort in speaking Spanish all the time and also forcing me to speak Spanish all the time and calling me out when I flip into English."

Even if your partner does speak the way you do, it's not easy to just leave English at the doorstep.

"I did a master's in dual immersion, so I was really passionate . . . 'Our children need to learn Spanish!'" says Christine, a teacher in Utah, whose husband Miguel is also Mexican. But with their busy work schedules, it was hard to keep up with. "I think I'm just tired and it's hard to express yourself always in [another] language," she says, regretfully. "I do have friends that are consistent, but it's very, very rare."

Here, Christine and Miguel count the people in their multicultural network who speak Spanish to their kids all the time. They come up with one name.

Hannah, an American, speaks French as much as possible to her young child, so the boy can stay connected to his large family in France. But she's found that language changes social dynamics. "If we're out in public, I'm always conscious and concerned that people are, oh, is she trying to be too much or showing off," she tells me over coffee.

Hannah recalls a time the couple took their son to a petting zoo in their California town. "My husband was fluently speaking French to him, as he always does, and I was speaking a mix of the two. And there was a mom with this little kid close by. All of a sudden she switched to '*Would you like some agua?*'"

■ ■ ■

When it comes to single-parent households, the family can adopt the heritage language as the family language.[53]

Experts say there is no one universally best strategy for becoming bilingual. It's a matter of what works for the individual family.[54]

No matter what strategy you pick, Grosjean writes in his book, "once bilingualism has started to take hold, the family has to keep monitoring the environment to ensure that the child has a real need for both languages, and that he or she is receiving enough exposure to both languages."[55]

Those moments of uninterrupted monolingual conversation are important. They teach kids to adapt their speech to the situation and carry on a conversation in one language.[56]

■ ■ ■

In the first few years of parenthood, I sometimes feel that bilingualism is an all-or-nothing proposition. The kid will either speak it, to the enthusiastic applause of relatives, or not at all. My efforts are either productive or hopeless.

But it doesn't have to be this way, I eventually realize. Perfectly balanced bilingualism is more of a myth, and language learning is a process that changes throughout one's lifetime. It's bigger than what we, the parents, desire.

Plus, humans are emotional beings. We don't deliver every single message in exactly the same way and language, be it praise or instruction.[57] It's not like you adjust the input in the "Settings" menu and, boom, you're now male Korean Siri.

So maybe the child won't read the original works of Tolstoy by the time she's in high school. Maybe she will. Maybe she already can (and if so, congratulations!). In the end, it's the foundation built on tiny discoveries and those adorable wobbly steps. We are teaching another human an entirely new way to think and communicate, when, statistically speaking, the odds are against us. Isn't that monumental?

Once I stop stressing out over whether I'm doing enough to teach Russian to Leah and Greg, I begin to notice how much they already know. And the more I marvel, the more they want to learn, on their own volition and with plenty of enthusiasm.

9. NANNIES AND DAYCARES AND GRANDMAS, OH MY!

They told jokes that didn't require explanation and debated arguments that were decades in the making. All of this was coupled with the familiarity and comfort of speaking in our native tongue.

—DINAW MENGESTU[1]

WHEN YOU MOVE somewhere new and it's not quite like the place you came from (I don't just mean the speed limit is different and people refer to their sandwiches as "grinders"), it may seem jarring at first. Even lonely.

But then, usually, compatriots start popping up around you, like mushrooms after the rain. You might recognize each other by the way you dress or talk when you're out and about, or by the groceries you buy when running errands.

That's what happened when I moved to the place where I currently live: I started bumping into other Russian speakers. This occurred naturally, without any plans to that effect, but am I glad that it did. (I meet one expat at the supermarket's seafood aisle because of the way we both pore over the smoked salmon options, while our children bounce in the shopping carts impatiently.)

Every new arrival is heartily welcomed to our town. It's like an invisible handshake, a reconnection with a long-lost acquaintance. Whatever the religion, whatever the city of birth, we share a language, we share a similar upbringing, and we share the intel.

Then comes the inevitable question.

"So, where are all the Russian childcares at?" the newcomer will ask, in person or on an online forum. The newcomer is looking for the big kahuna: the same hearty lunches she grew up eating, the soulful songs from the homeland, the language, and a bevy of academics and arts.

"There are none around here, actually" someone will answer, knowing all too well where this conversation is headed. The others listen plaintively.

"What do you mean, none? Like none at all?"

"That's right," the longtimer concedes. "None at all."

"But in the town where we lived before, there were so many Russian daycares."

"Yeah, well, not here. There's one almost thirty minutes south when it's not rush hour. And another close to an hour north in traffic. And there's a wait list," the old-timer cautions.

"Oh, I don't mind the drive!" declares the new person. "It's important for me to provide my child with the cultural immersion experience. I'll just leave work early and listen to podcasts in my car."

But after making the trek to check out the cultural immersion daycare, most usually give up. They enroll their progeny in whatever is available closer to home. Those, too, are competitive and packed.

■ ■ ■

It's not easy to find the right childcare arrangement in America. There are home and center options. There's Montessori versus Waldorf, play-based versus academic. Some offer yoga, a low teacher to student ratio, catered meals with non-GMO ingredients, and a hefty price tag. Others are budget friendly, but don't expect organic yogurt. There are nanny shares and relatives. And immigrant families have even more to consider.

I know this, of course, because I've been there.

Pete and I start looking for a local daycare for Leah before I go back to work. A Russian one would have been nice, but it's not in the cards.

No beets? No problem.

We just want a place that's loving and safe—we're easygoing and fairly reasonable people. At least I think so. We don't need Leah to master Latin and Mandarin by four years of age and perform violin concertos by five.

I research the options, gather recommendations, and make appointments to visit.

Maybe I'm just anxious, having never left Leah with a stranger outside the home before. But our daycare search turns into a gargantuan task. The options seem endless, yet availability is scarce, the costs are often out of reach, and the thought of leaving my kid in most places makes me want to grab her and run away.

First, we try a neighborhood daycare. On her first day, Leah comes back with food in her hair and a busted lip. Horrified, I ask what happened, but nobody knows. The main caregiver blots the wound with a crumpled napkin she fishes out of her pocket. "Better now!" she says, sunnily.

We keep searching. "Are you the grandmother?" asks the owner of another facility after inspecting my sleep-deprived visage. Admittedly, sleepless nights with a small child haven't been doing me any favors. The woman leads me through a tiny living room with peeling paint to the official daycare space, which smells like assorted diapers. There, children are tinkering with a pile of talking toys in the middle of a stained carpet.

There's also a corporate daycare chain tucked away in a suburban office park. I've heard good reviews. At the reception desk, I'm given a bulging folder with information and forms. During the tour, the administrator touts an iPad in every room and an app that sends play-by-play communication to parents about the child throughout the day. She points to the video cameras, which let adults keep an eye on their youngsters and on the classroom remotely, from the comfort of their office.

"Our parents say cameras make them feel comfortable, like they're right here!" she says, smiling. But as I walk through the industrial-sized foyer with fluorescent lighting, it does not feel comfortable. It feels creepy. Besides, the tuition is almost what Pete and I pay in monthly rent.

The protracted daycare search is starting to remind me of dating. I expand the criteria to widen the pool of opportunities. A shared heritage is no longer a "must have," just a "nice to have." Still, does it feel like a good match? Is it out of my league? Is one party too eager to seal the deal or, on the contrary, seemingly hard to get? Are they too busy right now and can't commit, unless it's only on a "part-time basis"? One is invited to plunk down $150 and keep in touch, except instead of a mediocre steak dinner date, it's called a deposit to hold your spot in the Tiny Turtles room.

Finally, we enroll Leah in a small daycare in our neighborhood. The owner is organized and her home is sparkling clean. Although she is American, she doesn't smile or mince words, which appeals to my Russian sensibilities. When we visit, it smells irresistibly like an Italian café inside.

"The secret to minestrone is you make the soup, then you make the pasta," she explains when I comment on the mouthwatering fragrance. "You never mix 'em." The kids get home-cooked lunches here, she adds.

We check a couple of references and sign Leah up.

Some time passes. Whenever I pick Leah up after work, I begin to find the owner in her kitchen, berating her children for flunking a school test again and fixing meals for her family (she no longer feeds the kids; they now bring their own lunch).

Meanwhile, her young charges are parked on the couch and strapped in the high chair in another room alone, in front of the TV.

"How did this munchkin do today?" I ask over the sounds of a commercial and yelling as I stuff Leah's arms in her jacket on our way out.

"What do you want to know?"

I wonder if Leah napped, if she finished her lunch.

"She did fine." She opens the door and waits for us to exit.

Every day, Leah seems more gloomy and less talkative at pickup. I know absolutely nothing about her day.

■　■　■

"You know how Americans are," my neighbor, an immigrant from Europe, says. Her children are older, so she's familiar with the system. "You can ask things, but never be direct about it. You need to smile, and do it in a sweet voice, like this [her intonation goes up] 'We *really love* this place and we're just *so very* grateful for everything, but I was just wondering . . .'" she instructs. "See?"

Am I being too picky, too privileged? At least my kid's physically safe, right?

"That's not okay," an American friend offers when I share my qualms with her. "Plus, everybody knows it's the parents who get to use TV for babysitting, not the daycare," she quips.

"I don't want to give advice or anything," another friend in our group adds demurely, removing an applesauce pouch from her bag, "but I probably wouldn't stay. It's not you, it's her. You guys deserve someone nice."

"Yeah," says another. "It took us awhile, too, but we fell in love with ours right away. Just keep looking. The perfect one is out there!"

This conversation is giving me encouragement, even if it's unfolding by a sandbox on a Saturday morning and not at a dim karaoke bar with scratchy speakers after a breakup.

Sure, it could be worse. Back in my Soviet kindergarten, children weren't allowed to get up from the table until our plates were empty, like Lenin's. (He ate every morsel on his plate, we were taught.) In my old kindergarten, kids were forced to stand in front of an open window in their undergarments as punishment for chatting during nap time.

But we're not in Soviet Russia anymore. And neither is my daughter.

The new daycare search is on again.

. . .

How do people decide on the right childcare arrangement for their tykes? Zero to Three, a nonprofit based in Washington, DC, working with early childhood issues, recommends checking if the childcare program is licensed, safe, and sanitary, the organization's website says.

"Young children need a schedule that is responsive to their needs, including appropriate stimulation and time to rest," the guidance adds. Infants and toddlers need to be played with and talked to, forming a "comfortable, secure relationship with a caregiver that will nurture their healthy emotional development."[2] Do the caregivers respect the cultural values of the families? Would you feel comfortable leaving the child here?

All excellent questions.

But on top of that, if you're an immigrant, will the grandparents fly in? What if they don't know how to drive in the American suburbs? Should we send the kid to a language immersion childcare? What if we speak multiple languages—which one do we pick?

It doesn't need pointing out that immigrants are not all the same. Some have lucrative white-collar careers and can hire a live-in nanny and a personal driver to shuttle the littles between extracurricular activities. Others work nights and weekends, barely able to pay a neighbor to watch the child. Some, like Edwin from El Salvador, raise their younger siblings while still teenagers themselves.

"The experiences the folks are having can vary so widely," says Maki Park, senior policy analyst for Early Education and Care at the Migration Policy Institute when we talk.[3]

Childcare is challenging for everyone in the United States, Park says, because it's not affordable for many families and not publicly provisioned. Many programs don't meet the needs of immigrants. Sometimes it's an issue of costs or transportation, or the fact that immigrants are more likely to hold multiple jobs and need flexible schedules that formally licensed places may not offer.

Many don't speak English well enough or lack the cultural or computer literacy, "to say nothing of mixed-status or undocumented families who might not be able to access any form of formal care," adds Park.

A friend in Washington, DC, where childcare is notoriously competitive, recommends parents to lobby daycare facilities by visiting in person while pregnant to make a good impression and staying in touch after getting on the waiting list. These techniques can help middle- and upper-class American households secure a spot. But try and imagine a recent arrival or an unacculturated immigrant researching reviews on listservs, striking that perfect balance between coolness and enthusiasm, and dropping names so hard that they generate a small tsunami.

Even those who've lived in America for years face tradeoffs.

"When most people think about high quality childcare, they're thinking of very normative standards . . . and do not consider some very important things, such as the ability to hold on to your heritage, the ability to develop a bicultural identity, the ability to gain support in your home language, and the ability to communicate with parents," Park tells me. "The system isn't responsive to a huge swath of the population. You know, one in four children now are young children of immigrants, so this is not a boutique issue."

Park hopes that eventually, daycares for the younger kids and preschools for the older ones won't separate the needs of the child from the needs of the family.

As I read and talk to people about their childcare arrangements, I get a bit of a sticker shock. If you think it's expensive to birth a child in America (starting at over $30,000, and more than $50,000 for a cesarean delivery, not to mention IVF), just wait till you send them to daycare.[4]

Infant care is pricier than tuition at four-year public colleges in more than half of the United States, writes Taryn Morrissey for *The Conversation*.[5] American couples shell out 20 percent of their household income on childcare (make that a third of the income for single parents), putting the US behind the majority of other developed nations. Couples in Denmark spend 11 percent of their income. In Korea, it's 3 percent, and just 2 in the Czech Republic.[6]

Part of it is the policies. America invests less in kids under five compared to other high-income nations, writes Ajay Chaudry, a research professor at New York University and former deputy assistant secretary at the US Department of Health and Human Services, in his book *Cradle to Kindergarten*.[7]

"Socioeconomic disparities early in life contribute to starkly different long-term adult outcomes," Chaudry and his colleagues report in their findings. "High-quality early care and education is in short supply, and when available, it is very expensive relative to most families' means."[8]

Some can swing it with one kid. Yet by the time a second one comes along, to say nothing of the third, a number of women I know cannot afford to work outside the home after becoming mothers, even if they've graduated from college, held stable jobs before, and volunteered for causes they believe in. Paradoxically, it is cheaper for many to care for the child at home than to be employed. They become priced out of the workforce.

This triggers a spiral effect: a longer gap on the resume and a more challenging, lower-paying entrance back into the workforce, assuming it happens at all.[9]

However, childcare workers are anything but wealthy. Their median hourly wage is below that of a parking attendant: $11.65 for the former compared to $12.09 for the latter in 2019,[10] according to the US Bureau of Labor Statistics.

The woman with the minestrone soup who watched Leah had a second job, I learned later. In the evenings, she'd rush over to a chain store as a salesclerk so she could have health insurance.

I should probably mention another daycare experience on our family's roster, albeit, unfortunately, a brief one. Its owner, an immigrant, worked long days, starting in the wee hours of the morning. She never spared hugs or snacks; she taught children how to hold a pencil, share toys, and not bite others; she changed diapers and gifted Disney books to every family for Christmas. She had three children of her own and a tradesman husband who worked all the time. What she didn't have was a house. When she was evicted from her rental home, she could not afford another one in her gentrifying town. She had no choice but to quit and move her family of five into a small apartment, where she tried to recoup the losses from operating a business by babysitting.

. . .

Despite the low wages, caring for a child is hard work. Just ask any full-time parent, or a work-from-home parent, or a nanny. Heck, ask me; I'll tell you the same thing. On top of being demanding, it's also incredibly impactful. Early experiences leave a lifelong mark. Children develop tremendously in the first three years, setting the stage for their future. By three, the brain reaches 80 percent of its adult volume, doubling in size in the first year alone.[11] Impressive, isn't it?

And yet the profession is not always seen this way. "I think this is why immigrants are so overrepresented in care work," says Maki Park, "because people don't think of it as being important, as being professional, as being skilled. But working with a baby successfully takes incredible skill."

Park and I speak as the COVID-19 pandemic rages across the world, and childcare providers in the United States are becoming rightly thought of as essential. They are "undergirding our economy," she emphasizes.

Beatriz, from El Salvador, raves about her grandson's daycare. She's elated that they found a place they like in their San Francisco Bay Area city, with a high population of immigrants from Latin America. (This demographic disproportionately lives in areas with an insufficient supply of licensed childcares, also known as childcare deserts.)[12]

But, Beatriz says, they figured out a way to get by, shuffling transportation, work schedules, and the commute from home, where three generations live together.

"It's very good! It's close to our house," says Beatriz, who cleans office buildings in downtown San Francisco during the week and client homes on weekends.

Beatriz explains that early every morning, they all get in the car. Her daughter drops Beatriz off at the train station, then brings her toddler to the daycare, then drives to work.

"She found work across the street from the daycare," Beatriz tells me, putting her hands together and thanking God.

I ask where her daughter works.

"At Burger King," she answers. "Next to the train station. We are so lucky."

■　■　■

On top of costs and availability, there's another piece to this childcare puzzle. Many families hope that the caregiver will help keep the heritage language alive.

Immigrants aren't alone in this desire. Many native-born families are also enrolling their children in bilingual programs, since they've become in vogue. As a result, these programs are becoming less available to the immigrants themselves, Maki Park points out.

Many parents covet bilingual childcare providers because of the cognitive and economic advantages of bilingualism.

Yet others aren't in it for any quantifiable reasons.

Such is the case with Carey, an American mom in Ohio. Since she was a teenager, Carey wanted to teach her future kids Spanish.

"I want my child to have more opportunities than I was given," says Carey, whose child attended a Spanish daycare until recently. She met the caregiver while pregnant and "fell in love with her" immediately. She also tries speaking to her child in Spanish at home. "The more experiences you can provide to your children, the more they will want to learn and not live in fear of people who they believe are different," Carey says.

Is having a bilingual caregiver enough to reap those sought-after language benefits?

That depends on what we mean by "benefits."

Just a few years ago, the thinking among many neurolinguists was that occasional nonnative language use doesn't offer many cognitive advantages for an individual.[13] But our understanding of bilingualism is changing. Even some language exposure is good for the brain, shows recent research by Ellen Bialystok of York University, a leading expert in the field.

"Any kind of bilingual experience has measurable benefits for cognitive function," Bialystok tells me. "The extent of these benefits varies with how long you've been learning another language—the earlier, the better; how proficient you've become—the more proficient the better; and how much time you spend using the other language—the more time, the better," she says. "It's the same as taking piano lessons. The more you practice, the better you will be."

That's cognitive benefits. But will a bilingual daycare make my kid fluent?

"It depends on how much support there is at home," Bialystok tells me. "Because if you do nothing beyond the Spanish daycare, there probably will be very little effect. As soon as you take the child out of Spanish daycare, there probably will be little evidence that there was Spanish daycare. But nobody knows for sure. There is no formula for the effect."

■   ■   ■

Nicole, an American, and her husband, born in Chile, hired a Spanish-speaking nanny to watch their baby. She used to come to their San Francisco home and bring her own child too.

When the couple moved to the suburbs and had a second kid, the costs got prohibitively expensive. For a while, Chilean relatives flew in to help them.

Then, Nicole and her husband hired an au pair. A young person came from Colombia to take care of their kids in exchange for room and board and a weekly stipend (plus a program fee for the au pair organization). Nicole, who works for a tech company in the San Francisco Bay Area, is delighted with this arrangement. Their youngest kid even said many first words in Spanish, thanks to the au pair.

"We needed someone that was Spanish speaking, not only for the kids but also to feel comfortable living in our home. We have Spanish music on all the time, eat and live like Chileans and Americans," she says. "It's a blended-culture home and we love it."

An au pair is not for everyone. She is practically a family member during the stay and needs a private room, something not all households can afford.

For Nicole, the cost "beats running late to daycare drop-off [and] having to be home from work for kid sick days," she says. "It's very cost effective for two or more kids in the Bay Area. And the benefits of teaching your kid about another culture are incredible."

As I learn about early childcare arrangements, I'm left wondering: What if someone doesn't want an outsider to watch their brood? Or can't? Many parents decide to stay home with the little one, while others have a dedicated network of aunties and grandparents for whom caring for the new family member isn't just an option but an assumed responsibility.

Grandparents tend to be the go-to childcare providers around the world, from Italy to China, where multiple generations often dwell under one roof.[14] The number of grandparent caregivers in America is on the rise too (sometimes assisting a parent who is deployed in military or in trouble with the law).[15]

And why not? It passes down the family values. It's free. It's convenient. You don't need to run a background check on Grandma.

That was the situation for Miguel and Christine in Utah. Miguel's mother visited from Mexico after the birth of her granddaughter, then returned and stayed for six more months. She spoke with the tot in Spanish, fixed home-cooked meals, and even helped around the house when she could. "We both have really crazy schedules," Christine says. "[Miguel's] nursing schedule is at night sometimes and I was going to school, and so it really was a big help."

Along with the meals and the stroller walks with Grandma, sometimes the babe is also served cultural values in a nostalgic time bubble.

"This creates kind of weird generational throwbacks," New York–based sociologist Philip Kasinitz tells me.

"The kids are a third generation out in the world, complete US citizens, living often in predominantly American communities. And yet they go home after school to babushka who is sitting there with the borscht, and is really making a world that is not only Russian or Jewish, or some combination of Russian and Jewish, but also sometimes Russian of, say, 1975. That's a Russia that doesn't exist in Russia anymore."

■   ■   ■

For Pete and me, help from the grandparents isn't logistically possible. And there's barely enough space for ourselves in our tiny apartment, much less for any au pair. So we keep looking for another daycare for Leah.

Curious how bilingual daycares work, I visit a Chinese-language provider in the San Francisco Bay Area.

There, Jia, the owner, teaches her Asian, Black, and white charges English and Chinese nursery rhymes. At circle time, I find the kids counting to ten in both languages and singing "Take Me Out to the Ball Game" and traditional Chinese songs. Starting at just a few months of age, they're exposed to Cantonese vocabulary like *milk, bread, wash hands*, and, my favorite, *eat noodles*.

Jia doesn't advertise, she tells me. Parents find her by word of mouth, and I can see why. She's got little turnover among families and her assistants. There's the cherished language exposure, especially for those with Chinese heritage; that's reason number two. And Jia is one of those genuinely warm people who'll never shame you for butchering the haircut you gave your kid over the weekend. She'll ask you about work troubles, then offer wise counsel, all while getting another parent to sign a form and breaking up a toddler scuffle at the same time.

Her husband, who works in construction, has personally put a permitted addition on the house for the daycare, complete with extra rooms for diaper changing and naps and a restroom outfitted with a tiny potty. He built the wooden cabinets for the toys. When he returns from work in the evenings, he waits until everyone's been picked up, then parks his truck in the driveway, smiling and waving to the stragglers toting their kids home in time for dinner.

Another draw, says a current parent I chat with, is the food, at a time when many American-run daycares often have parents pack their kids' lunches in boxes or little thermoses to keep the contents warm.

"They love my rice," Jia boasts. She tells me she serves beef and cabbage dumplings, homemade stir-fries, and noodles to the kids.

When I ask about cold sandwiches, she cringes.

During my visit, I find Jia's assistant bouncing a baby on her lap and singing to him in Cantonese, smiling. The older ones are playing with blocks and coloring on little tables in the main room, next to the

English alphabet posters. Balls of dough on the kitchen counter are rising to become buns and dumplings for lunch. Later, I learn that Jia gives a red envelope with a crisp bill for Chinese New Year to each child. To her, they are family.

Jia perfected her people skills back in the village where she grew up in China's Guangdong province, she tells me. As a little girl, she helped her parents, both vegetable farmers, sell produce at the market. When she got older, she worked with customers as a hairdresser.

Her family of six lived in a house with one bedroom, a living room, and a kitchen.

At some point, the government seized her father's land for development and evicted him, offering below-market compensation. Money got tight, and her mother went to work as a cook at a factory.

Then Jia's future husband came from the United States, where he was working in construction, to visit his family. The two met. He proposed. Jia eagerly accepted. "Absolutely, yes, right now!" she said.

Marriage meant moving to America. It meant financial stability, better education, and a brighter future for the next generation, she says. "Anything is much, much better than in China."

In California, Jia started from scratch. She didn't speak the language. She moved in with the in-laws, whom she'd never met before, in a house in Oakland with eleven people. She missed her family terribly.

She took classes at adult school, learned English, then got a degree in child development, while raising her own brood. A few years later, they saved up to buy a house on a tree-lined street and she opened her own business, a daycare for babies and toddlers.

I don't know if it's the dumplings that did it or the way we both straddle two worlds. Most likely, though, it's the effortless way in which she picks up Leah during our visit. Leah smiles back at her. The sight of it fills me with indescribable serenity and gratitude. I enroll her here, and later Greg. It turns out to be one of the best decisions I've ever made as a parent.

10. PROTESTS AND MYTHS

I had prided myself on being a chameleon, as many immigrant children do, but now I felt muddied by it—I felt like a liar.

—DINA NAYERI[1]

AFTER I GO BACK TO WORK, Leah, and then Greg, stop hearing Russian during the day. They're still exposed to it when they're home, of course, and when visiting my family on some weekends and socializing with other Russian-speaking families in town. From birthdays to picnics in the park, we share the same goal: to expose our American-born progeny to our heritage and to enjoy each other's company while we're at it. We take turns hosting playdates, where the adults chat over coffee, bagels with lox, and an occasional mimosa while the children play together. Around the holidays, we chip in to hire a Russian-speaking Santa Claus and his assistant, the wispy Snow Maiden, to sing songs, exchange presents, and play artificial snowballs with the kids. It's an idyllic, even if messy, scene.

There's a catch, though. Most of these two-parent households are like mine. One partner is a born and bred American. Our offspring discuss LEGO castles in the language they hear most: English. No adult wants to be that guy who crashes a kid fort party with "Now, everyone, one more English peep from you and this little shindig is over, I tell you. O-V-E-R. Is that clear? Well, go on now children, have a marvelous time!"

Extracurricular activities seem to be the answer. They're an opportunity for Leah to express herself creatively and to develop motor and social-emotional skills. And if that can be done in the native language, then all the better.

I take cues from her. Leah loves singing and making up her own lyrics. She'll ask to listen to anything from Beethoven to Broadway show tunes. By the time she's three, she's already made up her mind about which version of "New York, New York" she likes better, Frank Sinatra's or Liza Minnelli's (it's Liza Minnelli).

So I sign Leah up for weekly "Mom and Me" music sessions a few towns away. In this morning class, toddlers sing popular Russian songs, dance, and play coordination games. We attend every class in the session. But the drive is long and overwhelming, especially with a new baby. I scramble to pacify Greg, who accompanies us to class in his baby carrier and wails in the back seat when we get stuck in traffic.

A while later come piano lessons with a music instructor from Ukraine. She lives just a few blocks away. Her playful enthusiasm reminds me of my first piano teacher in St. Petersburg. I can hardly contain my excitement while waiting in her home piano studio, reminiscent of a Victorian sitting room with paintings in pretty frames, plants, and antique furniture. The teacher patiently shows Leah the notes and has her memorize finger numbers.

"Does this sound like a little hummingbird?" she trills the highest keys. "Or . . ." she lowers her voice, "like a big bad bear?"

"Hummingbird?" Leah answers.

"That's right! What about this one?" The teacher furrows her brows and presses chords on the low notes.

"Bear!" Leah is delighted.

I get so involved that I blurt out "Bear!" from my corner.

But after a few lessons, Leah loses focus. Instead of studying scales, she keeps running off to play with the teacher's cat. We decide to put piano off for a while.

Soon, an opportunity for a trial ballroom dance class in Russian comes along. Leah is already taking ballet in English once a week, but when she sees a video of a tango performance, she is transfixed and keeps asking for a lesson.

The dance teacher looks as if she'd just stepped off an international dance competition. She is muscular and graceful as she glides across the waiting room to welcome the children. She wears hoop earrings, and her shiny hair is pulled up in a high ponytail. Her Russian speech has no trace of an American accent, all of which boosts her credibility among the parents, eager for the old-country tutelage in just the way they remember it—or think they remember it.

The teacher ushers the students into the classroom. The adults stay in the waiting area, watching through the glass.

I hear the rhythm of the cha-cha. The instructor's words are muffled. The kids follow her lead and step right and left, backward and forward. They split up into couples, sometimes getting directions confused and bumping into one another or stepping on each other's toes. But the teacher quickly adjusts the tiny dancers and demos the steps again. They look adorably focused as they follow along.

The adults smile at one another and snap photos through the glass.

"Precious, aren't they?" one parent says.

"Oh look, look at how she fixes their posture! Our American ballet teacher last year just had them hop up and down," says a woman in a leopard print sweater. "*You twirled? Good job! You showed up to class? Great job!* No discipline at all," she shakes her head. She tries to get her daughter's attention on the other side of the glass and takes pictures with her phone.

That's right," someone else chimes in. "Children need authority, not finger painting. Dancing is not a game."

Others in the waiting room nod. In their words, I recognize my own anxiety. I, too, want my kids to learn extracurriculars from the experts, with a kind, yet firm teacher who likes discipline and doesn't congratulate them just for twirling or showing up. And preferably in the native language. I look around the room and feel understood. Maybe this is it. Maybe I've found this environment for Leah.

But then the mother in a leopard print sweater asks, "What's the teacher saying? Can anyone hear?"

Someone gets up and puts her ear against the door. "She is talking in English!"

People in the waiting room gasp. "English?"

"Yes, English."

There is a moment of silence. Then the room gets animated, as if someone pulled a fire alarm during a romantic dinner, just as the waiter brought out the escargot. Even the bespectacled father, who stepped out into the courtyard to do homework with his older son, returns to see what the commotion is about.

"Wait a minute, why English? This was supposed to be a Russian class, no?" the woman by the door asks.

"I didn't drive here all the way from San Francisco so my Alex can learn English! He does that plenty at school," someone adds.

"If this is how it's going be, I'm pulling Katerina out. We don't need this. English? *Tfu!*"

A parent knocks on the classroom door. The music inside stops. The teacher comes out.

"Yes?"

"Pardon me, but did we hear you speak in English in there?"

"Um, yes, I was instructing them in English." She seems surprised.

A chorus of voices joins in. "You see, we thought this would be a Russian class. And turns out it isn't. Would it be possible to conduct your instruction in Russian?"

The instructor considers this. "Umm, of course," she says. "It's just some of them don't seem to understand the language . . . too well." She explains this could get in the way of her ability to teach the material.

"But could you maybe try? They'll catch on."

She assures them she'll try. She smiles and goes back inside.

The cha-cha music starts up again and the kids practice their rock steps. The mom with her ear pressed against the door confirms that now the language is just right. The adults exhale in relief.

For all intents and purposes, my kids are growing up American. Their English is unaccented. They tell knock-knock jokes, attend American birthday parties, and know all the superheroes. Not to mention that's what their passports say.

The languages in my home are a hodgepodge, with plenty of code-switching. We watch family Disney movies and read *If You Give a Pig a Pancake* without fretting about stratified language input.

But there's an irrefutable other dimension to their lives. It's the family history and the idiomatic expressions, it's the native dishes and the language activity books, and beyond that, a sense of identity that's larger than the sum of its parts.

I try to read to them in the language almost daily and binge-buy many of the books used, from across the ocean. They arrive in thickly swaddled parcels dotted with foreign stamps. These books are the same vintage versions I'd left behind over two decades ago. The ornamental letters, the bright illustrations of witch houses on chicken legs—all of it is achingly familiar, even with bent corners and yellow washing across the paper. I hold my breath while turning the pages. Leah and Greg seem as fascinated as I once was.

I try to make time for uninterrupted Russian conversation at home. For the holidays, I show up at their preschool to make a presentation to their classmates about heritage customs, to make it all seem less weird and maybe even exciting. And as Leah gets older, I teach her to read and write in Russian. Soon, she can spot other Russian speakers at the park, even when I don't, and strikes up a conversation in their shared language. Her inflections are mismatched and her vocabulary is rudimentary, but as her interest grows, so does her knowledge.

And then—I should have seen it coming—it's her little brother's turn to rebel.

It begins soon after he transitions from Jia's daycare, where he was the oldest kid, to a large American preschool in our neighborhood. Now my three-year-old is surrounded by English-speaking peers.

In this new environment, Greg's vocabulary explodes in what feels like days. Up until recently, he understood English, Russian, and Cantonese to varying degrees. His English vocabulary was fairly basic, and Russian even more so. But now, all of a sudden, he's forming complex English sentences, even if only to inform Pete and me how he really feels about getting his hair cut. (Hint: not well.)

Soon, Greg is fidgety at preschool pickup when I greet him in Russian.

He continues to protest at the dinner table.

"No Russian! I don't like Russian!"

"Mommy and I speak Russian," Leah interjects nonchalantly, picking up a piece of broccoli with her fork, "because it makes our lives happier. May I have more broccoli, *Mama*?"

Greg throws pasta at her. Leah ignores him.

"Runglish is our secret language!" she adds.

When we read at bedtime, he scoffs at his favorite book about the circus, the one he's asked me to read probably a hundred times before.

I'm confused. "But why? You love this book."

"Because I don't want to read in Russian," he grumbles. He grabs an English picture book from the shelf and retreats to another room.

Boom. Denied.

I learned my lesson before, with Leah. It's what it is. I will meet him where he's at. Maybe he'll come back to it; maybe not. I follow Greg and we read the book that he's picked out.

Actually, it's not uncommon for toddlers with a school-aged brother or sister to have more advanced English compared to toddlers without such sibling. That older child acts like a bridge, bringing English home from school. That's what researchers Erika Hoff and Kelly Bridges discovered in studying Spanish-speaking bilingual families.[2]

Toddlers are more likely to interact with their older sibling in English than with others. English even rubs off on mothers. When a woman has a school-aged child, she ends up speaking more English with her kids, even with toddlers. This happens at the expense of the heritage language, which, not surprisingly, takes a dive.[3]

It's basically like a crafting party where someone brings glitter. Before you know it, glitter is everywhere. Except instead of glitter, it's English.

But just because you're learning English doesn't mean you can't learn another language at the same time, Hoff tells me. "There is no capacity limit in the brain that requires a tradeoff," she says. "It's just that in the US, as children get better and better at English, they hear and use Spanish less and less—with predictable consequences."

Greg's ambivalence doesn't last long. As COVID-19 puts the country under lockdown orders and children get tethered in front of computer screens for distance learning, I sign Leah up for an online Russian class. Greg, playing nearby, overhears it all: the sounds and the chattering of kids on the screen.

This type of secondhand exposure actually turns out to be a good thing. It makes the language less alien, more normalized. Soon Greg is articulating words and phrases on his own volition and asking for Russian stories again.

Besides, while sheltering in place, we're now spending all the time together, whether the kids like it or not. They both speak the language more—even at times when I don't.

. . .

I've read plenty of fiction about intergenerational conflicts, of children yearning to break free of the old-world bonds as they mature. I rebelled, too, back in the day. So did plenty of my peers from immigrant families. But now that we're older and at a different life stage, we're getting the taste of our own medicine. Sometimes, our children just don't find our heritage as cool or as necessary as we think it is—even if it's only a phase.

That's been the experience of Jia, the daycare owner from China.

"Should I celebrate Chinese New Year? Should I do Christmas?" she wondered after moving to the United States. "Then I decided, I want to do both. It was very hard from the very beginning," she says, referring to getting her kids to be on board with her customs. "I want them to know Chinese culture, and they learned their culture from their school and teachers and friends."

The children didn't like the Chinese classes their mom made them attend. They struggled with character writing. Jia's husband, who is from the same province as Jia, finally suggested letting them off the hook. "He said, it's okay, they can do good in their school and that's good enough and everybody's different."

To an exasperated parent, this refusal may make little sense. But why does resistance happen in the first place?

Usually, it's not personal. When the kids won't speak our language, it could mean they simply haven't had enough practice and exposure to the language, experts say.[4]

In fact, when the child won't respond in the heritage language, it's actually a good sign, says Erika Levy, Columbia University professor and trilingual speech-language pathologist, when I visit her in her office.

"That shows social awareness. Your child is socially healthy, knows who's in power," she says. If they won't reply in the language, talk to them anyway, and don't feel badly about bribes. "This is your time; this is before their brain has changed. They're hearing your accent, and they're getting something. Get those sounds in any way you can, early. They probably will come back later, grateful and wanting more."

But you can't force it, Levy adds.

Forcing a child to speak in a language that doesn't feel natural can be upsetting and make her resist it more.[5]

"Children who are punished for their errors will become self-conscious, ashamed, and quiet," Levy reminds parents in her book *Baby's First Words in French*. "The magic of children's rapid linguistic development has much to do with their uninhibited chattiness. . . . Conversations that are loving and rewarding work far better than anxiety-ridden sermons on how your baby should speak."[6]

Maybe the child is simply not ready at this point in her development, Levy writes. "No matter what you do, you will not be able to train your six-month-old to babble 'Oh, là là' or your two-year-old to recite Hamlet's soliloquy."[7]

Societal cues could also be the reason for kids shying away from the language, especially when English has a higher status (as mentioned in chapter 8). A child might also dislike it if she's witnessed her immigrant parents in an inferior position before.[8]

Whether the kids aren't on board with the language or the customs, it often triggers a classic response from the adults: *I left everything behind to give my children a better future, and now they're being ungrateful little pains in the neck.*

"That's the motivation and the story people bring with them: 'We're going to sacrifice for the sake of the next generation,'" says sociologist Nazli Kibria. "That can become a huge burden for people, because they feel the success of the whole immigrant project is on their shoulders."

Children just want to fit in, she explains.

"The hope is that the family itself would together develop some ways to be successful in the larger society but also preserve their identity and culture," Kibria tells me. "I see different families really negotiating well and some others not . . . It's not something that's written in stone. There is not one path. People just need to do the best they can to balance these things, . . . be willing to accept that things will not be the same."

And then one day, a child who rejects the ancestors' language might go off to college and decide to study it, she says.

Often, these tensions are just your basic parent-child relationship in a rapidly changing world, Kibria adds. Immigrants just have an added dimension to it.

She recommends joining heritage associations, language classes, and cultural hobbies like a choir, as well as trips home to maintain transnational ties.

And then there's the traditional food. "I think that's very American, but it's also very accepted of all the things that people do. There's the least resistance to keeping your food," she jokes.

. . .

Mei-Ling was born in China and lives in the Midwest with her American husband and two kids. She knows about resistance firsthand.

"They don't read as much as I used to when I was young," Mei-Ling says, disappointedly. "I would have rather them read extensively or do math or play outside more. I have a secret pleasure when I do math. I told my older one: every time I solve a math problem, I feel so giddy in my mind. He looked at me like I was a weirdo."

In over a decade that Mei-Ling has lived in America, she feels "very Westernized," she tells me. "My point of view sometimes is not a traditional Chinese way anymore. But there are times when I feel like I want to teach my boys what the Chinese would do."

Her sons, who attend elementary and middle schools, address the parents in English, even though her husband is fluent in Mandarin too.

When Mei-Ling was growing up, academic achievement came first. It's not what she's seeing around her, though. "I think in the US academics are being overlooked," she shares her concerns. "Maybe sports are being too emphasized. I feel like when my kids grow up, they're facing competition from kids that grew up in China or Russia or India."

Mei-Ling, who holds two graduate degrees, tried to engage her sons with tutors and Chinese school on weekends. "Like extra homework or self study, being ahead," she explains. But the kids wouldn't have it. One boy attends Chinese classes reluctantly. The other one stopped altogether. "It's actually just very short: a two-hour-long class, not that much," Mei-Ling tells me, baffled. "Of course, they do have homework . . ."

She works long hours at the office and doesn't always see eye to eye with her husband when it comes to the extracurriculars.

Eventually, the resistance got to be too much.

Now the boys are growing up in a more typical American way. Like their peers, they eagerly participate in sports teams and leagues year-round, from baseball and hockey to basketball. That means two to three practices per week for each child and at least one game on weekends.

Mei-Ling finds herself in a common immigrant predicament: cultural in-betweenness. She supports her children's passion but also wants them to know that their ancient heritage is more than just eating Chinese food.

"Celebrations and holidays, the food and stuff, it's very superficial. There are deeper levels of understanding," she says. "Kind of like holiness, sacredness. It's difficult to sense the gravity about those holidays: New Year, Mid-Autumn Festival. I wish they could understand. And when I try to explain why we do this, they're not interested," she sighs.

"Do you remember your cousin?" she asked one of her kids. "Last time we were in China, you guys played together. And he said, 'Who's that?'"

But Mei-Ling is not losing hope. Her son recently told her when he's older, he's going to have Mei-Ling live with him and support her, in a traditional way, she says.

In the end, all she can do is keep showing up. "I have no way to force it. What I can do is bring all the possibilities of the Chinese culture. Maybe when they're older, they can comprehend more." If her sons can learn to motivate themselves, "that's a bigger win," she explains using a sports reference.

When I touch base with Mei-Ling three years after we initially spoke, she has some updates. Her older son has been taking Chinese classes at his public high school for a year and enjoying them. "What he learned in Chinese school years ago helped him not only get placed into Level 2 class as a freshman but also handle the Chinese class with a lot ease," she shares in an email. And the younger one has agreed to take Chinese when he enters high school in a couple of years, she writes. "Surprisingly, they have less resistance to Chinese as they grow older, ha!"

I also ask Jaime Cárcamo, a clinical psychologist in New York, what he recommends when kids aren't interested in their parents' language and heritage.

Much of it goes back to the attitudes of the society. "They're receiving messages from the school and other peers, and from us, the parents, and so it creates a conflict in the child," says Cárcamo during our interview in his clinic. "Let's say a Hispanic-looking child that doesn't speak Spanish goes to school. His Hispanic peers may expect him to be Spanish speaking. So it creates an identity problem. Am I Hispanic, am I American, where do I fall in this?"

Parents should try to be proactive in understanding behavioral changes. But adults are often at a loss about what to make of their children's cultural identity issues. They may get frustrated or rigid, only adding to the problem.

"If you have more educated parents—let's say they tend to be more open-minded and receptive—they may be able to listen to their kids and guide them," says Cárcamo.

Yet all too often that's not the case, including for many of his clients in the New York area. "Many times, unfortunately, the parents that I've seen are very busy working: cleaning houses, those kinds of labor. They really don't pay attention to the mental health of the child. So kids are often neglected, not because their parents want to neglect them, but they have to take care of these basic needs first. They got to work, they have two jobs."

Conversations about "the realities of the world" go a long way, Cárcamo says. "This is where we live, we have to adapt and adjust to this culture. I mean, it goes back to Darwin . . . If you don't adapt, you perish. And at the same time, Mom and Dad bring these traditions, these belief systems. You cannot go one way or the other. You have to blend both of them."

Adopting a bicultural identity may be a healthier approach, Cárcamo tells me. "You have *that* identity, you know? I don't consider myself totally Salvadoran or totally American. I'm a bilingual individual with an accent, but I'm still American, I'm here, and I was raised here."

Younger children can't always express how they feel. In those cases, he recommends communicating through art. Ask your child to draw a person, a house, and a tree on separate pieces of paper, then inquire what that person is feeling, thinking, and doing, he says. Ask her to also describe the house and the tree. This exercise helps kids elaborate in their limited language. "And then you can really listen to what they really have to say," he adds.

Many immigrants, especially those with an undocumented status, don't always know about the resources available to them. Often, there are social workers and counselors at a child's school, family therapy, and nonprofit cultural organizations helping immigrants access services, Cárcamo says.

. . .

You know what else can get in the way of bilingualism? Misinformation.

Myth number one: bilingualism causes speech delays. It's not true. Bilingualism does not cause speech delays. Yet it's something we are often told by well-wishing relatives and sometimes even doctors. Sadly, this misconception is harmful. It can make families give up on their native language, as was the case of Mitali in Seattle, who wanted to teach Hindi to her sons from birth but was told to go all English.

But ask any bilingualism expert and they'll categorically tell you the same thing: bilingualism does not cause speech or language delays. Bilingual children, just as much as monolingual ones, vary in their rate of language acquisition, but they reach developmental milestones within the same time frame.[9] Bilingual and monolingual babies start babbling with repeated syllables (like *da-da-da*) at around the same age, between six and ten months.[10] The baby's first recognizable words might be spoken around the first birthday.[11]

Many children will differ in these averages, though. Naomi Steiner, author of 7 *Steps to Raising a Bilingual Child*, notes the range between eight and fifteen months for first words, for monolingual and for bilingual youngsters.[12] By eighteen months, they may be able to say roughly fifty words, though some may be hard for parents to understand.[13] At around eighteen months, many children might begin to make up two-word phrases.[14]

The myth about speech and language delay for bilingual kids is a pet peeve for Erika Levy. She even appeared on the *Today Show* to dispel it.[15] (Levy explains the difference between speech and language for me in layman's terms: speech is the physical way words and sentences are produced. Meanwhile, language is how we use words to communicate, including what words mean and how they can be combined to express ideas and wishes.)

"You don't end up with a disorder because you speak another language," she says emphatically. "People are told to stop speaking the second language when there is no reason to stop."

"There are people who say bilinguals are a little faster at saying their first words, others who say they're a little slower, but there's no big difference, regardless. It's something that we're very nervous about here. You go to Switzerland, and it would be weird to even have this conversation," says Levy, who's trained hundreds of Columbia Teachers College students to become bilingual speech-language pathologists. Many of them sought this school specifically because of its bilingual track option, one of the first in the country, and now work with immigrant populations in New York and nationwide.

There's a dearth of trained bilingual speech-language pathologists in the United States.[16] Children often get misdiagnosed as having a disorder just because they speak a different language, Levy adds. Or parents of bilingual kids who may actually have a disorder are sometimes incorrectly told everything's fine. "We need speech-language pathologists who can help bilingual children in the languages they speak," Levy says.

Oh, I get this worry about benchmarks, I do. Ours is a competitive culture that kicks in as soon as the baby is born. How long was labor, and how did it compare to that Instagram influencer for whom it took all of twenty minutes and was "all natural"? Is the newborn in the ninety-ninth percentile by weight, or only average? Is she nursing like a champ, like so-and-so's cousin's kid, or does it require the help of six lactation consultants? Is she sleeping through the night, like the baby of that Facebook acquaintance, or still waking up and crying every two hours?

When it comes to language acquisition, should my child be speaking by now? Okay, what about *now*? If I'm not worried, should I be?

∎ ∎ ∎

Exact milestones can vary, according to Levy. It's good to know them, but more important, look at the overall communication, even the nonverbal kind.

"If your child is pointing to objects, that's maybe more important than the first word," she tells me.

One potential red flag is if the child is not pointing around the age of one and doesn't seem to "intend to communicate." An example is if the child pulls a caregiver to the light switch to turn it on, without looking at that person. "So if they think of people as objects that need to do something, as opposed to communicating with them. When we see that intent to communicate doesn't seem to exist, that can be of concern. It's also important to know the variability of children, because there is so much," explains Levy, who is raising her own children bilingually, in French and English.

Some kids are late talkers. They may have more difficulty expressing themselves or understanding others compared to peers of the same age, says Levy. "Many of these children are considered simply late bloomers, who will catch up with their peers by the age of five."

Of these late talkers, a small subset might have more enduring language delays, "which may be an early sign of disorders, such as specific language impairment or a developmental disorder," explains Levy. "It's important to remember that bilingualism doesn't cause language disorders," she emphasizes. "And when monolingual or bilingual children do have specific language impairment or Down syndrome, for example, the bilinguals perform similarly to monolinguals on language tasks, suggesting that being bilingual does not make the language disorder more severe."

Remember that development benchmarks vary, Levy says, and try not to panic. Discuss your concerns with a pediatrician or a speech-language pathologist.

■ ■ ■

And that brings me to myth number two: bilingualism confuses children.

A well-traveled, multilingual American friend put off teaching her young child a second language. Her husband was adamantly against it: he thought it would confuse the kid. He was wrong. Now that the two are divorced, her preschooler is rapidly picking up Spanish in the bilingual preschool, the mom says, and has recently even started correcting her Spanish.

From their first moments, babies can already distinguish between languages they hear and not get confused. That's because the roots of bilingualism go back even before birth, in utero. In one study, newborns whose moms spoke only English while pregnant preferred hearing English to another language. Yet sure enough, infants who heard English and Tagalog in utero reacted to both of these languages similarly.[17]

And just when it hardly seems possible, researchers took it back even farther, all the way to the fetal stage. Using a noninvasive sensing technique, researchers at the University of Kansas observed expectant American mothers a month before their due date. They were interested in seeing how the fetuses responded when they heard an unfamiliar language—Japanese, in this case. Remarkably, the fetal heart rate changed when they heard a passage in an unfamiliar language played back.[18]

Young bilingual kids might mix languages—it's not a sign of confusion and actually quite normal. They're just learning and experimenting and will soon see these languages as separate, writes bilingualism researcher and author Colin Baker. If they code-switch at home, that's likely because they're taking cues from family members. When families keep the languages separate, the children code-switch less.[19]

I ask Fernanda from Brazil how her three-and-a-half-year-old is juggling Portuguese, German, and English.

"She's not confused," says Fernanda, a little taken aback by my question. I get a sense that to her and her kid, it's not a juggling act but a normal part of life, not unlike eating breakfast and brushing teeth. She tells her daughter something in Portuguese and the girl responds in Portuguese, nodding and climbing off the swing set. I give her chocolate.

"Thank you," her daughter tells me politely, in unaccented English. We help her open the box of sweets. Then she stuffs a piece of chocolate in her mouth and dashes across the field with the rest, as Fernanda and I chase after her.

Fernanda is calling out to her as we run. I don't speak Portuguese, but I'm fairly certain she's saying, "Come back! Don't eat all the chocolate! Do you hear me?" I guess, what else is a mother to say in these circumstances, regardless of where she's from?

11. LIVE AND LEARN

*We share much more in common with
one another than we have in difference.*

—VIET THANH NGUYEN[1]

THE WORKDAY IS DONE. I'm rushing to pick up the kids from preschool. We enrolled Leah here, then Greg, after they aged out of Jia's daycare, following emotional good-byes.

Greg's lunchbox will probably return home with the contents barely eaten. Today it's buckwheat groats and ground chicken patties. Like yesterday's lunch of carrot pancakes with sour cream, most will be discarded.

His predominantly American classmates eat sandwiches for lunch, Greg wistfully explains at home. The ones with sunflower-seed butter inside (a low-allergen alternative to peanut butter). He asks for a peanut butter and jelly sandwich for dinner, in English.

I look at Pete.

"Sure, bud, I'll make you one," Pete says, not looking at me. He knows that as an Eastern European immigrant, I still struggle with the concept of a cold dessert sandwich being a meal, especially when referring to a nut paste smothered between two slabs of presliced bread.

I begin to fantasize about transferring my kids to a Russian preschool. The closest one would add nearly two hours of travel per day on a congested highway, on top of our existing commutes. But maybe it's worth it? My kids would sing songs about nesting dolls. They'd eat soup for lunch, made by a doting grandma in the nearby kitchen. They'd learn the language and study music and art. The more I dwell on it, the guiltier I feel about denying my children the cultural bedrocks of my forebears. In that preschool of my imagination, Greg would learn to recite the Cyrillic alphabet, forward and backward. Maybe he'd casually mention the elements from Mendeleev's periodic table during pickup. He might even ask to be put on the phone with his grandparents, to recite a Russian poem, whereupon they would weep with joy.

"Finally!" my parents would exclaim. "Aren't you glad you're nurturing your child's potential, the way it was *meant* to be nurtured? What did they even teach at that American preschool—making art out of toilet paper rolls? We told you so."

My daydream is over. I join Pete in fixing that peanut butter jelly sandwich and make an extra one for myself. Because like any forbidden fruit, it's damn delicious.

The next day, I pack a lunch sandwich in Greg's lunchbox. And chicken nuggets the day after that. I hold his hand as we walk into the brightly lit preschool building. With his backpack with Disney cartoon characters, he dashes into the classroom, the door closing behind him.

■　■　■

The desire to give the next generation our cultural learning experience can be visceral and unrelenting. And yet the preschools many immigrants settle on often look and sound very different.

Why is that? Is it a matter of cost? Availability? The personality fit? It's a little bit of everything, I'm seeing.

Some argue that when there's a will, there's a way, and preschools are no exception. I hear all kinds of heroic stories about families moving just to be near a desirable preschool. Or they enroll the child somewhere near their work, trekking together an hour each way as the kid finishes breakfast and does art projects in the car. Or one parent—usually the mother—quits her office job to drive the kids. Sometimes, those with resources even invest in a second home, biding weeknights there and weekends back on the home turf.

But we, for the time being, are staying put. After touring a few local facilities, Pete and I find one in the neighborhood that fits most criteria we're looking for and, most important, feels like home.

Leah and Greg's American preschool becomes an indelible part of our family for many years. It's where they tend to a garden and learn to color inside the lines and talk about their feelings. On holidays, they perform in a little neighborhood amphitheater next door, dancing to "Thriller" for Halloween and belting out "This Land Is Your Land" and "Feliz Navidad" in adorable reindeer ears, as parents huddle in the audience, snapping pictures and blotting their eyes. It's where I volunteer for sing-along and know the name of their every classmate. It's where families participate in community potlucks, complete with pasta salads and hot dogs.

Even our morning walk to the preschool turns into a magical quest, first in a red pull wagon, then by foot in slow strides, then on a scooter. The trek is filled with familiar mileposts: a decorative ball in the neighbor's yard that needs waving to, a wooden fairy door affixed to the trunk of a tree, a row of bushes you can press your palm against and feel the branches recoil against the fingers as you move. The routine of our walks and the attentiveness of the teachers are the things they will remember more than anything else, I tell myself. They are happy. They are loved. What can be more important than that?

■ ■ ■

But I'd be lying if I said that I didn't wonder if I'd made the right choice during these formative years.

Keeping the family legacy and language was also important for Yael, who moved from Israel with her husband and children. She wanted her kids to hold on to their Hebrew. In addition, she wanted an environment that offered plenty of playtime, similar to what she was used to in Israel. Back home, her daughter could show up "with a magic wand, in wings and high heels, and nobody would tell her it's not allowed," recalls Yael, a mother of four.

She visited a few preschools in Silicon Valley, but the ones she saw felt too regimented for her taste. "It's all sort of uptight—they don't let kids monkey around and just be kids," Yael says. She says she also didn't expect the high level of oversight, like "don't wipe the butts, don't touch the child." Back home, there'd be one form to fill out. But in America, you need twelve forms and signatures from all the doctors, she says. "It's crazy."

Yael eventually enrolled two of her kids in a preschool founded by an Israeli expat. They sang in Hebrew, danced traditional dances, and celebrated Shabbat, on top of American holidays. When Chinese and

Indian families enrolled their kids, they would quickly pick up Hebrew too.

"Everybody says, 'Oh, the kids are being spoiled,'" Yael says. "But what does it mean, spoiled? These children join the army at eighteen. I didn't care at all whether they're learning to read, write, and count. It was important for me that they had this playtime, and lots of it."

· · ·

Other families, on the contrary, report they want little to do with the early learning from their homeland.

One immigrant mother I know sent her child to an American preschool, even though she had other options nearby. After years of living in the US, she still sometimes feels like an outsider, she confides. She doesn't want the same for her daughter. "I want her to fit in," she explains. "She lives in America."

Then there's Elena, who emigrated from Georgia, a nation formerly under the Soviet rule. She wasn't keen on a Russian-speaking preschool for her child. Elena still gets flashbacks to the tough-love schooling she'd witnessed back home in lower elementary grades. "Got a math problem wrong? You get paraded in front of the class as an idiot who can't do math. Made some other mistake? You're shamed in front of other teachers," she recalls.

Though she's no longer in Georgia, Elena worried the steamrolling style from the old country might follow all the way to Portland, where she lived at the time. "My kid and my paranoia will stick to our *Portlandia*-style preschool," she decided, "with a climbing wall and a vegetable garden."

· · ·

Amandine, from France, shares a similar reluctance with me about the learning from her homeland. After arriving from France, she enrolled her young son in first grade of a local French elementary school on the East Coast. It was familiar. It celebrated the heritage. It seemed *très fantastique*.

But it was a rude awakening. "Even if you're a good student, you can always do better. They acted toward my son—he has to adapt to the school, the school doesn't have to adapt to the child," she says.

"The teacher will come and hand you back the papers, and they will start with the highest grade and then go down until the very last grade, during which it would be a real humiliation, torture!"

She ended up pulling him out and placing him in an American elementary school instead. There, the boy blossomed and made friends.

So when time came for her younger daughter to head to elementary school, Amandine briefly considered the French option, then concluded *non*. "I'm not gonna sacrifice another one," she tells me.

•   •   •

Here, I should probably point out a secret early-learning ingredient for many immigrant families. It's not the cost. It's not the location. It's not even the mother tongue.

It's academics.

To be fair, academics have taken the front seat in many American preschools. In an attempt to close the achievement gap and prepare children for kindergarten, there's a nationwide trend of teaching reading, memorization, and "seat work" type tasks at earlier ages.[2]

"There's just more of a sense that you'll fall behind if you aren't doing those things in earlier years," says Maki Park, senior policy analyst for Early Education and Care at the Migration Policy Institute, when we talk. Preschool enrollment for three- and four-year-olds has become more of a norm in recent years, even when the family has a stay-at-home parent, she says. "At the same time, we know from research that immigrant families are less likely to be participating in those kinds of programs."

The achievement gap is getting wider, but the reason isn't necessarily that students from low-income families have fallen behind. "It's because those who are well-to-do are coming in at higher and higher achievement levels even before kindergarten because of the way that parenting and early childhood education is now being pursued," Park explains.

For foreign-born parents, education isn't just a way to keep up with the Joneses, whether it starts before kindergarten or after. It's a ticket out of poverty. It's the immigrant's currency.

The babe may still be in diapers, but the elders can already see his future. They know for certain that once he's come of age, if not before, he will have a real vocation, not just a pastime to express his innermost feelings. Under no circumstance will he be permitted to wait till his late twenties to self-actualize on some backpacking trip to Europe or discover a higher calling on a mushroom-fueled vision quest. None of that liberal arts nonsense. He will have a real job, with a respectable purpose: to pay the bills. Beginning at a tender age, the immigrant child's educational events are primed toward survival.

"Ah, so you're Russian?" notes an enrollment coordinator at a French early education center when I call to ask about their waitlist. On the other end of the line, I imagine a French headmistress gazing over her pince-nez. Her voice softens when I mention my birth country. "Our cultures share the same love of learning!" she adds. She encourages me to apply.

This expectation follows immigrant kids from cradle to college and beyond.

Back in college, an immigrant friend was told by her father she could study anything she wanted. ("It's a free country!" he announced to her.) But the only major her parents would be willing to support financially was molecular biology. That or computer science.

After moving to New York for graduate school, I saw an apartment in Brooklyn for rent. The landlord called me soon after. But he didn't call to offer a lease. With an Italian accent, he insisted that I speak to his daughter, who, in spite of his best intentions, was refusing to go to law school.

"Just tell her," he urged. "Tell her why being a lawyer will give her a good life. You're from a nice immigrant family, the both of you. You're the same age. She'll listen to you."

"But I'm not studying to be a lawyer," I tried to explain. "My family is just as disappointed as you are." (Maybe even more disappointed, I almost added, because I wasn't studying to be a doctor or an engineer either.)

The Italian dad wouldn't budge. Graduate schools were all the same to him. And his daughter had to go to one. The law one.

"I hate law!" his daughter sniffled on the phone when we talked. "I want to be an artist. I'm sick of playing by their rules."

I don't remember my exact words, but they probably sounded something like "You and me both, sister! Don't let the ancestors jerk you around. You do you."

In the end, I failed at convincing her to choose a practical career. I also didn't get the apartment.

■ ■ ■

Pragmatic education is something sociologist Philip Kasinitz and his colleagues observed in their study of the children of immigrants and those who arrived in the US at a young age, published in a book *Inheriting the City: The Children of Immigrants Come of Age.* "Those respondents who grew up with immigrant and native born minority parents had less option to think about education in terms of personal fulfillment," the researchers write. "Almost all these respondents thought that education was the only route out of poverty." For instance, many working-class Chinese parents in the study may not have had a lot of schooling themselves, Kasinitz writes, but they had high educational ambitions for their children. Chinese American respondents "often mentioned how their parents would compare them—usually unfavorably—with the children of relatives and friends who were doing well."[3]

The authors found that young people from immigrant households and from native-born families of color reported the same message from the elders: "They would have to work harder than other groups to get ahead."[4]

It turns out these great academic expectations, coupled with immigrant resourcefulness and the tendency for young adult children to live at home, deliver results. No wonder the children of immigrants (and those who arrived as kids) outdo their parents and, often, their American peers in most measurable markers of success. There's even a name for this phenomenon: the second generation advantage.

Kasinitz's study of New Yorkers from immigrant families found them to be overwhelmingly fluent in English, compared to their parents. They also have higher incomes and educational attainment. More exceptional is the fact that they often do better than their native-born peers.[5]

A 2013 Pew Research study captures similar findings for the country as a whole. Second-generation Americans are outperforming their parents, earning more, and graduating from high school and college at higher rates. More of them are homeowners and fewer live in poverty.[6]

"The ability to select the best traits from their immigrant parents and their native born peers yields distinct *second generation advantages*," wrote Kasinitz and his coauthors in their findings. ". . . In developing a strategy for navigating challenges, second generation youngsters do not have to choose whether being foreign or being American is 'better.' They can draw on both cultures."[7]

The native-born population is taking notice. Some worry about what this second-generation advantage could mean for them, Kasinitz tells me.

"A lot of upper-class Americans feel the children of immigrants are eating their lunch," Kasinitz adds. "Some of the hysteria among natives has to do with the fact that they feel they're being competed against. The arms race is getting ratcheted up."

Could our vigilance, or that of our parents, and all that nagging in multiple languages have a silver lining, in that it's doing the next generation good? At least *measurably* so?

. . .

Academic achievement is held in extra high regard in many immigrant communities. That includes mine.

Discussions about it often pop up in my conversations and on social media. "Is twenty hours of extracurricular activities per week enough?" asks a woman in one of my online groups. Her child is seven.

Another mom is seeking online recommendations for a coding class for her five-year-old—and gets bombarded with recommendations.

. . .

Sasha, who moved from Ukraine to go to college in the Northeast, has two kids. In her household, education is paramount.

She tells her eight-year-old daughter that "math is the most important thing on earth if she wants to be a successful professional," says Sasha, who holds an MBA and works for the federal government.

When her daughter was just three years old, Sasha started doing math with her daily. Although the girl is in third grade, she's already placed out of fifth-grade math in her public elementary school in California. Luckily, Sasha says, she spoke to the teacher and the school principal and they excused her from most of the school math.

"I said, if you guys want to, keep giving her the next level, but they were not interested. The reason why I even reached out to them is not to brag, but she started really complaining this year that she is really bored," Sasha explains to me. "Even if you look at textbooks online, the third grade level starts to diverge pretty significantly in terms of what is done in Ukraine." (She calls it "simple American math.")

Sasha found a tutor in Kyiv, who does a video class with her daughter twice a week and assigns daily homework. Now the girl does her Ukrainian math homework during class.

Her daughter also takes piano classes and practices daily. She attends gymnastics and judo weekly, and, until recently, also contemporary dance and silks class. The last two weren't difficult, Sasha clarifies: it was one lesson after another on a weekend. "I only had to drive her once. She really loves it."

Russian language is also important for the family heritage. The girl enjoys reading, but Sasha also encourages her to write. "I just tell her maybe to copy something or write a little essay."

Recently, when her grades were not perfect in English writing, Sasha she hired a high school student to work with her in the summer. Her daughter is now above her grade level in spelling and English grammar, so there is no more need for a tutor, Sasha explains.

Sasha manages all of these activities while working full time.

The kids (she also has a younger son) hardly watch TV. "Maybe she watches one little cartoon with her little brother for five minutes, which we use as positive reinforcement for him to brush his teeth. She is an easy kid," Sasha says. But it's not just busy work, she explains. "The reason why we signed her up for so many sports is she was awkward. She would sit on a chair and suddenly fall and chip her tooth. Now it's night and day, a complete turnaround."

Her brother is a total opposite. "I think I'll sign him up for sports, I'll have no choice. Everything else, oh, I can already foresee a struggle!" Sasha says, laughing.

Recently, someone in an online discussion group called her a "crazy mom." "I don't feel that way," Sasha says. "Maybe there have been times I was a little extreme, but we found a balance and she has time to play and read a book. You need to get them to do something. It's not hard for us."

. . .

My children are far from clocking in twenty hours of extracurricular activities a week, like in that online group. Still, I'm feeling the pressure. My own upbringing with its focus on education and grit—the antidote to starting over—is staring me in the face.

How do people manage to get the kids to multiple classes a week if they both work full time? Is it better, as the mom of Leah's American friend puts it, to just let her "play outside to get her wiggles out" in the afternoons? Am I setting my children up for success or beleaguering them with the collective expectations of family and immigrant classmates?

I'm still sorting that one out. I'm also figuring out the interests and the learning style of each child. And our own abilities to make it happen.

As the new school year begins, we've got a few activities lined up for the kids. Now that Leah is six, she also wants to study piano again, so I sign her up at a local music school. We begin practicing together every day and, oddly, entirely in Russian. As I teach her the scales, the hand positions, and her first pieces, reviving them from memory, piano becomes more than an extracurricular. It turns into a journey for us both.

. . .

I'm still curious to see what a bilingual preschool looks like. Not just from hearsay but from the inside.

A friend raves about a daily Persian immersion program located in El Cerrito, next to the progressive city of Berkeley. It's also the first of its kind in the United States. I decide to go and visit.

I walk up a set of stairs painted with a Middle Eastern motif until I reach the entrance of the school, called Golestan, meaning "a garden of flowers" in Persian.[8]

Like many endeavors, the idea for Golestan Education sprang up from a parent who saw a larger need not being met. Yalda Modabber, cofounder and executive director of this nonprofit, grew up in Iran and worried about her American-born children losing the connection to their heritage. So with a few like-minded friends, she started an informal playgroup. It quickly grew. They invited a teacher, then a teacher's aide, then moved into a historic house in Berkeley. Soon, even that wasn't large enough.

Today, Golestan is a sprawling eighteen thousand square-foot green campus, with bird feeders, sun-drenched classrooms, wooden desks (no plastic is allowed on campus, for the most part), Persian wool rugs, and an Alice Waters–inspired edible school yard. Kids grow their food, then eat it in the school kitchen, learning about the food cycle. Green plums, pomegranates, and tangerines from Iran grow here. The house chef prepares the meals right on site with organic ingredients and seasonal and local produce.

"It is a place that smells like baked bread, tastes like fresh greens, and sounds like the United Nations," reads Golestan's website. It certainly seems that way as I walk past the classrooms, each equipped with a large sliding door and an outdoor patio. In one, a group of toddlers is doing circle time: they've linked hands and are walking and singing a Persian song with the teachers.

"Nima-Joon!" I hear the teacher calling out to one of the toddlers. (*Joon* is a term of endearment.) Many students here have a Persian family member, but not all.

Children in the next group are busy inspecting the ground with little magnifying glasses. They are learning about sharing the planet, explains Yalda.

The American play structures have minimized risk, necessary for healthy child development, Yalda tells me, but left the hazards. Golestan designed their playground to offer "risk, but no hazard," she says as we pass by youngsters climbing through a mesh net tunnel, jumping on bales of hay, and enthusiastically rolling barrels in the spacious yard.

I notice a music room stocked with beanbags and musical instruments, from piano to the traditional *daf* drum and the stringed *tar* and *santoor*.

Yalda's own immigration story, in part, is what brought the school idea to fruition. After coming to Massachusetts as a nine-year-old, she was physically bullied by classmates.

The American girls around her dressed in pants, but she wore skirts and had an accent. She also happened to come during the Iranian hostage crisis, when militants stormed the US Embassy in Tehran and took dozens of Americans hostage for more than a year. "It was really a hard time for the Iranians," recalls Yalda, who speaks three languages and went on to graduate from Harvard Medical School and became a molecular immunologist.

Her school is now so popular that women sign up for the waitlist while pregnant; the list ran three binders long before they digitized it. Some families move just to be closer; one would even drive over seventy miles one way daily to bring their two children there, Yalda tells me.

On top of teaching, Golestan advises educators across the world on language immersion and hands-on teaching techniques.

"Any child I ever met has a love of learning," says Yalda. "You can teach a two-year-old about the universe—the sun doesn't move, the earth rotates about the sun—very easily but through play. But if you sit them in a classroom with desks, they're not going to want to know more about it."

The preschool is taught entirely in Persian. Weekend classes alone, Yalda says, are not enough.

"I have a tremendous respect for weekend language schools [but] one of the biggest challenges is the parents don't speak the language at home during the week, and every week [the weekend school] has to start all over again."

The school recently added elementary classes, and Yalda wanted more languages for the older cohort. But which ones?

One day she was listening to Barack Obama's United Nations assembly speech. "All of a sudden, I had this lightbulb moment when I realized I wanted it to be Persian, Hebrew, and Arabic. It was this click. I ran upstairs to my husband saying, 'I got it! I got it!'"

People have tears in their eyes when they find out about their language offerings, Yalda says. "Our cultures are actually the same. Our languages are similar. Our rituals are almost identical. Yet these three groups perceive themselves to be so different." Now all elementary school students are learning all three languages, with the rest of instruction conducted in English.

Persian-language education isn't the school's only goal, Yalda says. She wants to cultivate a love of learning and empathy in children and raise responsible change makers. Much of it boils down to her immigration experience and personal philosophy. "As a parent," Yalda says, "my priority was that my kids be kind."

12. "THEY SAY LITTLE RACIST THINGS"

Do you know what a foreign accent is?
It's a sign of bravery.

—AMY CHUA[1]

IT'S TOUGH to be an interpreter when you're a kid. But that's what Amira had to do after immigrating from Iraq to Michigan with her family. She helped her mother, who was still learning English, navigate their new life in the West.

"You live in America! What the hell are you speaking?" a woman lashed out when Amira was out shopping with her mom one day. "Tell her to speak in English!"

Amira was barely ten years old at the time, but she mustered all the courage she had and held her own. "I speak English," she countered. "And my mother doesn't have to speak English. We live in this country and we belong here."

The woman pressed on. "People are gonna think you're talking about us. How do I know she's not talking about me?"

"You must be really unhappy to think my mother is talking about you," Amira retorted.

"People would hear us and they would say very, very rude things," Amira tells me about speaking Arabic and Chaldean with her parents in public when growing up. "I was subject to ridicule and criticism. It just showcases someone's lack of evolution and intellect. And frankly, we still live in that time."

She hasn't had these run-ins as an adult. Her English, her third language, is unaccented, and she didn't stand out much as a foreigner growing up, she explains. Another reason is the company she keeps.

"I surround myself with a tremendous amount of diversity. I have friends who are Indian, I have friends who are Black, I have friends who are Jewish. Many of them are immigrants. All are well educated. That changes the dynamic."

. . .

Just as for Amira, it doesn't take much to make foreign-born folk aware of their difference. People mistrust what they don't know, no matter their ideology. Progressives can get weirded out by foreign accents just as conservatives can rally around immigrant causes.

And contrary to popular perceptions, not all immigrants are liberal. Those from the former Soviet Union, Cuban Americans, and Vietnamese Americans, just to name a few, are a sizable conservative voting bloc, even though politicians often lump Latinos and Asians in one homogenous category.[2]

My acquaintance Deborah, a US military officer and a liberal, tells me how worried she was after hearing a security guard at work speak with a Russian-sounding accent.

Deborah's no stranger to accents, mind you. She grew up in a Spanish-speaking household (though her parents stopped talking to her in Spanish "because of the looks they got from other people," she says).

But the security guard made Deborah uncomfortable. There she was, handling classified information as the Russian-American relationship was tanking following the 2016 election meddling scandal. Could this Russian-sounding guy be up to something shady?

"I didn't say or do anything," Deborah assures me, "but was wary."

She soon found out the security guard was not Russian but Ukrainian, with "a very different perspective entirely," she says. "It reminded me that we never really know a person's story solely based on one data point."

. . .

I often get questions about my heritage.

Questions like "Where are you from? No, I mean, where are you really from, before that?"

"Wow, your government is pretty screwed up. Any plans to move back?"

"My housekeeper is Russian too! But she's so nice. Do you know her?"

"Funny, you don't look like the girls from your country. What are you?"

I don't take it personally. The strangers doing the asking usually don't mean to call me out or to reduce me to a line on a birth certificate. They might be curious and eager to connect.

Still, even the most well-intentioned inquiry can sometimes thrust the foreign-born folk squarely in the limelight as de facto spokespersons for their ethnicity. Social structures come toppling, with the blaze detectible only by those who'd gotten burned, now waving away the smoke.

■　■　■

"So where are you from?" a Lyft driver in Chicago booms from the front seat during our drive through the Windy City as we chat about the tourist attractions.

"I'm from California."

"And before then?" he continues.

I hesitate. "Oh, Eastern Europe."

"Like, where?"

I answer, somewhat reluctantly.

This makes the driver animated. "Oh, you hacked our election! I should report you to Lyft!" I feel the vehicle speeding up.

These taunts from strangers have gotten tiring in the past few years. They're no longer funny. Maybe they never were. I've got no energy to explain.

The driver picks up on my silence in the back seat.

"Hey, I was only kiddin'. I know you didn't mess with our election," he says. "Or did you?" he adds, just to make sure.

"Nope," I answer. "That's why I'm an immigrant. I live here, not there."

He talks about the Navy Pier and the merits of Lou Malnati's versus Giordano's. Despite my love of Chicago-style pizza, I'm having a hard time paying attention. I'm ready to be done with this ride.

■　■　■

There are deeper layers to these dynamics, multiple undercurrents. I think back to a dinner date in San Francisco before I met my husband.

"Can we swap tables and move down that way?" my date asks the restaurant busboy.

"What?" asks the busboy.

"Swap seating arrangements?" my date repeats, growing a little impatient. "Like, switch?"

The busboy stands there, confused.

I recognize it all: anguish, pride, a desire to pretend to understand *swap* and *switch*, even though he really doesn't. Not that long ago, I'd also wondered why the heck English has so many synonyms for a word as simple as *change*.

My date isn't trying to be an asshole. He is kind, and like so many people on earth, he's battling his own demons and invisible illnesses. He just happens to be a monolingual native English speaker who grew up in the suburbs around other native speakers. In college, he studied liberal arts with native speakers, in addition to being tall, white, and male. The way he shows up in his world, at job interviews, at happy hours, makes it easy for people to pronounce his name. Girls usually swipe right for him. His résumé is more likely go to in the pile with the Jennifers and Stephens, as opposed to the other pile with Svetlanas and Jamals. He'll probably never know what it's like to be in that other pile.

"You know, like, switcheroo?" my date keeps trying to explain in his booming voice.

"Sorry, I don't understand," the busboy finally says.

"If he doesn't understand 'switch,'" I quietly say, "he won't understand 'switcheroo.'"

I turn to the busboy and ask him about changing the tables, with sparse words and body language, all of which takes one second. This is my other language, my phantom limb, the one I've had the privilege of carrying for over twenty years. Spoken by millions in this country, this utilitarian tongue's got no dictionary or a writing system in its name, because it's designed to convey the basic facts as efficiently as possible. It's bare-boned, stripped of tenses, articles, and phrasal verbs, loosely held together with gestures and smiles for connective tissue.

"Okay, it's okay," the man says, smiling, and leads us to a different table.

My date didn't catch what happened. He pulls the chair out for me and recommends his favorite items from the happy hour menu.

But I'm struggling to bring myself back into his Anglo-centric worldview, with its bison sliders and an oyster selection "to die for." Suddenly, I am the busboy, and not this woman wearing a J.Crew sheath dress and a pearl necklace, even if the pearls aren't real. Not too long ago I, too, didn't know what *switch* and *seating arrangements* meant and wondered why someone *tears* the paper yet has *tears* in his eyes.

I think about my relatives who are regularly told, in a kindly sort of way, "Still didn't lose the accent, huh?" at ticket booths and ice cream parlors and questioned about their allegiances.

I think about the doctor who'd interrupt my grandmother whenever she read her symptoms off the paper she'd prepared the night before, writing out words from the dictionary in her neat teacher's handwriting.

"Look, I don't have time for this," the doctor would say to me, tapping the pen against his clipboard. "Can you just have her tell you and then translate?"

English, for my grandmother, is a beast, but having survived the war and immigrated in her golden years, my grandmother is unafraid to wrangle it. Apologetic and eager to connect, she practices at every opportunity—with bus drivers, librarians, and neighbors flinging their garages open for sidewalk sales. Most people smile back, engaging and welcoming her efforts.

"Is *stomach* in English *STOH*-much or stoh-*MUCH*? It's all in my note for the doctor right here," my grandmother tells me at the next appointment. "How do you say: 'Doctor, may God give your family a long prosperous life and good health?' You must always be prepared. You live almost eighty years, you'll understand."

I get her glasses and we work on pronunciation until the doctor enters the exam room. He quickly nods at me. He doesn't look at her at all.

．　．　．

Francis, a documentary filmmaker, emigrated from Brazil to the United States when he was seven years old. People still ask him what he is.

At a recent party in New York, a wealthy American tried to peg his background.

"'You're Brazilian? No, you're white, you're white!'" that person exclaimed, Francis says. "He kind of added me to the white team without me asking for it. All of a sudden he's giving me a pass to be his friend. Sure, I'm white Brazilian, but I'm still Latino. I didn't feel like I was part of the white crowd in Pittsburgh," he points out, referring to the place he lived after immigrating.

His ethnicity tends to crop up in strange ways. "If I say what people agree with, I'm on their team. The moment I say something they disagree with, they say, 'Oh, you're Brazilian.'"

■   ■   ■

I also talk to Vlada, a teacher in San Francisco. Occasionally, when others hear a trace of an accent in her speech, they assume she doesn't speak good English. But she does.

"I have an MA in English from Stanford, thank you very much," she wants to say but holds her tongue.

Instead, she explains that she was born in Moldova. The reply sometimes is "Great job. You speak a lot of English."

Vlada is also Jewish; she left Moldova to escape anti-Semitism. But her heritage isn't easy to peg in one sentence. "Being from Moldova entails understanding of where Moldova is," says Vlada. Besides which, her native language isn't Moldovan. It's Russian, since Moldova was under the Soviet rule for many decades. It's sort of like the Russian Manifest Destiny, explains Vlada, who also knows Spanish and Hebrew.

"I want them to know that there is a reason why I speak Russian but don't really speak Moldovan. This, however, involves a long lecture and very quickly becomes dry," says Vlada, who also founded a nonprofit organization for teen leadership, cultural competency, and social justice at the San Francisco high school for immigrants, where she teaches.

Regardless of where she is or what language she is using, she often gets asked the same question: "Where are you from?"

Explaining her story is emotionally fraught. "Only now, thinking about this question, I am also for the first time realizing that it holds emotional labor," she says. "I wish that I wasn't a refugee and didn't have to lose my homeland."

. . .

I've also asked strangers where they are from. I've gotten political regimes and dictators confused. Accidentally butchered foreign names, no matter how hard I tried to get them right. Attempted to guess someone's place of birth by the sound of their accent.

Unless there is respectful dialogue, how will we understand difference and discover our shared humanity? How will we repair the disconnect unless we talk and ask questions?

Curiosity is inevitable.

Carelessness and cruelty, however, are not.

Like that sign in my high school: *Welcome to California. Now Go Back Home.*

Sorry, we don't rent to Russians here.

Why do you even want to teach English Composition at our school? Just stick to your language.

No offense, but I don't date people with your background.

I don't need to explain how dehumanizing it feels to be told to go back to where you came from. To be denied jobs or housing based on your origins. To be pressured into reciting your family tree just to satisfy a stranger's fleeting curiosity or unpack generational trauma for the sake of a job interview.

It's no surprise that few like to talk about being treated differently as an immigrant. When in the course of my interviews this topic comes up, most people go quiet. Some look at their partner for support. Or say they don't remember. They point out that it's just a part of life, a requisite stumbling block on their American path that's otherwise filled with optimism and tenacity.

I understand what's behind this reluctance. Hashing it out won't change the past, so what's the use in dwelling on it? It's not like the others will understand anyway. It's been a part of the immigrant survival experience for centuries. Just keep your nose to the grindstone. Just keep going.

. . .

Miguel and Christine, the couple in Utah have also run into stereotypes.

After the couple got married, Christine's dad was worried that Miguel, an immigrant from Mexico, was "only trying to get papers," Christine says.

Her family members still struggle to understand his Spanish accent, she says. "They're like, what? What are you trying to say? But it hasn't happened a lot lately," she adds.

The first year they got married, the couple decided to start a holiday tradition. They headed to Walmart in Salt Lake City to buy a Christmas tree.

"It was right after Halloween," says Christine. "And I thought, oh, we should start getting decorations for Christmas up. And so we went and it was in November. They had Christmas things ready."

Miguel asked a saleswoman on the floor where the Christmas trees are located.

The saleswoman responded with, "What did you say?"

Miguel repeated, "A Christmas tree."

"What is that?"

Christine overheard the exchange from another aisle. She yelled out, "A Christmas tree!"

"Oh, Christmas trees! Down this aisle," the saleslady offered, to Christine.

I ask if Miguel's accent threw the saleswoman off.

Nope, that isn't it, Christine says. "She did understand it, because she repeated: Christmas tree? She was acting like, oh, you don't know what you're talking about."

Miguel interjects. "Let me say it: a Christmas tree." He waits for my reaction.

"Yeah, that sounded like Christmas tree to me," I say. And it did. The three syllables, the vowels, the consonants are all there, even with an accent.

There's the issue of trust, which comes up for Miguel at the hospital where he works.

"Sometimes people take time to trust me," he says. "I don't know if it's because I'm a guy or Latin. So sometimes the people that are confused, they say little racist things or be like, you're not my nurse, or I don't want you here, I don't want you in my bed with me."

It doesn't happen much, he assures me. And when it does, he just calls another nurse over, he says.

The other day, he was going to administer a narcotic to a patient and the patient's wife wanted to know "Where's the other person that's going to double-check? I was like, well, we don't do that here. The only double-check we do is for insulin here. And she was like, oh, okay," Miguel says. "So she was looking at me, whatever I did. And it gave me the impression that she was making sure I wasn't stealing it, that she was trying to make sure I gave the morphine to her husband. So that was kind of weird. I don't know," Miguel shrugs.

Another patient on his shift wanted to know where Miguel is from. When Miguel told him, the man asked, "Don't they need nurses in Mexico? And I'm like, I'm sure they do, but I live here."

Patients sometimes ask if Miguel is a citizen. They share their views on immigration as he brings them food, administers their medication, and cleans them up.

"What do they say?" I ask.

"Just comments about, oh, Trump, whatever. I can't remember," Miguel brushes it off. "I think they're just trying to make conversation. They're mostly disoriented people."

Other nurses also get mistreated and yelled at sometimes; it's part of the job, he tries to explain. He tells them he doesn't know much about politics and keeps working.

And when patients get "really, really mean," he pretends to not understand what they're saying.

■ ■ ■

Meanwhile, Denis, an IT professional from Cameroon, has had people make fun of his accent. He says he doesn't let it bother him.

"Everywhere that I went, most my life, I was an outsider," he says. As a child, he's lived in different parts of Cameroon for schooling, where people spoke different languages, just a few being Ewondo, French, and English (he is fluent in all three).

"I don't let it affect me," he states, confidently. "And that's actually the reaction that I always tell: oh, you're making fun of me? I speak three languages and you only speak one."

. . .

Then there's Antonio, a Mexican man married to Ruth, an American, who isn't sure how to respond when I ask if he's experienced prejudice due to being an immigrant.

"Maybe the times I've been applying for jobs it might have hurt my chances that I have a Spanish name," he speculates. "I can't be sure of that or prove that. I'm also not dark skinned, so that's also something that I've never had that a lot of people face because of their skin color."

But Ruth, his wife, does deal with some of it. She's been asked if Antonio is with her "just to get his green card."

"I just say yes. If you ask me a funny question, I'm gonna give you a funny answer."

It also comes up when they travel to visit family in Mexico. "There's this perception of Mexico as if there's constant violence. People are comfortable with the idea of going to Cancún and the beaches, but [with] Mexico City, people would ask is it safe for you to go?" she notes.

His immigration status comes up too. "Normally it's from a good place. They do it in a way that they are concerned about what's happening with Latinos," Ruth says, referring to recent immigration reforms in the United States. "They want to know if my husband and my son are protected."

But a few conservative acquaintances slip in remarks about her husband's Mexican heritage. "Oh, his name is Antonio; maybe he doesn't speak English fully, even though they know he does," she says. "They use [the fact that] my spouse is from Mexico as a way to belittle him."

My friend Irina in California has navigated prejudice outside her community and also within it. Irina was raised in Russia by a single mother, a public school teacher who sometimes wouldn't get paid for months on end. Her mother was able to put food on the table by teaching English classes on the side for adults who'd planned to move out West.

When the Soviet economy collapsed, some of her girlfriends continued studying. Those whose parents got into the burgeoning private sector were able to make ends meet. Others found husbands who supported them. But Irina had her eyes set on America. "Live your life," friends said to her.

"Go if you want, but I won't be able to help you financially," her mother told her, recalls Irina. "People think you come to America, and everything will be easy. But my mom understands."

So when Irina turned eighteen, she moved to the United States to study. "I was going through hell the first six months. I was crying every day. I wanted to go back home."

But she was determined to make the best of it. She went to a community college, then got accepted into a four-year college and worked her way up. She got a visa through her employer and eventually a green card. Her citizenship ceremony was on a Tuesday. On Friday of that same week, her daughter Simone was born. "She was not an anchor baby!" Irina jokes.

Now Irina is ensuring that her biracial daughter is educated and proud of who she is.

"'My dad has brown skin, you have white skin, and I have milk chocolate skin'" is how Simone describes her family. They've already had the talk about discrimination and slavery in the United States. "I need to raise a Black woman," she says. "We talk honestly about race. It's something I'm struggling with myself, how to explain. She knows that she can always, always come to me and ask a question. Language doesn't matter."

When Simone was still little, Irina, whose hair is straight and blond, realized she had no idea how to care for her daughter's curls. So she took her to a salon with a Black stylist, who showed her brushing techniques and recommended hair products. She also watched YouTube videos and read articles to learn how to do it herself. Now Irina brushes her daughter's hair for fifteen minutes in the morning.

A white student in her kindergarten class recently told a Black classmate that people like her shouldn't be allowed to attend their public school.

Simone relayed the incident to her mom. "She said, what does it mean? How can someone even say something like that?"

Irina immediately contacted the teacher and is now working with the principal to bring a diversity and equity program into the school curriculum to help manage their multifaceted student body and resolve conflict.

Irina's family back home adores Simone. However, race issues sometimes rear their ugly head within her immigrant community.

One acquaintance suggested Irina should straighten her daughter's curls. Another asked if she's adopted. Another friend, showing them around town, cautioned to avoid a certain neighborhood because "Black people live here." Irina hasn't seen that person since.

"They don't even realize my daughter is here, standing right there!" she says, throwing her arms up. "They think 'she's okay, but the others are bad.'"

She's lost friends over this and has no regrets.

Instead, she's constantly reinforcing Simone's multifaceted background.

"Believe me, when I see Beyoncé on the magazine, I bring it home. When I see Michelle Obama on the cover of the magazine, believe me, I bring it home. So she sees it, that that's normal," she tells me.

On top of Russian language education and multiple extracurriculars, Simone reads multicultural books, watches Russian cartoons, eats buckwheat, or *kasha*, and visits Afro-Cuban and Afro-Brazilian dance events with her mom, a former dancer.

"It's hard to keep it all in mind but it becomes sort of a habit," Irina explains. "She'll be a combination of all of that. I want her to feel it's her country."

Prejudice lurks within the immigrant enclaves too.

When Casey, a second-generation immigrant from the Philippines, was a baby, family members pinched her nose to try to give it a bridge and "raise it," she says, "so it's not super flat, like Filipino."

"A lot of colonial attitudes are in play," says Casey about the mentality she grew up with, a painful residue from the time when her ancestral homeland was colonized by Spain for over three hundred years, then by the United States. "That's a lot of colorism. And there is definitely the belief that the lighter skinned you are, the better," she tells me. "The immigrant community still very much subscribes to the idea that why would you tan? When I would spend too much time in the sun, I would hear, 'Oh, you're getting darker. That's not good.'"

So as a teen, Casey avoided the sun. She also began using whitening creams and soaps. When visiting the Philippines, her family would even go to a dermatologist for a whitening scrub, then bring products back to America, she says.

"I saw [in the Philippines] just how adored and glorified these women are, who were part Spanish or part white American or part white Australian. So I was like, oh, that's what beauty is, that's standard . . . Growing up as a high schooler, that was hard to take."

All that changed when she went away to college. "I learned to really love the skin that I was in," says Casey. "I was like, oh, I actually look great tanned."

Yet the colorism issue came knocking after Casey started dating her now husband, a white American.

"Are you sure you want to date outside of our culture?" her immigrant family probed, as immigrant families are wont to do. But there was an additional message. "I remember hearing, 'Oh, I'm glad he's white because you're improving the race.'"[3]

Now that she's a mom of two young biracial boys, this topic still looms large. "One happens to have features that are more Caucasian, and the other one happens to have features that are more Filipino," she tells me. "And for my family, they don't say it directly, but they'll always kind of highlight, 'He looks so American. Or his nose, he has such a great nose. He's so light.' So you just hear that constantly being said about your kids and it's very disheartening."

Casey cherishes her heritage. She grew up surrounded by a large family network, on whom she can always count for support. To her it's a blessing, she explains.

But she is raising her children a little differently. "You are a good, amazing, intelligent, smart boy," she and her husband tell their sons. "How you treat people is way more important than how you look. It's beautiful that his skin is the way that it is."

■　■　■

Same-sex marriage became legal in the United States in 2015, but prejudice against LGBTQ relationships remains.

Aleksey, from Ukraine, and Edwin, from El Salvador, have confronted this prejudice from within their own diasporic communities.

"In addition to being quite sexist, the [Ukrainian] culture is also fairly insensitive to gay relationships," Aleksey tells me. During Soviet times, such relationships were criminalized with a prison sentence.[4] In today's neighboring Russia, things aren't much better, and so-called homosexual propaganda is punishable by law.

"In the part of America that we live, our relationship is very accepted. We adopted the American culture and became proud of being American," says Aleksey. "Coming out in the US was something that was very different than it would have been in Russia or El Salvador. America gave a great opportunity for us to be together." But he has noticed a change since the 2016 presidential election. "How much more intolerance is being tolerated now seems to be so inconsistent with the American values," he says. "It is something we have to be aware of, because we need to protect ourselves."

Edwin's Salvadoran family, which is Catholic, has wholeheartedly welcomed Edwin's husband and their daughter. His grandparents have accepted his relationship, "though they're not accepting of anyone else's gayness, at all," Edwin tells me.

During the time of our interview, the couple is preparing a second birthday party for their daughter. But there's also another milestone they're anxiously awaiting: the arrival of baby number two. They're scrambling to get the house ready.

The couple spent years dreaming of having a child together. This finally became a reality with the help of a surrogate.

Edwin was apprehensive about his family's reaction to conceiving as a gay couple. "I feared that they were not going to welcome our daughter with open arms just because she was 'made in a lab' per se, as opposed to a conventional method," Edwin says. "They love her to pieces, all of them. But they still sometimes refer to the pregnancy as 'not being real.'"

"Yours doesn't count," remarked one of his cousins about the child.

"We're like, really?" Aleksey exclaims. "Our parenthood feels pretty real to us. We don't have any secrets. But because the element of a woman being pregnant who's part of the couple is missing, for some people that's hard."

A sense of humor has been their way of dealing with prejudice, uncertainty, and ignorance. "I don't know if all of it, but certainly with a lot of it," says Aleksey. "These things can get very, very complicated. We want to do everything right, but gosh, there's no prescription. We just sort laugh about it and move on."

13. BETWEEN TWO WORLDS

The funny thing is, the moment I am in
one country, I am homesick for the other.

—ALLEN SAY[1]

SIX WEEKS AFTER GREG IS BORN, I get the green light to exercise from the doctor. I can't wait. Contrary to celebrities with flat midriffs weeks after birthing a human, my pregnancy weight hasn't really gone anywhere. Strangers still congratulate me and ask when I'm due.

I relish every moment spent with the new baby, whether we're at home or out on a walk around the neighborhood. I'm also craving meaningful interactions with adults outside my immediate family and the saleslady at Target. Pete and I have recently moved, and I begin looking for a community in the place we now call home.

In a little over a decade leading up to my son's birth, I've relocated over a dozen times (not counting temporary sublets or friends' couches). This includes three back-and-forth moves across the country, for all the usual reasons: schooling, work, and relationships, in no particular order. By my early thirties, I dread ordering bank checkbooks to avoid committing to an address. It will probably change again before too long. At one point, I begrudgingly realize that I know most IKEAs in the San Francisco Bay Area and along the Eastern Seaboard and can put together a Billy bookcase at a moment's notice. At my age, the pressure to grow up and invest in serious furniture, settle in what adults call a "forever home," and develop lasting relationships with other families in the neighborhood—where even the spouses and the children get along—is on.

Forging new friendships is relatively easy for a single person in the city. You can mingle at trivia nights and talk shop at networking events. There are cultural and religious groups for young adults to join. You can even bond with strangers from the internet over your shared love of urban farming.

But good luck pulling that off in a new suburban town with a baby, where distances expand and free time dwindles. With a two-year-old and a newborn in tow, making friends and even acquaintances is taking me significantly longer.

So after the doctor's sign-off, I find myself by a lake in Oakland, at a stroller workout group for mothers. The gray winter sky hangs low over the water. The grass is frosty from the overnight cold.

Baby Greg is snoozing in his car seat, bundled in a one-piece suit with bear ears. I click the seat into the stroller base and off we walk to the meeting point.

I see women trailing in with their strollers from the parking lot. Their outfits are similar to mine: leggings, pullovers, hair up in a messy bun. Many, like me, must have slept for about three hours total the night before. Water bottles and coffee cups are propped up in the stroller cup holders.

In a cloud of euphoria, I feel like these women could be my long-lost sisters. They probably worry about the same things: whether their babies are getting enough milk or formula, where to find good childcare for when they return to work, whether they'll ever want to have sex again.

A dozen of us gather in a circle next to the coach, whose name is Kaylee, and begin with introductions and stretches.

"My name is Stephanie," says the first woman, picking up a pacifier her baby threw from the stroller. "I have a seven-month-old and I'm trying to get back in shape. Whatever that means, right?" she rolls her eyes.

We all chuckle in agreement.

The next woman says she joined the workout to heal her abdominal muscles.

The group nods in understanding, fawning over her infant.

The next person needed a reason to get out of the house in the mornings, especially with a colicky newborn. The rest of us murmur supportively.

"I'm Jen and I'm a manager at Facebook," says a woman next to me, in a hoodie with a large Facebook logo on it. "We have an awesome maternity policy at Facebook, so I'm here, like, every day, till I return in the fall. Kaylee and I go way back." She waves at Kaylee and jogs in one place.

My company's maternity leave policy isn't awesome, but I feel affinity with these women. Maybe after the workout, we'll stroll over to a local café and get to know each other and our babies better, having bonded over bench presses and mountain climbers.

"Alright," Kaylee says. "Now let's get that heart rate pumping! Jumping jacks!"

We jump and count, sneakers pounding the dirt in unison. The sun peaks out from behind the clouds.

For the icebreaker, we're asked to share what sports we played in high school.

"Cheerleading and swim team," someone says, leaping up.

"I was on the soccer! Varsity! Team!" the Facebook mom says, her sneakers thumping against the ground.

"Nice!" says Kaylee, jumping in tandem. "What position?"

"Center striker. You?"

"I was the sweeper!"

"Sweet!"

The woman next to me ran track and field and played softball.

Then comes my turn.

But I've got nothing. I didn't play sports in high school. Or ever.

Just about every American-born person I know was involved in team sports in school, even if they didn't become athletes in adulthood. But when I was growing up, competitive team sports, for an average kid, was not a thing. At least not in my family. I was always doing something after school: ballet (until I was deemed to have neither a ballerina's bone structure nor focus), piano lessons three times a week, English classes once my family started planning to leave the country. One day my literature teacher took our class on a field trip to a horse stable in the woody outskirts of St. Petersburg to read poetry and ride. I became a barn rat after that, taking the train every weekend to clean the stable and practice riding. So did half the girls in my class. But other than that, I was woefully unathletic.

"I never played high school sports," I say.

Kaylee and the moms glance at me in between jumping jacks.

"No sports?" Kaylee repeats.

"Not really."

"That's okay," she offers. "Just wasn't sure I heard you right the first time."

"I rode horses, though. Not competitively or anything," I add. "It was actually in Russia. I grew up there."

My brain is mush from sleep deprivation. My limbs are sore from exercise for the first time in weeks.

"Yeah, where I'm from, we didn't do a lot of school team sports," I hear myself carrying on, egged on by the presence of real adults. "I mean Russia's got ballet and gymnastics, and skiing is mandatory at school, oh, and there's also chess—though technically that's not a sport. I think. Or is it?"

Thump. Thump. Thump. Thump.

"I *was* pretty okay at badminton," I conclude.

Someone's baby starts to cry.

"Now, everyone, squats!" Kaylee shouts. "For an icebreaker, go around and say what your favorite Girl Scout cookie is. Go!"

The women banter about the merits of Thin Mints versus Samoas and share childhood memories of being a Brownie. Me? I'm neutral about Girl Scout cookies. I'd love to contribute, really, I would, but I can't conjure up any meaningful recollection of selling or buying the product, and though I tried a few, the flavors didn't evoke any feeling. All that comes to mind is the memories of old Soviet propaganda hammered into us about how money is the root of all evil, and how children handling money is basically the devil in blue jeans stirring the flames in a pit of capitalist sin.

"All of them!" I pipe in, sunnily. "All those cookies are so good!"

"Okay then! Moving on to lunges, mamas!" Kaylee directs.

Kaylee has everyone name their favorite TV shows growing up.

The women chat about the formative series of their childhoods. *Inspector Gadget. Sesame Street. The Magic School Bus. Mister Rogers' Neighborhood, The Powerpuff Girls.* They hum theme songs and discuss how hot Uncle Jesse from *Full House* used to be, reminiscing about Saturday morning cartoons and old commercial jingles.

Then comes my turn.

On my US citizenship test, I correctly identified the three branches of the government and Francis Scott Key, the man who penned "The Star-Spangled Banner."

But this workout, with its Americana icebreakers and TV programs, most of which I haven't seen, also feels like a test, one I'm not really passing.

"Well," I respond, trying to quickly manufacture a culturally fitting answer. "I was really into *The Crow* after moving. . ."

Silence.

"Isn't that with Bruce Lee's son?" another woman asks.

"Yeah! Did you watch it too?"

"Oh, not me!" she shakes her head. "It was a little dark for me!"

"Alright!" Kaylee calls out. "Grab your strollers, mamas. Get ready to run!"

One by one, the women whisk away their strollers and jog gracefully down the muddy path, then disappear into the woods. Baby Greg is asleep. I take the stroller and follow along, trying to keep up with the group.

The song from Russian *Winnie the Pooh*, one of my favorite cartoons growing up, is on repeat in my head. The plot is the like the English one. The characters are too: there's Piglet, there's honey.

And yet they seem a world apart.

Having lived in the United States most of my life, I've raised dozens of champagne and vodka toasts to America at every major family function, from New Year's Eve parties to birthdays. I've voted in every presidential election since becoming a citizen. I've baked Flag Cakes on Fourth of July and for friends receiving their green cards. (It's basically a frosted rectangular sheet cake festooned with strawberries and blueberries in a stars and stripes pattern. It's quite good, actually.) This is where my children were born and where I've lived most of my life. This is home.

But no amount of patriotic cake and country music can erase that occasional feeling of statelessness.

Don't get me wrong: there's plenty to love about being multicultural. You've got a shapeshifter's flexibility and the richness and support of two or more traditions. You can swear in at least two languages, on top of the other perks of bilingualism, like the ability to relate to people from various walks of life, cognitive advantages, and access to books in their original form. People call you worldly. At potlucks, you can hold your own with so-called exotic dishes, even if it's a recipe your aunt taught you by throwing together three ingredients and one of them is mayonnaise.

But the search for that corner of the world to call your own is sometimes a journey, particularly after becoming a parent.

While still pregnant, I marvel at the gentle, almost philosophical way mothers address their toddlers in the park ("Do you want to leave now, Riley, or in five minutes?"). I try to tell baby bouncers apart from swings on the bountiful must-have lists for the nursery. American childhood feels practically nothing like the one I've experienced.

In contrast, I grew up when most people didn't own cars, washing machines, or diapers. They didn't debate attachment versus helicopter parenting, because they didn't know what that meant. They gathered baby-related information from family, friends, and the translation of Benjamin Spock's *Baby and Childcare.* They owned the same prams and watched the same three TV stations, government controlled and propaganda laden. (They also had state-subsidized childcare to support them with home and work responsibilities, I should add.)

Now, except for the subsidized childcare, that's not a life I'd want for myself, but this lack of options did make some things a little simpler. For one, it created a sense of community, even if it meant being scolded by somebody's grandma on the street. A stranger might rock the pram outside a grocery store so the mother could stand in line for bread inside.

American child-rearing was simpler, too, until roughly the 1970s. The baby boom generation was raised on that same wildly popular *Baby and Childcare* book (allegedly a second bestseller in the US after the Bible).[2]

Today, parenting is way more intensive. Parents are offered a plethora of philosophies and social media platforms, but rather than boost morale, it can be confusing and lonely.

In her bestseller *Bringing Up Bébé: One American Mother Discovers the Wisdom of French Parenting*, Pamela Druckerman writes, "The Americans I know also believe that pregnancy—and then motherhood—comes with homework. The first assignment is choosing from among myriad parenting styles," she writes. "But instead of making me feel more prepared, having so much conflicting advice makes babies themselves seem enigmatic and unknowable. Who they are, and what they need, seems to depend on which book you read."[3]

At the same time, a growing number of adults are raising kids without family support, says Juli Fraga, a San Francisco–based licensed psychologist who specializes in maternal mental health and parenthood education.

"In that regard, the village has disbanded. In many cases, it's been replaced with online support groups, Instagram pages addressing the pitfalls of parenthood, and webinars," says Fraga, who is experienced with culturally sensitive therapy, including working with Asian and Asian American women. Social media can be helpful, but it can't replace the intimacy of in-person relationships, she tells me.

Multiple studies suggest that new mothers lack the social support they need.[4] Those with limited social networks and a lack of familiarity with cultural norms are at a risk of psychological distress and isolation, research shows.[5]

Yet parents are often expected to pull themselves up by their own bootstraps. "Relying on others is sometimes seen as a burden or a weakness," says Fraga. This individualistic, high-pressure approach makes it harder to ask for help and leads to burnout.

For sure, a village is important. But what about those of us who aren't intimately familiar with the local norms, yet already too "Western" for those from our birthplace? Where is the village for folks like us?

I wonder about this especially in the earliest months and years of parenthood. It's on my mind as I attend playdates in the park and beer gardens with California mothers, watch my baby play in the sandbox next to immigrant nannies in Central Park in Manhattan, and wait behind vans full of kids in a double drive-through lane for Chick-fil-A in Ohio.

Talking to other immigrants, I'm noticing that this state of inbetweenness is actually quite common. Even for those with a green card or a US passport. Even for those who churn out long legal briefs in English and laugh at jokes on late-night comedy shows on TV.

Take Amandine. She grew up in a multicultural household in France and moved around quite a bit as an adult, "either because of studies or love," she explains.

After arriving in America as a new mom, Amandine found herself in a crossfire between cultures.

The first thing she tells me is her children, now young adults, still make fun of her French accent, especially the way she pronounces *juice* and *lettuce* ("I would say *lett-OOS*," she says). "I mispronounce it just for the pleasure of them rolling their eyes over and going 'Mom'!"

One stark difference was the child-rearing approach. Amandine's own mother was "a typical, very strict French mother," but Amandine wanted to be more lenient with her children. "Maybe I wasn't strict enough, even though my kids say I was really, really strict—my son called me gestapo. If he had known my mother!"

She was struck by how encouraging and involved the American parents were, particularly when it came to education and volunteering.

"In France, no teacher would allow parents to come and spend hours in the elementary school. [But] here, they said, 'I spent the morning in school with Audrey!'"

Amandine, too, began to volunteer at her children's schools. After getting a full-time job, she'd still volunteer in the evenings. She had both kids join the American Boy Scouts and Girl Scouts (though not before trying the French scouting organization), and helped her daughter sell Girl Scout cookies.

Still, Amandine doesn't quite feel like an American mother. "I didn't become as encouraging as I wanted," she reflects.

For example, she didn't attend all of the games of her son, an avid athlete who'd get up before dawn for hockey practice.

"Why couldn't you be more of an American mom?" her son probed later. "You never attended any matches!"

"I said, yes, I attended two. He said, no, it was not enough. He said I never came to his wrestling match or lacrosse match. I said, I needed to work and, unfortunately, we were not rich enough for me to be the homemaker and baking cookies."

As much as she doesn't fit neatly the American parenting mold, Amandine doesn't feel "one hundred percent French" either.

"The French, they always complain about the fact that people are organized in the forms of community. And then when they come to the United States, well, that's what they do. They stick together," she observes.

Her family took notice too. "My son accused me of not perpetuating the French culture enough in the family," she complains. "I tried to explain to him it would have been easier for me if my husband had been French, because then I obviously would be speaking French all the time."

Recently her French colleague told a joke from a popular movie. Everyone laughed, but Amandine didn't. She missed the reference.

This grated on her immensely.

"I find myself tormented by the fact that I could be an impostor," she confesses. "The next day I call my colleague and tell him how I felt and he, very reassuringly, [tells] me that no, I am not an impostor."

.   .   .

Fernanda, a biologist from Brazil, also occasionally feels like an outsider, especially when people try to guess where she's from.

"Oh, you look Mexican," some tell her. "Are you Puerto Rican?"

At a former job, a colleague would refer to her as "that Mexican girl over there."

These assumptions make her feel invisible.

"Today I wouldn't care," Fernanda says, "but I was so offended because it was like my country doesn't exist. I think it's the way I look. I'll always have an accent. I feel completely Brazilian. It's where I'm from. I would like my culture not to be erased."

That fear of erasure was so strong that Fernanda hesitated taking her baby daughter to a sing-along at a local public library. She feared for her child's Portuguese being taken over by English. The new rituals felt foreign, making her nostalgic for her homeland. "I didn't learn these songs," she tells me. "I learned others."

Looking back, she wonders if she should have been more open.

Today, Fernanda's friends are a mix, though most are native-born Americans. "I love other cultures. When I meet somebody from somewhere else, I want to hear that. I think first we're moms before a certain nationality, right?" she says, and talks to me about Russian ballet.

*   *   *

Denis, from Cameroon, describes his social circle in Washington, DC, as "fifty-fifty." "I have American friends and I have African friends," he says. "From Africa, most of the people that I know that I'm close to are from Nigeria and Cameroon."

To get a better sense of how immigrants across the board feel about home and identity, I head over to a farm near America's Salad Bowl on the central coast of California, where most of the country's—and the world's—supply of lettuce, broccoli, and other vegetables is grown. The majority of crop farmworkers in America are immigrants.[6]

I take the picturesque winding Highway 17 to Lakeside Organic Gardens in Watsonville. Fittingly, this vegetable farm is owned and operated by a grandson of a Portuguese potato farmer who immigrated to America at the turn of the twentieth century.

I'm standing in the middle of a two-hundred-fifty-acre field, bountiful rows of cabbage, artichokes, and cauliflower stretching as far as the eye can see, with morning mist gently enveloping the crops.

There, I find Lalo, the foreman of the cabbage crews. We meet by a dirt road marked with tractor tire treads. He's keeping an eye on his crew as they harvest and pack the produce. In his twenty years of living in the United States, he's been an employee of this farm for sixteen.

Lalo is wearing a baseball cap, jeans, and an orange work vest on top of his T-shirt. His sneakers are caked in mud from working in the soil. He stands tall as he surveys the fields.

He tells me he came to the United States at eighteen from Mexico with his uncle, leaving his mother and four brothers behind. His father is now in the US. The woman he eventually married followed him from the town where they grew up. They now have three kids.

Keeping his language isn't hard in the Watsonville area, with a large Spanish-speaking population. Most of Lalo's colleagues on the field speak Spanish too. He feels comfortable holding on to his culture, or *cultura*, he tells me through an interpreter, another farmworker.

His kids, however, throw in English words when they speak to him in Spanish.

"The best is for them to keep speaking both languages," Lalo says. "I don't want it to be based on the Mexican culture, because they will deal with English too."

Where do you feel your home is?, I ask.

It's in both places, "because I spent a lot of time here too." Lalo's family is here, and his work is here, he explains. "Here there are more opportunities to succeed," he pauses. "You miss your homeland, but you're here to make progress."

When I ask if he goes back to visit family, his answer is curt. "No more," he replies.

.   .   .

All these conversations get me thinking about how different people adapt in the new land. We all know it happens, one way or another. But how?

It's not like we have a script on how to assimilate.

There is no playbook, but there are theories. You've probably heard the term *melting pot*, which used to be the yardstick of immigrant adaptation. The idea is various cultures "melt together" and produce a homogenous group of people with similar behaviors and beliefs.[7] Immigrants and their descendants, according to the melting pot notion, assimilate and absorb the majority's norms overtime.[8]

The Ford Motor Company is a fitting example of how this expectation played out. Starting in 1914, immigrant workers at the Ford Plant attended mandatory English classes, which also taught them hard work, how to spend their wages, and "the right way to live" (by then, nearly three quarters of the Ford employees were foreign born). "Ask anyone of [the graduates] what nationality he is, and the reply will come quickly, 'American!' 'Polish-American?' you might ask.[9] 'No, American,' would be the answer. For they are taught in the Ford English School that the hyphen is a minus sign," is how the *Ford Times* magazine described it.[10]

But assimilation is nuanced, researchers have since pointed out. What does *mainstream* mean, anyway? Is it someone middle class and white, with Protestant values?

Disadvantaged immigrants often bump into structural barriers of the new society, from employment and racial discrimination to underfunded schools. Succumbing to some of these problems, their children might join a street gang, for example.[11] In reality, assimilation isn't always a straight path to success.

Interestingly, a 2015 study by the National Academies of Sciences, Engineering, and Medicine found that immigrants tend to have better health, longer life expectancy, and lower incidence of alcohol use than the native-born population and less crime in their neighborhoods than in comparable nonimmigrant neighborhoods. (Next time your uncle or high school friend rails against "those criminal immigrants," please cite this study for him. No, really, please do.) One unintended side effect of assimilation is the longer immigrants live in America, the more similar they become to native-born peers in those parameters.[12]

.   .   .

Even when people want to assimilate completely, it isn't always possible. They may unconsciously hold on to their heritage values, notes Mercedes Fernández Oromendia, a clinical psychology postdoctoral fellow who works with transracial adoptions and has expertise in bicultural identity development.

Say a person's been in the US since childhood—going to public schools and speaking without an accent. But as an adult, he might have a hard time asking the boss for a raise. "His apprehension may be associated with his culture of origin's more hierarchical structure, emphasis on respect and collectivist values," Oromendia tells me.[13]

.   .   .

The social psychologist John W. Berry spent many years studying how our beliefs and behaviors change when we're in contact with other cultures, a process known as *acculturation*. He came up with not just one but four different scenarios of how people acculturate.

Assimilation is what happens when an immigrant identifies with the new culture and rejects (or is forced to give up) the heritage culture. But, Berry pointed out, a person might go the opposite route instead: reject the new society and hold on to the original culture. Berry calls this *separation*. The third possibility is for the immigrant to withdraw from both the old and the new. Perhaps this person feels hostility from the new community and lacks the support of the old network. Such a fringe strategy, which Berry calls *marginalization*, tends to be the least successful. Finally, there is biculturalism, when one stays rooted in the old community and participates in the new one too. This hybrid can lead to the greatest psychological well-being These four ways of coping aren't set in stone, of course: an immigrant might try on various ones before settling on the method that's most satisfying.[14]

But acculturation is a two-way road. For newcomers to integrate and assimilate, the new society must welcome them. It can happen only "when the dominant society is open and inclusive in its orientation towards cultural diversity" Berry writes.[15]

Young children, for the most part, acculturate relatively smoothly. Adolescents usually have a rough time after immigrating, and it's hard on the older generations too, Berry writes. For adults, higher education makes the adaptation easier for all the obvious reasons, from financial to social. At the same time, though, when someone's "departure status" is higher than their "arrival status" and the newcomer is devalued in the new society, the process will likely be psychologically fraught.[16]

It's easy to see why. How many people realize that their cab driver might have a PhD in physics? That the aesthetician waxing their eyebrows used to be a respected physician whose credentials have little value here, and their housekeeper was a teacher in her past life? Phlebotomists and nannies, waiters and movers with accents—does anyone ever wonder about their past?

■ ■ ■

Once I start digging into texts about cultural psychology, I can't stop. Things begin to click.

For example, did you ever get a sense that, culturally speaking, you're expected to be either one or the other? Turns out this "us" versus "them" worldview is common. Being culturally unmoored is seen as a transient state, something people don't always know what to make of.[17]

But a bicultural person's identity can change over time and shift back and forth, writes psycholinguist François Grosjean in his book *Bilingual: Life and Reality*. You can "deactivate" one culture and fit into another one while handling a range of situations—from entertaining guests to dealing with monocultural family members and dressing according to local norms, Grosjean writes. But unlike with language, turning off cultural traits at the drop of a hat isn't always possible. Sometimes you're just stuck with a mix of both.[18]

Grosjean himself has changed his dominant culture four times (English, French, American, and Swiss). Figuring this out can be a "long and sometimes trying process." Though a dual identity isn't simple, many come to accept their biculturalism—even if their own cultures might not.[19]

Some feel like they don't belong to any group at all. "They feel estranged from their cultures, particularly at turning points in their lives, for example, when they return 'home,' which is no longer home," writes Grosjean.[20]

In the end, folks juggling multiple traditions may have an easier time relating to others who are like them.

"Biculturals will invariably say that life is easier when they are in a bicultural mode—that is, with other biculturals like themselves. These are precious moments, when the bicultural person can relax and not have to worry about getting things right each time," he writes.[21]

I also bring up biculturalism with Monika, born in Puerto Rico, and Paula, born in Colombia, when we talk. Both work in the English-speaking media, host an English-language podcast, and have American-born partners and children. But they're also inextricably connected to where they came from.

"I'm Puerto Rican to the core," Monika states. "I'm so proud of where I grew up; it's where my ancestors are buried. And it's a place that I can call my own."

Her husband was raised in a Puerto Rican family on the US mainland, but, Monika says, didn't reflect on his roots much until the two met. "I think he was encouraged to suppress his Puerto Rican-ness . . . I mean, yes, you're coming in as a citizen. Politically, you're American. But that's not how people see you. And then he meets this very proud Puerto Rican person. Now we all say we're Puerto Rican."

Growing up in Miami, her daughter is exposed to children from all over Latin America. She knows what they eat and what holidays they celebrate. Monika seeks out family activities in places where Spanish is spoken.

"I'm not intentional about that," she tells me, "but now that I'm thinking about it, speaking about it, clearly I gravitate toward that!"

It's a little different for her friend Paula, who'd moved to another city with her husband shortly before having a baby. She ended up joining a mom's group with American-born mothers, organized by her doula; these women became her social circle.

After a while, Paula found herself gravitating toward families like hers. It wasn't intentional. "You know, oh, you're from Colombia and then that's immediately a common ground that you build on. And you might hit it off, you might not, but in this case, we have been fortunate."

Last December, she joined with other Colombian families from her daughter's school to celebrate the Day of the Little Candles, or Día de las Velitas, the start of the Christmas season in the country. Many families were like hers: one partner is American born; the other one is Colombian. They prepared traditional dishes and the children lit the candles.

"It made me realize that it's not only about the language. When you have other families that understand [these customs] and value it the same way that you do, it becomes more of a communal thing," Paula says. "It's not just something that we do because mama is from Colombia."

■   ■   ■

So how does culture affect our socializing patterns? And how does one begin to look for that village?

I reach out to Anya Dashevsky, a clinical psychologist with a private practice in Massachusetts.[22] She's spent over fifteen years working with families and children. As an immigrant, Dashevsky is no stranger to culturally sensitive issues: her immigration experience is one of the reasons she went into psychology.

"I do feel like I'm very integrated at this point, but I think I can relate more because I know what it's like to be an outsider," she explains.

"I think the biggest problem that sometimes happens in a different culture is isolation, whether their family of origin is far away or they don't quite feel comfortable in this society yet. When they have the baby, they don't really have a huge support system or anyone to ask, what should I do, how should I do this?" Isolation isn't just a multicultural issue, Dashevsky, a mother of four, emphasizes.

Some are uncomfortable about interacting with the school system and the medical system. It doesn't always correlate with how long they've lived in the country or how good their English is.

She shares a story about a former client. The woman had lived in America for a decade and her English was excellent. Her child felt isolated and wanted to make more friends.

Dashevsky suggested setting up a playdate. But the woman was not familiar with the concept and it frightened her, Dashevsky recalls. "The mom said, 'How do I do that? How do I ask an American parent for a playdate?'"

Unfortunately, when it comes to communicating one's needs, many immigrant communities frown upon expressing difficult emotions. *Toughen up, buttercup* is what many of us grow up hearing.

"We had to cheer up and keep going," one foreign-born client told Dashevsky about her upbringing. "I would have never said to my mother, 'I'm depressed,'" the client said.

To find a community, try joining activities where you can meet other parents, from children's sports to youth theater to music lessons. And reach out to the existing network for support, Dashevsky recommends.

"It can be a great way for parents to get engaged and meet other parents. There is that common activity or common goal, which gives parents an easy topic for a conversation, and it could be a great equalizer." The kids will also enjoy having the adults involved.

Some parents do gravitate toward those who share their background. "In my experience," she adds, "many mothers feel more comfortable joining groups of other mothers from their own culture."

In the end, her practice is all about relationships. "If they are coming because they can't relate to their kids, regardless of their reason, the recommendation would be very similar: Why don't you listen to your kids? Why don't you play with them?" says Dashevsky. "Get to know their child's world even if it's different from what they grew up with."

. . .

Parent groups aren't always easy, notes Juli Fraga, the psychologist from San Francisco. They're just like any group and relationship. "People may feel judged, left out, misunderstood," she says.

Start by figuring out what you want in a community, she recommends. "What do you want to share with the group? What needs do you want the group to meet? By defining what you're looking for, you're in a better position to find the right type of support."

For immigrants, "finding parents who understand what they're going through can be tricky." Fraga suggests connecting with others who share similar experiences. And if that type of support doesn't seem to exist, create your own.

■ ■ ■

But back to that stroller workout by the lake in Oakland. Baby Greg and I attend a couple more times. I learn some good ab strengthening exercises and get a jump start on our daily routine, but I don't hit it off with any of the members.

Still, I keep looking for opportunities to socialize with new mothers. Because when you've got a new baby, there are few other people in the world who'll revel with you in the joys of new parenthood and share tips on dealing with colic and mastitis. They'll seek companionship as much as you do. And in the luckiest of circumstances, those people might even bring you a meal if you're recovering from labor and end up in your photo albums over the years.

The process seems pretty straightforward. Just pack a diaper bag full of necessities; chug coffee; apply under-eye concealer; feed, change, and burp the crying baby; put on a spit-up-free shirt; repeat. Then, if there's still enough time left in the day and caffeine in your bloodstream, leave the house for an organized activity.

The good news is I'm finding plenty of opportunities to meet other mothers and babies. There are nursing support groups out there, stroller walks, picnics in the park, even family potlucks at a clubhouse of someone's apartment complex.

The bad news is socializing with strangers as a new parent is not always easy, much like anything that people swear to be easy and is anything but (see: folding a fitted sheet, making a soufflé).

So here we all are, a dozen strangers, a little bit petrified, yet also hopeful to find their version of a "mom crew" glamorized in the movies and on the internet. We want to make friends. Maybe our babies will befriend each other too, so that years later, when asked how they met, they'll respond, "Our mothers met at a baby yoga class, and we've been BFFs before we could walk!"

But unlike in the movies, this process takes longer than getting to the bottom of the popcorn bag. Sometimes it's more awkward than the social media pictures would have one believe. Rather than a power posse of smiling women wearing pastels, with matching aerodynamic strollers and lattes in hand, it may instead feel more like the back of the high school cafeteria, and you're that lone, teenage math whiz doing calculus homework. Or the goth poet with headphones. Anyway, you get the idea.

I attend the American spaces for socializing with new parents. I also learn that a local university campus hosts get-togethers for Russian-speaking women. One morning, I head over with the baby.

Most are wives of postdoctoral students and visiting scholars, having only recently come to California. Our exchange is courteous and pleasant. And yet it's as if we're speaking two different languages. Their idiom is ebullient and fresh, while my Russian is stuck in the early 1990s. I miss some references and fight the urge to switch to English when discussing local restaurants and abstract ideas. It feels like I'm sporting a pair of Mickey Mouse ears on my head: distinctly American and also just a strange thing to wear around adults on a Wednesday morning.

As time passes, I realize that new parent friendships aren't that different from other types of friendships. You either like each other or you feel nothing about each other, or worse. A shared zip code, parenthood, and time may bring people closer, or, alas, they may not.

Eventually I find my tribe in the place I now call home. More like a few different tribes, in two languages. Some trace their lineage to this continent for generations; others are immigrants like me. Our children become acquaintances and, sometimes, friends. Occasionally, even our spouses get along.

It doesn't happen right away. There are no pastels, fancy matching strollers, and lattes in hand. Nonetheless, this parenting thing is finally beginning to feel like a village, and it's quite exhilarating.

14. FINDING HOME

*Some may derive enjoyment from hybridity and
relativity of their existence and others may feel that
they inhabit distinct and at times incommensurable
lifeworlds and experience pain and anguish over this
condition. Yet this is not an aberration on their part but
a part of what makes us human.*

—ANETA PAVLENKO[1]

I'M GOING to New York soon.

Before the trip, I get in touch with Alex and Olga, whom I first met well over a decade ago. I knew them back when they'd organized events for New York's young Russian-speaking Jewish folk, who often felt disconnected from their roots due to anti-Semitism in the Soviet Union. We'd attend music gigs and book readings by compatriots and meet for special holidays, singing old songs to the strumming of a guitar.

Alex and Olga live in Brooklyn now. I'm only happy to have a reason to return to the borough.

Brooklyn, a patchwork of neighborhoods and ethnicities, has been a beacon of hope for immigrants across generations. Ethiopian-born Dinaw Mengestu, one of my favorite authors, professes his love for his neighborhood: "We can remake and rebuild ourselves and our communities, over and over again, in no small part because there have always been corners in Brooklyn to do so on."[2]

Just like neighborhoods change, people's relationships with their heritage also transforms, often in unpredictable ways.

■ ■ ■

Before heading over to Alex and Olga's house, I hop on the Q train and take a detour to the southern tip of the borough. Next to me is a sign from the Metropolitan Transportation Authority: "Hate has no place in our transit system." I notice that the smooth face of Dr. Zizmor, the dermatologist whose ads graced subway cars for over a quarter century, is missing. Much has changed since I left, like it always does in the city. My Sicilian landlords, who owned a pizzeria beneath my apartment in the northern part of Brooklyn, have shuttered it long ago. Now it's a liquor store. Across the street, the bustling old-school diner has been replaced by a vintage co-op "for the modern bohemian." The busy off-track betting parlor down the street is long gone.

Some forty-five minutes later, I'm in Brighton Beach, a Russian-speaking immigrant enclave formerly known as Little Odessa, named so after the influx of Jewish refugees from the USSR in the 1970s.

Back when I lived in New York, Brighton Beach had been my hide-away whenever I felt homesick or overwhelmed with adult responsibilities. It's not the real Russia. Still, here I could fill up on fragrant *plov*, an Uzbek rice and beef dish, at a café beneath the rumbling elevated railway. I'd stock up on rye bread, black-currant tea, and books at shops lining Brighton Beach Avenue and eagerly speak Russian with the salespeople. Then I'd head over to the waterfront on the boardwalk, wandering past the grandmas gossiping on the benches and men playing chess, as seagulls flew overhead.

On overcast days, when the sun sets without much fanfare and the steel-colored sky seems to blend with the ocean, you can look out at the water and imagine different worlds on the opposite shore. Then suddenly it's no longer 2019 or 1992, but say, 1890, when steamships take two weeks to chug across the Atlantic, carrying anxious passengers toward the Ellis Island immigration line. Soon, they'll clutch their trunks and featherbeds and step onto land.

If you squint long enough into the windy gray space ahead, on the other side of the water, you might glimpse an apartment with a crystal chandelier and a creaky rocking chair, gone long ago but suddenly beckoning and bright; or perhaps you'll dream up wholly unfamiliar sights with grazing sheep and cobblestone alleys across the ocean. There's estrangement and longing here on the edge of the water. It teeters between the familiar and the unknown with the ebb and flow of the waves.

And then, like a specter from another life, a woman in a fur coat will walk by carrying a plastic shopping bag with potatoes and leaving a trail of Chanel perfume in her wake.

I look around Brighton Beach, taking stock of what's changed and what's still the same since my last visit. For the most part, it is just as I remember it. The scent of vegetable stands and piroshki intermingle with cigarette smoke and car exhaust in the cold. Snippets of conversation in my native tongue fill the streets and the stores, often with expletives that are both jarring and pulsating with life. I walk through my language, excluded and enchanted by it, caressed by it.

"*Bol'shoe spasibo!*" I thank the grocery store clerk and beam in a way that probably doesn't befit the transaction. Balancing plastic shopping bags in the crook of my elbow, I snap pictures of the neighborhood, as if committing it to a digital file will safeguard it from ever changing.

· · ·

Alex and Olga live just a few subway stops away from Brighton Beach. Exiting the station in their neighborhood, I'm in a whole new microcosm. The streets are lined with brick apartment buildings, manicured family homes, and a few synagogues. I pass by the men in head coverings and women in long skirts.

I find the couple in their driveway, unloading Costco groceries from their car. Last time I saw them, they'd just had a baby. Now they have four. I help carry the fish and a box of diapers upstairs.

Typical of large households, the home is abuzz with activity yet hemmed in by self-sustaining orderliness. We catch up in the kitchen as the couple rushes to put the perishables in the refrigerator. One of their children plays "Bohemian Rhapsody" on the piano, two others retreat to read and do homework, and the littlest one wants to nurse.

And yet when we sit down to talk, it's like I'm watching the romantic couple cameos from *When Harry Met Sally*.

Alex and Olga do that thing couples do where they effortlessly finish each other's sentences—even when they disagree. And they have a ton in common. Both were nine years old as new refugees in the early eighties, and both settled in New York with their families. With just a handful of other Russian speakers around at the time, they acculturated fast. "We had to very quickly figure it out," says Olga, who is about to start a new job as a product manager.

In Russia, both grew up mostly secular. Olga's grandmother celebrated Passover and spoke Yiddish. And Alex's parents had a secret Jewish wedding with a chuppah. But for the most part, that was that.

As young adults, Alex and Olga, with a few exceptions, dated Americans who weren't Jewish.

"There were things I worked so hard to get away from, everything having to do with my Russian identity and my immigrant identity," says Alex, who works for a technology company. "I just wanted to fit in and be like everyone else."

In fact, Alex almost married an American woman. But as the big day approached, he panicked. The question of "Who the hell am I?" was gnawing on him. He couldn't shake the sudden feeling that he was letting go of something important.

"I realized late in the relationship—we were about to send out the invitations, we had reserved the boathouse in Central Park, were ready to go—and I realized that it wasn't actually okay with me to not marry somebody Jewish," Alex says.

He was mortified. The breakup was devastating for the bride and for him. So was the recovery.

To try and make sense of what happened, Alex began studying the faith of his ancestors and attending services at a local synagogue. There he discovered a deep-seated connection to Judaism.

Eventually, he began going on dates with American Jewish women. Still, those dynamics felt foreign.

But once he started meeting Russian and Russian Jewish women, everything changed.

"That was interesting and strange and uncomfortable," he explains. "I couldn't put on all the various masks that I have that I learned as an American. There was nowhere to hide. I couldn't quite express myself, because my Russian wasn't strong enough anymore. And I also didn't even need to express myself, because there were things that were just like home."

In the company of those who shared his background, whether as romantic prospects or platonic friends, he felt exposed. "You immediately were among others who were just like you," Alex says. "You may have some variations or differences in your immigration story, but you were also culturally the same. Try as you might, you had to just be yourself."

Like Alex, they'd gone through the trauma of being uprooted. "None of us had the opportunity to process it. We just went on with our lives," Alex adds. "All of that came flooding back" and was healing, he says.

He decided to start a social group to bring people with a similar background together.

Meanwhile, on the other side of the country, Olga was thinking of doing the same thing.

Maybe you two should talk, their sisters decided, and introduced them.

Alex flew to New York and the two met for afternoon tea.

"We wound up hanging out until three in the morning," Olga remembers. They cancelled their respective evening plans. They also realized they had friends in common.

"We were like, what?" Alex exclaims. "It was all just the worlds colliding. I knew that many people [in the group] would meet their soulmates or their best friends. I knew I would meet mine. I didn't know how and when it would happen when I met her. It was so clear, and it was so powerful. I just knew. We both just knew . . ."

"Right away," Olga adds.

Everyone falls silent for a moment.

"Mama, I want a crocodile!" their youngest child announces in Russian, waddling up to Olga and plopping a picture book on her lap. "I'll read to you in a moment," Alex promises him.

The serendipity didn't stop here. Even their ancestors knew each other, the couple discovered. Olga's grandmother used to frequent Alex's great-grandfather's store in the same Ukrainian shtetl.

"Isn't that insane?" Olga exclaims.

"It's insane!" Alex replies.

Linking all their identity pieces together, the couple settled in a largely Jewish neighborhood near a Russian one, with the requisite piano and ballet classes and Russian-speaking nannies for the kids.

As busy working parents, they're still involved with the community, organizing Jewish learning events for families.

"Everyone's thinking about what it is am I going to pass down to my children," Alex says. "Our community has such a tremendous pent-up demand for learning. We don't have practices. We don't have the knowledge. People are thinking about continuity and what they want their kids to take away."

■   ■   ■

Olga and Alex's return to their roots after a period of estrangement is not uncommon.

But it's not the only scenario. Others I know have drifted away from tradition or find themselves always in flux. Perhaps it's a part of the universal narrative about belonging, the yearning to carve out a new path and to safeguard the old ways, like a snow globe. All it takes is a shake, we hope, and the universe as we once knew it will come to life, sparkling and bountiful, again and again.

Lakshmi, who grew up in Tamil Nadu, a state in the south of India, dutifully studied in a Christian convent school as a little girl, as did many of her Indian peers, even though her parents are practicing Hindus. In college she triple-majored in math, physics, and chemistry. She then became an engineer, one of the first to enter the burgeoning IT scene in India.

"Growing up in India, you either became an engineer or a doctor. You really had no choice," explains Lakshmi, a writer and business analyst who lives in Pennsylvania with her husband and three children. "Art is for losers," she remembers the adage from childhood.

After college graduation, her parents placed a matrimonial ad in a newspaper. She met her match, got married "much to the relief of my family," and headed to America with her new husband.

Keeping the customs wasn't difficult for Lakshmi: she and her husband share the language, come from the same geographical area, and are both Brahmins by caste.

But then the couple adopted twins with European and Navajo ancestry and Lakshmi gave birth. Three kids and a cultural amalgam prompted her to consider her identity in new ways.

"Adopting children who were born here or giving birth to a baby here tethers you to this land," she says.

Then the 2016 presidential election divided the country, bringing with it a spike in anti-immigrant rhetoric, hate crimes, and social protests. Lakshmi felt personally affected.[3]

"Two of my children are white and one is brown. And when we go out as a family, I have no idea of what people around me are thinking," she says. "Up until 2016, I've never given a single thought as to what my neighbors think of me or my family. But now, even when they are not talking about it, I'm wondering, you know, are they thinking in their head that I don't belong here or my children don't belong here?"

This awakened her politically.

"I feel fiercely protective of the world that I want to leave my children," Lakshmi tells me. "So if until now, I had the privilege of being apolitical of not wearing my politics on my sleeve, now I have yard signs, I'm active."

She also got involved with mobilizing South Asian voters ahead of the 2020 presidential election. Many of her compatriots were primarily concerned with the effect of US policies on their birth country, Lakshmi remembers. "I feel like if you've sworn the oath of allegiance, you better put America first," she counters.

Becoming a mother changed her socializing patterns too. As a new immigrant, Lakshmi felt drawn to other South Indians. She wouldn't actively go out of her comfort zone. "There's a certain comfort in knowing your shared foods, you share a certain language," she says. "I still am in a very Brown bubble and a very Indian bubble, and that is something I'm actively working to change."

"But ever since adopting the children, I'm like, I need my children to know that our circle is not entirely Brown. So I have to put myself in spaces where I'm probably the only Brown person, and that makes me extremely uncomfortable because it's not my natural state of being," she admits.

This branching out isn't without challenges. "Many times conversations like book clubs or wherever, where I feel like I'm the only person of color, the burden of representing all of BIPOC [Black, Indigenous, and people of color] falls on me," Lakshmi says.

Reconnecting to one's heritage—or disconnecting from it—is not linear. A heritage isn't a cable company (though wouldn't life be remarkably simpler if it were?).

Besides, folks don't represent their cultures in homogenous ways. We are not all the same, regardless of our birthplace. "We sometimes have expectations that you come from X group, so you're supposed to do Y thing," says sociologist Philip Kasinitz, when we speak in his office at the Graduate Center at the City University of New York. "And there's some truth to that. But it's also true that within X group, there's lots of variation." The individuals involved "may really love some parts of the traditional culture, and they have other parts that they can't stand."

We're always picking and choosing from our culture's characteristics and traditions. "They're a repertoire; they're not a mandate," Kasinitz says. "In fact, anybody who was completely the perfect embodiment of their culture would strike other people as pretty weird, you know?"

.   .   .

On my flight back to California, I think of the lessons I'm learning, and of that which I've only recently found the words to verbalize.

1. That the world won't end and family won't disown me if I break traditions. Nor will it end if I keep them.
2. That parents, including immigrants, are figuring out the ropes as they go. The "immigrant parent of the year" award doesn't exist. Who'd get to be the judge of that show, anyway?
3. That perfect bilingualism is rare. For immigrant families in America, it is a work in progress. If our kids are, in fact, growing up bilingual, let's celebrate by popping open a bottle of bubbly and letting them scrawl on the wall in both languages with nonwashable markers. And if they aren't bilingual, they might just be later. There's no need to be seduced into parental guilt.
4. That language education isn't a labor camp; I can't force my children to say what they don't want to say. All I can do is keep showing up, making adjustments, and meeting them where they're at.
5. That it's fabulous if the kid can have a childcare provider that speaks our language. But if it's not in the cards, there are other ways to stay connected to the roots. Are our children safe

and loved? Well fed? Thriving? We must be doing something right.

6. That the problems immigrants face are not always related to immigration. Then again, many of them are.

7. That a mistrust of immigrants has always existed, and today is no exception.

8. That every culture has that one *dish that must be explained*, much like herring under a fur coat salad. We must hold on to such salads with reckless abandon and immortalize them with poetry, even if others butcher their names, wrinkle their noses when they get a whiff, and dub them "interesting."

9. That loneliness is a cold companion, particularly when you have no language to express it. There's probably not a single person on earth who wouldn't want to hear "Hey! I'm glad you're here" when showing up somewhere new.

10. That living between two worlds offers the best seats in the house, even if it takes time to see anything at all.

* * *

Thanksgiving and the winter holiday season is here. This time of year is a big production for just about every family. But my immigrant kind of stress is fermented in triple guilt.

No matter how many activities are on the list, one aspect of my family's heritage always seems to get less playtime, like in a game of musical chairs.

Will my children's Russianness be adequately represented or probed by relatives? Will the kids experience traditions of their birth country and of their father, or will they feel as if they're stuck in a bunker somewhere in the Arctic? How can my Hanukkah story about rationing oil even begin to compare with the spectacle of Santa Claus and presents under a tree?

A group of local families will get together for our annual Russian New Year's event. Russian Santa, Ded Moroz, and his female assistant will play games and riddles with the children and sing classic holiday repertoire (invoking "Jingle Bells" in English as needed). There'll be presents from the North Pole and a mouthwatering spread of nostalgic dishes, next to the mac and cheese.

On that same day, there's an outdoor menorah lighting. The local rabbi will be there. So will the town mayor and a fire juggler, and hundreds of jelly-filled donuts and fried potato latkes for the attendees.

Leah and Greg will show my parents how to glaze cookies shaped like snowflakes and gingerbread men. There'll be *Nutcracker* recitals, preschool concerts, and white elephant gift exchanges where the adults will talk until we close the bar. There'll be Christmas dinners, Hanukkah, and strolls by the holiday lights, culminating with New Year's Eve.

It won't all go smoothly, of course.

Someone will dump flour all over the kitchen floor and I'll forget to buy important gifts. The store-bought pie a guest brings to a family function will be written off as "too sweet and too American." A tribunal of relatives will look heavenward and shake their heads about so-and-so's still-single nephew, then share stories about favorite vacation spots and toast to America. A small child might projectile vomit, making everyone wonder if it's because someone flipped him upside down after a meal—or if he's got a contagious stomach bug.

But for the first time since becoming a parent, this holiday season I ditch the stress about whether the balance is right. I'm no longer anxious that a wrong move will sever the link with one tradition or another, because traditions are so much more than a performance or a checkmark. I realize it's impossible—and quite unnecessary, actually—to do it all.

It's Christmas Eve. Everyone in the house is asleep. The kitchen sink is full of dishes. I'm binging on cookies left over after Santa got his share and inspecting the holiday tree with presents and mismatched ornaments.

This ornament is shaped like the Star of David. That one Pete glued together back in elementary school. Here's a glimmering orb, just like the one I left behind years ago. There's the Cheerios garland my daughter has strung together and my son tried to eat.

By the time this calendar year is over, my family will have had multiple present-opening ceremonies in different languages, with cookies, latkes, and beet salads, in the company of people who matter. All of the pieces will fit somehow.

But right now the house is still.

I think back to that thirteen-year-old, rushed off by a train from the snowy midnight platform, convinced that nothing will ever feel like home again.

And you know what? It turns out I was wrong.

ACKNOWLEDGMENTS

THERE ARE SO MANY people and organizations I am indebted to. I am thankful to my literary agents Katelyn Hales and Robin Straus at the Robin Straus Agency for their unwavering optimism and patience. I thank my amazing editor Rachael Marks and the entire team at Beacon Press, including Alison Rodriguez, Caitlin Meyer, Priyanka Ray, Bella Sanchez, Sanj Kharbanda, and Marcy Barnes, as well as Andrea Lee and Susan Lumenello for the careful edits and Louis Roe for the gorgeous cover design.

I want to thank Milana Khodorkovskaya, Kimberly Chase, Veronika Short, Anna Kaydanovskaya, and the Russian-speaking Alameda crew for their support in the form of advice, beverages, couches to crash on, and letting me bounce ideas and grow from their wisdom.

My readers Mona Rizzardi, Anna Dvigubski, and Olga Zilberbourg provided generous feedback. Olga and Yelena Furman also gave me an opportunity to read a chapter in its still-gestational form in San Francisco and to discuss this project online via *Punctured Lines*.

The book would absolutely not be the same without the generosity of the following individuals, families, and organizations: Zewditu Fesseha, Teacher Tadesse, the St. Mary's of Zion Amharic Church, Bi Yu Lin and family, Lakshmi Iyer, Lakeside Organic Gardens and their hardworking employees, Yalda Modabber and Golestan, Casey Wells, Anders Lee, Fernando Acosta, Francis Corby Ceschin, Brooke Bernold, Pedro Leon de la Barra Vega, Aihua, Lenny and Anna Gusel and RJeneration, Monika Leal, Paula Niño Kehr, Patrick, Sara, Roxanna Asgarian, Sarah Diligenti, Hema Nataraju, the Ceballos family, Glauce, Vlada Teper, Elizabeth Merkowitz, Ruchika, Altayeb Abdulrahim, Tatiana Vechniakova, Pollyanna, Sathab, Anindita Dutta,

Edwin A., Aleksey K., Jaclyn K., Ada Gurevich, Miriam Ward, Alla Z., Alexandra Onosova, Naomi Kaye Honova, and those who shared their experiences anonymously. I'm honored you entrusted me to retell your stories.

I am immensely grateful for the expertise of the following individuals: Dr. Ellen Bialystok, Dr. Erika Levy, Dr. Erika Hoff, Dr. Anya Dashevsky and Growing Minds, Maki Park, Dr. Philip Kasinitz, Dr. Jaime Cárcamo and the Psychological and Stress Management, Dr. Nazli Kibria, Dr. Mercedes Oromendia, Dr. Monika Schmid, Dr. Juli Fraga, and Dr. Catherine Crowley.

I am thankful to Julia Scheeres for her proposal writing class at the Writers Grotto in San Francisco, which jump-started this entire project, and for her support throughout.

Thanks to Adam Beck for letting me include several insights from his fantastic book on bilingualism.

Thanks to Dr. Barlow Der Mugrdechian for reviewing the background on Armenia.

Thanks to Julie Schwietert Collazo for checking facts.

The resourceful Sandra Barbulescu, Kristen Hodges, and Olga Livshin provided connections.

Thanks to those who've kindly given a first home to my writing on the topic of immigrant identity, including Sarah Todd at *Quartz*, Anna Halkidis at *Parents*, Amy Joyce at the *Washington Post*, and Lisa Keys at *Kveller*.

I thank the Alameda Free Library not only for being the perfect office space but also for its ever-resourceful librarians and their unwavering patience when asked, "But can I borrow it for longer?"

Thanks to Julie's Coffee and Tea Garden and the Beanery for being marvelous places to write and get sustenance.

Thanks to the Russian Vodka Room for making a killer herring under a fur coat.

A part of this book was written during the COVID-19 pandemic, a time of isolation, challenges, and loss, as well as a year the nation confronted racial injustice. I'd be remiss if I didn't thank those who worked tirelessly during this period: teachers and caregivers, store employees, food delivery folks, restaurant workers, political organizers, first responders, and medical workers. Specifically, thanks to Dr.

Grace Mitchell, to Lori Mihalich-Levin for her grounding "Calls for Calm," to Cassandra Caron for her ingenious craft kits that kept our family entertained during the lockdown, to Rising Star Preschool, Starbright School, Alameda Ballet Academy, and Rabbi Meir and Mushki Shmotkin.

Social media can be hit or miss, but I am immensely grateful for my Twitter and Facebook communities for providing a wealth of connections and conversations about translation and nostalgic foods, as well as to my Facebook writing groups.

The Simon family offered much encouragement with their care packages and well wishes. Thanks to Heather Reynolds for nurturing our whole household with books representing its many traditions and for her volunteer work with immigrant communities.

I am thankful to my parents, who believe in my work and dreams even though I didn't become a lawyer, and who taught me so much about the meaning of family, resilience, and cherishing my heritage. Thanks to Alex for being an unwitting tech-support guru. So much gratitude to my *dedushka* for his enthusiasm about my book and his treasure trove of stories, and to Luba. Here's also to the enduring memory of my other grandparents, the trailblazing immigrants, fighters, and role models.

Thanks to my children, my heart and soul and the inspiration for this project.

Special thanks to Paul, who has served as a generous advisor, a willing editor, a purveyor of late-night snacks, and the greatest cheerleader anyone could ever hope for. Without him, this book would not have been possible.

NOTES

PREFACE

1. Abby Budiman, "Key Findings About US Immigrants," Pew Research Center, August 20, 2020, https://www.pewresearch.org/fact-tank/2019/06/17/key-findings-abou t-u-s-immigrants/. Percentage-wise, the immigrant share of the overall US population today is still just below what it was near the turn of the twentieth century. Today, immigrants make up 13.7 percent of the US population compared to 14.8 percent in 1890.

2. "Fam4: Children of at Least One Foreign-Born Parent: Percentage of Children Ages 0–17 by Nativity of Child and Parents," Federal Interagency Forum on Child and Family Statistics, https://www.childstats.gov/americaschildren/tables/fam4.asp.

3. Sarah Pierce and Jessica Bolter, *Dismantling and Reconstructing the U.S. Immigration System: A Catalog of Changes Under the Trump Presidency* (Washington, DC: Migration Policy Institute, July 2020), https://www.migrationpolicy.org/research/us -immigration-system-changes-trump-presidency.

CHAPTER 1: I AM THE GRINCH WHO STOLE CHRISTMAS

1. Anzia Yezierska, *Bread Givers*, 3rd ed. (New York: Persea Books, 2003), 9.

2. Masha Rumer, "A Lot of Our Ideas About Bilingual Children Are Total Myths," *Quartz*, August 13, 2017, https://qz.com/1051986/a-lot-of-our-ideas-about-bilingual -children-are-total-myths.

3. Libby Denkmann, "California's Prop 187 Vote Damaged GOP Relations with Immigrants," NPR, November 8, 2019, https://www.npr.org/2019/11/08/777466912 /californias-prop-187-vote-damaged-gop-relations-with-immigrants.

4. Paul Reps and Nyogen Senzaki, *Zen Flesh, Zen Bones: A Collection of Zen and Pre-Zen Writings* (North Clarendon, VT: Tuttle Publishing, 1998), 23.

5. American Immigration Council, "Did My Family Really Come 'Legally'?," August 10, 2016, https://www.americanimmigrationcouncil.org/research/did-my-family -really-come-legally-todays-immigration-laws-created-a-new-reality.

6. Alejandro Portes and Rubén G. Rumbaut, *Immigrant America: A Portrait*, 4th ed. (Oakland: University of California Press, 2014), 212.

7. Portes and Rumbaut, *Immigrant America*, 1–2.

8. Portes and Rumbaut, *Immigrant America*, 2.

9. David W. Haines, *Immigration Structures and Immigrant Lives: An Introduction to the US Experience* (Lanham, MD: Rowman & Littlefield, 2017). Haines writes that with the brief exception of the Alien and Sedition Acts of 1798, when deportations

temporarily became easier and the wait to become a citizen grew, "migration to the United States was initially largely unregulated at the US receiving end. . . . During the early 1800s, then, there were few barriers to those seeking the opportunities that the United States had to offer," 23.

10. D'Vera Cohn, "How U.S. Immigration Laws and Rules Have Changed Through History," September 30, 2015, Pew Research Center, https://www.pew research.org/fact-tank/2015/09/30/how-u-s-immigration-laws-and-rules-have -changed-through-history.

11. American Immigration Council, "Did My Family Really Come 'Legally'?"

12. Statue of Liberty—Ellis Island Foundation, Inc., "Overview + History: Ellis Island," https://www.statueofliberty.org/ellis-island/overview-history.

13. Haines, *Immigration Structures and Immigrant Lives*, 19–21.

14. Haines, *Immigration Structures and Immigrant Lives*, 19–20. For more about the treatment of the Indigenous population by the colonial settlers, see Roxanne Dunbar-Ortiz, *An Indigenous Peoples' History of the United States* (Boston: Beacon Press, 2015).

15. Haines, *Immigration Structures and Immigrant Lives*, 22. The original letter can be found at https://founders.archives.gov/documents/Washington/99-01-02-12127.

16. Haines, *Immigration Structures and Immigrant Lives*, 22. Franklin wrote this in a letter to Peter Collinson in 1753. Some historians have doubted the authenticity of the letter, which is available in its entire form at https://founders.archives.gov/documents /Franklin/01-04-02-0173. Still, in another pamphlet, titled "Information to Those Who Would Remove to America," Franklin reflected on the benefits of immigration: "Strangers are welcome because there is room enough for them all," http://blog.yale books.com/2017/04/12/benjamin-franklin-on-immigration.

17. Dunbar-Ortiz, *An Indigenous Peoples' History of the United States*; Haines, *Immigration Structures and Immigrant Lives*, 22. Original emphasis. Franklin's statements came from his "Observations Concerning the Increase of Mankind" essay, first published in 1751 and available in its entirety at https://founders.archives.gov/documents /Franklin/01-04-02-0080.

18. Katie Reilly, "Here Are All the Times Donald Trump Insulted Mexico," *Time*, August 31, 2016, https://time.com/4473972/donald-trump-mexico-meeting-insult.

19. Haines, *Immigration Structures and Immigrant Lives*, 23–27.

20. Portes and Rumbaut, *Immigrant America*, 7–8.

21. Brigit Katz, "New Orleans Apologizes for 1891 Lynching of Italian-Americans," *Smithsonian Magazine*, April 15, 2019, https://www.smithsonianmag.com/smart-news /new-orleans-apologizes-1891-lynching-italian-americans-180971959.

22. *New York Times*, March 16, 1891, https://timesmachine.nytimes.com/times machine/1891/03/16/103299119.pdf.

23. Portes and Rumbaut, *Immigrant America*, 12.

24. Gary Kamiya, "How Early SF Kept Chinese Children Out of the Schoolhouse," *San Francisco Chronicle*, April 15, 2017, https://www.sfchronicle.com/bayarea /article/How-early-SF-kept-Chinese-children-out-of-the-11074408.php; and Gary Kamiya, "How Chinese Americans Won Right to Attend SF Schools," *San Francisco Chronicle*, April 29, 2017, https://www.sfchronicle.com/bayarea/article/How-Chinese -Americans-won-right-to-attend-SF-11107543.php.

25. Tom Rea, "The Rock Springs Massacre," Wyoming State Historical Society, November 8, 2014, https://www.wyohistory.org/encyclopedia/rock-springs-massacre.

26. "Repeal of the Chinese Exclusion Act, 1943," Office of the Historian, Foreign Service Institute, United States Department of State, https://history.state.gov/milestones /1937-1945/chinese-exclusion-act-repeal.

27. "Hang the Jew, Hang the Jew," Anti-Defamation League, August 6, 2015, https://www.adl.org/news/article/hang-the-jew-hang-the-jew.

28. During the twentieth century, tens of thousands of federally funded sterilizations occurred in thirty-two states, often without the victims' consent or knowledge. Inspired by the eugenics movement, many of those procedures were performed on women and girls of color and Native Americans. Some of the victims were mentally ill, many were poor. These procedures were widespread in California and also in the South, targeting the Black community. See Lisa Ko, "Unwanted Sterilization and Eugenics Programs in the United States," *Independent Lens*, PBS, January 29, 2016, https://www.pbs.org/independentlens/blog/unwanted-sterilization-and-eugenics -programs-in-the-united-states.

29. Edward Alsworth Ross, *The Old World in the New* (New York: Century Co., 1914), 293.

30. Ross, *The Old World in the New*, 113, 154, 291.

31. Daniel Okrent, *The Guarded Gate: Bigotry, Eugenics, and the Law That Kept Two Generations of Jews, Italians, and Other European Immigrants Out of America* (New York: Scribner, 2019), 211.

32. Timothy W. Ryback, "A Disquieting Book from Hitler's Library," *New York Times*, December 7, 2011, https://www.nytimes.com/2011/12/08/opinion/a-disquieting -book-from-hitlers-library.html.

33. Okrent, *The Guarded Gate*, 153–58.

34. Okrent, *The Guarded Gate*, 158.

35. Sixty-Fourth Congress, Session II, Chs. 27–29, 1917, Library of Congress, 885–87, https://www.loc.gov/law/help/statutes-at-large/64th-congress/session-2 /c64s2ch29.pdf.

36. Haines, *Immigration Structures and Immigrant Lives*, 32.

37. Haines, *Immigration Structures and Immigrant Lives*, 25.

38. Portes and Rumbaut, *Immigrant America*, 13–14.

39. Haines, *Immigration Structures and Immigrant Lives*, 28.

40. Portes and Rumbaut, *Immigrant America*, 14.

41. Mae M. Ngai, *Impossible Subjects: Illegal Aliens and the Making of Modern America* (Princeton, NJ: Princeton University Press, 2014), 72.

42. Portes and Rumbaut, *Immigrant America*, 21, 24. Portes and Rumbaut call the Bracero Program "one of the largest state-managed labor migrations in history."

43. Douglas S. Massey and Karen A. Pren, "Unintended Consequences of US Immigration Policy: Explaining the Post-1965 Surge from Latin America," *Population and Development Review* 38, no. 1 (2012): 1–29, https://www.ncbi.nlm.nih.gov/pmc/articles /PMC3407978. The number of temporary workers during the Bracero Program and the number of undocumented Mexican migrants soon after the Bracero Program are surprisingly similar. These numbers may be referring to the same people, just calling them different names.

44. Dara Lind, "How America's Rejection of Jews Fleeing Nazi Germany Haunts Our Refugee Policy Today," *Vox*, January 27, 2017, https://www.vox.com/policy-and -politics/2017/1/27/14412082/refugees-history-holocaust.

45. Okrent, *The Guarded Gate*, 374.

46. Haines, *Immigration Structures and Immigrant Lives*, 35–40.

47. Haines, *Immigration Structures and Immigrant Lives*, 40–43.

48. Haines, *Immigration Structures and Immigrant Lives*, 42–43. Also, Portes and Rumbaut, *Immigrant America*, 23–25.

49. Since 2016, immigrants have been referred to as "thugs," immigration as "invasion," and some of their countries of origin as "shithole countries" by President Donald Trump, with a wall between the US and Mexico becoming a core premise of the 2016 presidential election. Hate crimes have spiked alongside this rhetoric. For details, see Eugene Scott, "Trump's Most Insulting—and Violent—Language Is Often Reserved for Immigrants," *Washington Post*, October 2, 2019, https://www.washington post.com/politics/2019/10/02/trumps-most-insulting-violent-language-is-often -reserved-immigrants. Also Vanessa Williamson and Isabella Gelfand, "Trump and Racism: What Do the Data Say?," *Brookings Institution*, August 14, 2019, https://www .brookings.edu/blog/fixgov/2019/08/14/trump-and-racism-what-do-the-data-say.

50. "Deferred Action for Childhood Arrivals (DACA) Data Tools," Migration Policy Institute, https://www.migrationpolicy.org/programs/data-hub/deferred-action -childhood-arrivals-daca-profiles.

51. Nicole Goodkind, "Trump Administration Argues Detained Migrant Children Don't Need Toothbrushes, Soap," *Newsweek*, June 20, 2019, https://www.newsweek .com/migrant-children-border-trump-administration-1445090.

52. Masha Rumer, "Queens Detention Center Welcomes Asylum Seekers," *The Advocate, The Newspaper of The Graduate Center, City University of New York*, April 2004.

CHAPTER 2: THE BEET TEST

1. Marcel Proust, *Swann's Way: In Search of Lost Time*, vol. 1, trans. Lydia Davis (New York: Penguin, 2004), 45.

2. One harrowing example of a 1930s Soviet-era famine is Holodomor, when Joseph Stalin deliberately starved millions of Ukrainians by collectivizing farms and confiscating their harvest, then closing off borders so residents could not escape. It's widely considered to be an act of genocide. "Holodomor: Memories of Ukraine's Silent Massacre," *BBC News*, November 23, 2013, https://www.bbc.com/news/world -europe-25058256.

3. Nancy Foner, *Across Generations: Immigrant Families in America* (New York: New York University Press, 2009). Tensions between generations are not new, but they "often become intensified when the parents come from another country and culture and are unfamiliar with or disapprove of dominant American values and practices," writes sociologist Nancy Foner. "A further source of conflict is parental pressure to marry within the ethnic group, which second-generation young people may resent— and resist," 4, 6.

4. Mary C. Waters and Marisa Gerstein Pineau, eds., "The Integration of Im- migrants into American Society," National Academies of Sciences, Engineering, and

Medicine (Washington, DC: National Academies Press, 2015), 346, https://www.nap .edu/catalog/21746/the-integration-of-immigrants-into-american-society.

5. Waters and Pineau, "The Integration of Immigrants into American Society," 347–48.

6. Waters and Pineau, "The Integration of Immigrants into American Society," 348–49.

7. Waters and Pineau, "The Integration of Immigrants into American Society," 357.

8. Waters and Pineau, "The Integration of Immigrants into American Society," 6.

9. Nazli Kibria, phone interview with author, January 22, 2020.

10. Nazli Kibria, "Marry into a Good Family," in Foner, *Across Generations: Immigrant Families in America*, 98–113.

11. Kibria, "Marry into a Good Family," 101.

12. Philip Kasinitz, John H. Mollenkopf, Mary C. Waters, and Jennifer Holdaway, *Inheriting the City: The Children of Immigrants Come of Age* (New York: Russell Sage Foundation, 2008).

13. Philip Kasinitz, interview with author, February 3, 2020.

14. Unless noted otherwise, second generation and generation 1.5 will be used interchangeably in this chapter.

15. Kasinitz, Mollenkopf, Waters, and Holdaway, *Inheriting the City*, 232.

16. Kasinitz, Mollenkopf, Waters, and Holdaway, *Inheriting the City*, 232.

17. Kasinitz, Mollenkopf, Waters, and Holdaway, *Inheriting the City*, 229–31.

18. Kasinitz, Mollenkopf, Waters, and Holdaway, *Inheriting the City*, 235.

CHAPTER 3: THEN COMES BABY IN A BABY CARRIAGE

1. Daniel José Older, "I Rejected Spanish as a Kid. Now I Wish We'd Embrace Our Native Languages," *Time*, February 14, 2019, https://time.com/5528434/daniel -jose-older-spanish.

2. Masha Rumer, "On Finding the Perfect Name for My Russian American Jewish Son," *Kveller*, August 4, 2016, https://www.kveller.com/on-finding-the-perfect-name -for-my-russian-american-jewish-son.

3. Foner, *Across Generations: Immigrant Families in America*, 15.

4. Lauren Pardee and Nicole Harris, "What's Your Parenting Style?," *Parents*, October 12, 2018, https://www.parents.com/parenting/better-parenting/style/parenting -styles-explained.

5. Jessica McCrory Calarco, "'Free Range' Parenting's Unfair Double Standard," *Atlantic*, April 3, 2018, https://www.theatlantic.com/family/archive/2018/04/free-range -parenting/557051. Free-range parenting often exposes a double standard, especially when it comes to poor and working-class parents and Black mothers.

6. Christine Gross-Loh, *Parenting Without Borders: Surprising Lessons Parents Around the World Can Teach Us* (New York: Avery, 2013), 5–6.

7. Claire Cain Miller, "The Relentlessness of Modern Parenting," *New York Times*, December 25, 2018, https://www.nytimes.com/2018/12/25/upshot/the-relentlessness -of-modern-parenting.html.

8. Parenting in America," Pew Research Center, December 17, 2015, https:// www.pewsocialtrends.org/2015/12/17/parenting-in-america.

9. Cain Miller, "The Relentlessness of Modern Parenting."

10. "Why Is Karva Chauth Celebrated and Its Vrat Vidhi, Timings and Dishes You Can Eat," *Times of India*, October 16, 2019, https://timesofindia.indiatimes.com /life-style/food-news/why-is-karva-chauth-celebrated-and-its-vrat-vidhi-timings-and -dishes-you-can-eat/articleshow/71599205.cms.

11. Jaime Cárcamo, interview with author, January 31, 2020.

12. "Death of Mexican 9/11 Worker Raises Questions," Associated Press, January 16, 2012, https://www.cbsnews.com/news/death-of-mexican-9-11-worker-raises -questions.

13. Gordon C. Nagayama Hall, "Familismo," *Psychology Today*, April 13, 2017, https://www.psychologytoday.com/us/blog/life-in-the-intersection/201704/familismo.

14. This certainly isn't true for every American family, especially when financial crises force the youngest generation to move back in with their parents, such as during the 2007–2009 recession and the COVID-19 pandemic.

15. Foner, *Across Generations: Immigrant Families in America*, 4.

16. Denver Nicks, "Hitting Your Kids Is Legal in All 50 States," *Time*, September 17, 2014, https://time.com/3379862/child-abuse.

17. Christina M. Rodriguez, "Parental and Abuse Potential Affects on Child Depression, Anxiety, and Attributions," *Journal of Marriage and Family* 65, no. 4 (2003): 809–17, http://libres.uncg.edu/ir/uncg/f/c_rodriguez_parental_2003.pdf.

18. "Working with Immigrant-Origin Clients: An Update for Mental Health Professionals," American Psychological Association, 2013, https://www.apa.org/topics /immigration/immigration-report-professionals.pdf.

19. Katherine Ponte, "Mental Health Challenges in Immigrant Communities," National Alliance on Mental Illness, July 22, 2019, https://www.nami.org/Blogs /NAMI-Blog/July-2019/Mental-Health-Challenges-in-Immigrant-Communities.

20. Colleen de Bellefonds, "Cry It Out Method of Sleep Training," What to Expect, February 24, 2020, https://www.whattoexpect.com/first-year/crying-it-out.aspx.

21. Robert LeVine and Sarah LeVine, "It's OK to Sleep Next to Your Infant Child. It's Even Beneficial," op-ed, *Los Angeles Times*, September 16, 2016, https://www .latimes.com/opinion/op-ed/la-oe-levine-cosleeping-bedsharing-global-20160916 -snap-story.html.

CHAPTER 4: VODKA RUBS AND OTHER FAMILY ADVICE

1. Roxanne Gay, in *American Like Me: Reflections on Life Between Cultures*, ed. America Ferrera (New York: Gallery Books, 2018), 62.

2. Northwell Health, "Grandparents Who Practice Outdated Health Myths May Pose Safety Threat on Grandchildren," *Science Daily*, May 4, 2017, https://www .sciencedaily.com/releases/2017/05/170504083052.htm.

3. Emanuella Grinberg, "Swaddling and SIDS: About that Alarming Study . . . ," CNN, May 10, 2016, https://www.cnn.com/2016/05/10/health/swaddling-sids-study /index.html.

4. Amy S. Choi, "How Cultures Around the World Think About Parenting," TED Ideas, July 15, 2014, https://ideas.ted.com/how-cultures-around-the-world-think -about-parenting.

5. Caitlyn Collins, "Why American Moms Can't Get Enough Expert Parenting Advice," *The Atlantic*, May 12, 2019, https://www.theatlantic.com/family/archive/2019 /05/american-parents-obsession-expert-advice/589132.

6. "West East," *China Daily*, August 30, 2011, http://www.chinadaily.com.cn/cndy /2011-08/30/content_13215642.htm.

7. Ashley May, "Pregnant During the Eclipse? Superstitions Say It Could Harm the Baby," *USA Today*, August 18, 2017, https://www.usatoday.com/story/news/nation -now/2017/08/18/pregnant-during-eclipse-superstitions-say-could-harm-baby/579196001.

8. Lourdes Alcañiz, "Bringing Back the Hispanic Tradition of 'Cuarentena' After Childbirth," BabyCenter, https://www.babycenter.com/0_bringing-back-the-hispanic -tradition-of-cuarentena-after-chi_10346386.bc.

9. Malin Eberhard-Gran, Susan Garthus-Niegel, Kristian Garthus-Niegel, et al., "Postnatal Care: A Cross-Cultural and Historical Perspective," *Archives of Women's Mental Health* 13, (2010): 459–66, https://doi.org/10.1007/s00737-010-0175-1.

10. "Foods—for Mothers," La Leche League International, https://www.llli.org /breastfeeding-info/foods.

11. Grinberg, "Swaddling and SIDS."

12. Beth A. Choby and Shefaa George, "Toilet Training," *American Family Physician* 78, no. 9 (November 1, 2008): 1059–64, https://www.aafp.org/afp/2008/1101 /p1059.html.

CHAPTER 5: THE POLYGLOT BOARDINGHOUSE

1. Eva Hoffman, *Lost in Translation* (New York: Penguin, 1989), 273.

2. François Grosjean, "How Many Are We?," *Psychology Today*, September 19, 2012, updated April 4, 2020, https://www.psychologytoday.com/us/blog/life-bilingual /201209/how-many-are-we.

3. David M. Eberhard, Gary F. Simons, and Charles D. Fennig, eds., "How Many Languages Are There in the World?," *Ethnologue: Languages of the World*, 2021, https:// www.ethnologue.com/guides/how-many-languages; David M. Eberhard, Gary F. Simons, and Charles D. Fennig, eds., "Top 10 Most Spoken Languages, 2020," *Ethnologue: Languages of the World*, 2021, https://www.ethnologue.com/guides/ethnologue200.

4. This book uses the term *bilingual* interchangeably with *multilingual* where they are similar.

5. François Grosjean, *Bilingual: Life and Reality* (Cambridge, MA: Harvard University Press, 2010), 19.

6. Quoted in Grosjean, *Bilingual: Life and Reality*, 19–20; Christophe Thiery, "True Bilingualism and Second Language Learning," in *Language Interpretation and Communication*, ed. David Gerver and H. Wallace Sinaiko (New York: Plenum, 1978), 145–53, quotation on 146.

7. Colin Baker and Wayne E. Wright, *Foundations of Bilingual Education and Bilingualism*, 6th ed. (Bristol, UK: Multilingual Matters, 2017), 13–14.

8. Grosjean, *Bilingual: Life and Reality*, 20.

9. Grosjean, *Bilingual: Life and Reality*, 21, 22.

10. Harmeet Kaur, "FYI: English Isn't the Official Language of the United States," CNN, June 15, 2018, https://www.cnn.com/2018/05/20/us/english-us-official -language-trnd/index.html.

11. Claude Goldenberg and Kirstin Wagner, "Bilingual Education: Reviving an American Tradition," *American Educator* (Fall 2015), https://www.aft.org/ae/fall2015 /goldenberg_wagner.

12. Baker and Wright, *Foundations of Bilingual Education and Bilingualism*, 173.

13. "Boarding Schools: Struggling with Cultural Repression," chap. 3 in *Native Words, Native Warriors*, National Museum of the American Indian Education Office, https://americanindian.si.edu/nk360/code-talkers/boarding-schools/.

14. Kumari Devarajan, "Ready for a Linguistic Controversy? Say 'Mmhmm,'" August 17, 2018, https://www.npr.org/sections/codeswitch/2018/08/17/606002607 /ready-for-a-linguistic-controversy-say-mhmm.

15. Vasiliki Fouka, "Backlash: The Unintended Effects of Language Prohibition in U.S. Schools After World War I," working paper no. 591, Stanford Center for International Development, December 2016, https://siepr.stanford.edu/sites/default /files/publications/591wp_0_6.pdf.

16. "Babel Proclamation, May 1918," Iowa Department of Cultural Affairs, https://iowaculture.gov/history/education/educator-resources/primary-source-sets /immigration-regulation-response-and/babel-proclamation.

17. Portes and Rumbaut, *Immigrant America*, 216.

18. Portes and Rumbaut, *Immigrant America*, 216.

19. "Roosevelt Bars the Hyphenated: No Room in This Country for Dual Nationality, He Tells Knights of Columbus," *New York Times*, October 13, 1915, https:// timesmachine.nytimes.com/timesmachine/1915/10/13/105042745.pdf.

20. "Sauerkraut May Be 'Liberty Cabbage': Dealers Think Camouflaged Name Is Better Suited to American Sensibility," *New York Times*, April 25, 1918, https://times machine.nytimes.com/timesmachine/1918/04/25/96864971.html.

21. Kenji Hakuta and Rafael M. Diaz, "The Relationship Between Degree of Bilingualism and Cognitive Ability: A Critical Discussion and Some Longitudinal Data," in *Children's Language*, vol. 5, ed. Keith Nelson (New York: Psychology Press, 1985), 319–44, https://web.stanford.edu/~hakuta/www/research/publications/(1985)%20 -%20THE%20RELATIONSHIP%20BETWEEN%20DEGREE%20OF%20 BILINGUALISM%20AND.pdf.

22. Quoted in Ellen Bialystok, Fergus I. M. Craik, and Gigi Luk, "Bilingualism: Consequences for Mind and Brain, *Trends in Cognitive Sciences* 16, no. 4 (April 2012): 240–50, https://www.ncbi.nlm.nih.gov/pmc/articles/PMC3322418.

23. Hakuta and Diaz, "The Relationship Between Degree of Bilingualism and Cognitive Ability." Some of these early bilingualism studies were conducted in a child's weaker language and the groups were not controlled for socioeconomic status, so the results were unreliable.

24. Hakuta and Diaz, "The Relationship Between Degree of Bilingualism and Cognitive Ability."

25. Grosjean, *Bilingual: Life and Reality*, 105–6.

26. Take, for instance, Donald Trump remarking during his 2016 presidential campaign, "This is a country where we speak English," Beatriz Díez, "'English Only': The Movement to Limit Spanish Speaking in US," *BBC News*, December 3, 2019, https://www.bbc.com/news/world-us-canada-50550742.

27. Juliana Menasce Horowitz, "Americans See Advantages and Challenges in Country's Growing Racial and Ethnic Diversity," Pew Research Center, May 8, 2019, https://www.pewsocialtrends.org/2019/05/08/americans-see-advantages-and-challenges -in-countrys-growing-racial-and-ethnic-diversity.

28. Christopher Ingraham, "Nearly Half of White Republicans Say It Bothers Them to Hear People Speaking Foreign Languages," *Washington Post*, May 8, 2019, https://www.washingtonpost.com/business/2019/05/08/nearly-half-white-republicans -say-it-bothers-them-hear-people-speaking-foreign-languages.

29. "FAM4 Children of at Least One Foreign-Born Parent," Federal Interagency Forum on Child and Family Statistics, https://www.childstats.gov/americaschildren /tables/fam4.asp.

30. "Selected Social Characteristics in the United States," US Census Bureau, 2018, Federal Interagency Forum on Child and Family Statistics, https://data.census .gov/cedsci/table?d=ACS%205-Year%20Estimates%20Data%20Profiles&table =DP02&tid=ACSDP5Y2018.DP02&y=2018&hidePreview=true.

31. Samantha P. Fan, Zoe Liberman, Boaz Keysar, and Katherine D. Kinzler, "The Exposure Advantage: Early Exposure to a Multilingual Environment Promotes Effective Communication," *Psychological Science* 26, no. 7 (July 2015): 1090–97, https:// www.ncbi.nlm.nih.gov/pmc/articles/PMC4791950. For highlights, also see Jann Ingmire, "Children Exposed to Multiple Languages May Be Better Natural Communicators," *UChicago News*, May 11, 2015, https://news.uchicago.edu/story/children-exposed -multiple-languages-may-be-better-natural-communicators.

32. Fan, Liberman, Keysar, and D. Kinzler, "The Exposure Advantage."

33. Baker and Wright, *Foundations of Bilingual Education and Bilingualism*, 149–50.

34. Baker and Wright, *Foundations of Bilingual Education and Bilingualism*, 142.

35. Baker and Wright, *Foundations of Bilingual Education and Bilingualism*, 146–48. This benefit has been noted in multiple studies among bilingual kids with advanced proficiency in both languages.

36. "If Your Child Is Bilingual, Learning Additional Languages Later Might Be Easier," news release, Georgetown University Medical Center, October 2, 2017, https:// gumc.georgetown.edu/news-release/does_being_bilingual_help_your_brain_learn _additional_languages.

37. Ellen Bialystok, phone interviews with author, May 2, 2017, and January 16, 2020.

38. Fergus I. M. Craik, Ellen Bialystok, and Morris Freedman, "Delaying the Onset of Alzheimer Disease: Bilingualism as a Form of Cognitive Reserve," *Neurology* 75, no. 19 (November 9, 2010), https://n.neurology.org/content/75/19/1726.abstract.

39. Ellen Bialystok, Kathleen F. Peets, and Sylvain Moreno, "Producing Bilinguals Through Immersion Education: Development of Metalinguistic Awareness," *Applied Psycholinguistics* 35, no. 1 (April 2014): 177–91, https://www.ncbi.nlm.nih.gov/pmc /articles/PMC3987956.

40. Ayleen Barbel Fattal, "Research Rules Out Mental Flexibility, Attention as Advantages for Some Bilingual Children," *Florida International University News*, May 20, 2019, https://news.fiu.edu/2019/research-rules-out-mental-flexibility-attention -as-advantages-for-some-bilingual-children. This study from Florida International University looked at a larger sample size of children and did not find the previously reported executive function benefits.

41. Rumer, "A Lot of Our Ideas About Bilingual Children Are Total Myths."

42. Kyle J. Comishen, Ellen Bialystok, and Scott A. Adler, "The Impact of Bilingual Environments on Selective Attention in Infancy," *Developmental Science* 22, no. 4,

(July 2019): e12797, https://onlinelibrary.wiley.com/doi/full/10.1111/desc.12797. The highlights of this study can also be found at https://www.sciencedaily.com/releases/2019/01/190130103825.htm.

43. I was interviewed for this podcast as a guest, with the episode airing on August 6, 2020.

44. Monika Leal and Paula Niño Kehr, "Spanish Is Like a Warm Croqueta," *Entre Dos Podcast*, May 21, 2018, https://entredospodcast.com/2018/05/21/spanish-is-like-a-warm-croqueta.

CHAPTER 6: BILINGUALISM: AN UPHILL BATTLE, SOMETIMES

1. Nelson Mandela," *BBC Learning English*, https://www.bbc.co.uk/worldservice/learningenglish/movingwords/shortlist/mandela.shtml.

2. Lily Wong Fillmore, "Loss of Family Languages: Should Educators Be Concerned?," *Theory into Practice* 39, no. 4 (Fall 2000): 203–10, https://www.oise.utoronto.ca/eslinfusion/UserFiles/File/Home/Streamed_Vid_Resource/ESLInfusion/Comp_docs/Appendices_.pdf.

3. Robbins Burling, "Language Development of a Garo and English Speaking Child," *Word* 15, no. 1 (1959): 45–68, https://www.tandfonline.com/doi/pdf/10.1080/00437956.1959.11659683.

4. Quoted in Portes and Rumbaut, *Immigrant America*, 219.

5. Baker and Wright, *Foundations of Bilingual Education and Bilingualism*, 68–70. There are few exceptions to this general rule, like the Amish community, Spanish speakers in small rural communities along the US-Mexico border, as well as in Yiddish-speaking ultra-Orthodox Jewish communities.

6. Waters and Pineau, "The Integration of Immigrants into American Society," 6.

7. Erika Hoff, phone interview with author, April 24, 2017. Email interview with author, March 24, 2018.

8. Masha Rumer, "Bilingual Parenting Matters—Even If the White House Says It Doesn't," *SheKnows*, August 21, 2018, https://www.sheknows.com/parenting/articles/1140865/bilingual-parenting-matters.

9. Vladimir Nabokov, *Lolita* (New York: Vintage Books, 1997), 316–17.

10. Владимир Набоков, «Лолита» (Москва: АСТ, 1998), 380 [Vladimir Nabokov, *Lolita* (Moscow, AST, 1998), 380]. Translation mine.

11. Monika Schmid, email interview with author, May 6, 2020.

12. For more about language attrition, see Monika Schmid's website, https://languageattrition.org.

13. Monika S. Schmid, *First Language Attrition, Use and Maintenance: The Case of German Jews in Anglophone Countries* (Amsterdam: John Benjamins, 2002).

14. Asya Pereltsvaig, "The Disappearance of Yiddish in Russia and Elsewhere in the FSU," *Languages of the World*, November 22, 2015, https://www.languagesoftheworld.info/geolinguistics/endangered-languages/the-disappearance-of-yiddish-in-russia-and-elsewhere-in-the-fsu.html.

15. Annick De Houwer, "Parental Language Input Patterns and Children's Bilingual Use," *Applied Psycholinguistics* 28, no. 3 (2007): 411–24, https://www.researchgate.net/publication/228667112_Parental_language_input_patterns_and_children's_bilingual_use.

16. David M. Eberhard, Gary F. Simons, and Charles D. Fennig, eds., "What Is the Most Spoken Language?," *Ethnologue: Languages of the World*, https://www .ethnologue.com/guides/most-spoken-languages.

17. Baker and Wright, *Foundations of Bilingual Education and Bilingualism*, 78–79.

CHAPTER 7: STANDING WATCH

1. Henry Roth, *Call It Sleep* (New York: Picador, 2005), 9.

2. "About" webpage, Arab Cultural and Community Center, https://www.arab culturecenter.org/about.

3. Altayeb "Tayeb" Abdulrahim, phone interview with author, July 20, 2020.

4. "Arab Cultural and Community Center," *Bay Area Focus*, KPIX CBS SF Bay Area, March 25, 2015, https://www.youtube.com/watch?v=PErIao4cb-s.

CHAPTER 8: THE EXPERTS WEIGH IN

1. "A Spoonful of Sugar," *Mary Poppins*, Richard M. and Robert B. Sherman, 1964, https://www.loc.gov/item/smor.1964-1.

2. Erika Levy, interview with author, February 3, 2020.

3. Baker and Wright, *Foundations of Bilingual Education and Bilingualism*, 89.

4. François Grosjean, "Myths About Bilingualism," personal website, https://www .francoisgrosjean.ch/myths_en.html.

5. Baker and Wright, *Foundations of Bilingual Education and Bilingualism*, 57; Grosjean, *Bilingual: Life and Reality*, 210. For linguist Joshua A. Fishman, for example, minority language also should be present at school and after school, in the neighborhood and in the community. Otherwise, the bilingually educated kids are less likely to pass their language on to the following generation. In Baker and Wright, *Foundations of Bilingual Education and Bilingualism*, 54–55.

6. Erika Levy, *Baby's First Words in French* (New York: Living Language, 2007), 18–20.

7. Kim Eckart, "Not Just 'Baby Talk': Parentese Helps Parents, Babies Make 'Conversation' and Boosts Language Development," *UWNews*, University of Washington, February 3, 2020, https://www.washington.edu/news/2020/02/03/not-just -baby-talk-parentese-helps-parents-babies-make-conversation-and-boosts-language -development. The study was authored by Naja Ferjan Ramírez, Sarah Roseberry Lytle, and Patricia K. Kuhl and published in the *Proceedings of the National Academy of Sciences*, https://www.pnas.org/content/117/7/3484.

8. Erika Hoff, "Why Bilingual Development Is Not Easy," *Advances in Child Development and Behavior*, vol. 61, ed. J. Lockman (Amsterdam: Elsevier, forthcoming), shared with permission of the author.

9. Baker and Wright, *Foundations of Bilingual Education and Bilingualism*, 69. Adapted from a study by Nancy Faires Conklin and Margaret A. Lourie, 1983.

10. Nancy Conklin and Margaret A. Lourie, *A Host of Tongues* (New York: Free Press, 1983), adapted by and cited in Baker and Wright, *Foundations of Bilingual Education and Bilingualism*, 69.

11. Baker and Wright, *Foundations of Bilingual Education and Bilingualism*, 63, 119–20.

12. Conklin and Lourie, *A Host of Tongues*, adapted by and cited in Baker and Wright, *Foundations of Bilingual Education and Bilingualism*, 69.

13. Colin Baker, quoted in Levy, *Baby's First Words in French*, 16.

14. Adam Beck, *Maximize Your Child's Bilingual Ability* (Hiroshima, Japan: Bilingual Adventures, 2016), 47.

15. Beck, *Maximize Your Child's Bilingual Ability*, 185–86.

16. Beck, *Maximize Your Child's Bilingual Ability*, 29, 31. It is true that English is a high-status language, whereas many immigrants in America are up against very different challenges, including the fact that their languages lack the power and the status of English. This affects language transmission. Still, Beck's methodology, described in the book and on his website, *Bilingual Monkeys*, is consistent with research recommendations and has been popular with families around the world.

17. Rumer, "A Lot of Our Ideas About Bilingual Children Are Total Myths."

18. Ellen Bialystok and Xiaojia Feng, "Language Proficiency and Executive Control in Proactive Interference: Evidence from Monolingual and Bilingual Children and Adults," *Brain and Language* 109, nos. 2–3 (May–June 2009): 93–100, https://www.ncbi .nlm.nih.gov/pmc/articles/PMC2699211.

19. Erika Hoff, Cynthia Core, Silvia Place, Rosario Rumiche, Melissa Señor, and Marisol Parra, "Dual Language Exposure and Early Bilingual Development," *Journal of Child Language* 39, no. 1 (January 2012): 1–27, https://www.ncbi.nlm.nih.gov/pmc /articles/PMC4323282.

20. Hoff, "Why Bilingual Development Is Not Easy."

21. Ellen Bialystok and Xiaojia Feng, "Language Proficiency and Executive Control in Proactive Interference: Evidence from Monolingual and Bilingual Children and Adults."

22. Beck, *Maximize Your Child's Bilingual Ability*, 75.

23. Baker and Wright. *Foundations of Bilingual Education and Bilingualism*, 121. Another term for this concept is *family language planning*, necessary to establish and maintain childhood bilingualism, writes Baker.

24. Baker and Wright. *Foundations of Bilingual Education and Bilingualism*, 93.

25. Patricia K. Kuhl, "How Babies Learn Language," *Scientific American*, November 2015, https://www.scientificamerican.com/article/how-babies-learn-language.

26. "Bilingual Babies' Vocabulary Linked to Early Brain Differentiation," *Science Daily*, August 29, 2011, https://www.sciencedaily.com/releases/2011/08/110829070559 .htm. This study was coauthored by Patricia K. Kuhl, Adrian Garcia-Sierra, Maritza Rivera-Gaxiola, Cherie R. Percaccio, Barbara T. Conboy, Harriett Romo, Lindsay Klarman, and Sophia Ortiz, titled "Bilingual Language Learning: An ERP Study Relating Early Brain Responses to Speech, Language Input, and Later Word Production," and published in the *Journal of Phonetics* in October 2011.

27. Levy, *Baby's First Words in French*, 2.

28. Baker and Wright, *Foundations of Bilingual Education and Bilingualism*, 116–18.

29. Grosjean, *Bilingual: Life and Reality*, 77.

30. Baker and Wright, *Foundations of Bilingual Education and Bilingualism*, 117–18.

31. De Houwer, "Parental Language Input Patterns and Children's Bilingual Use."

32. François Grosjean, "The Languages You Speak to Your Bilingual Child," *Psychology Today*, October 24, 2014, https://www.psychologytoday.com/us/blog/life -bilingual/201410/the-languages-you-speak-your-bilingual-child.

33. Annick De Houwer, "Trilingual Input and Children's Language Use in Trilingual Families in Flanders," chap. 6 in *Trilingualism in Family, School and Community*, ed. Charlotte Hoffmann and Jehannes Ytsma (Clevedon, UK: Multilingual Matters,

2004), https://www.researchgate.net/publication/330658856_Chapter_6_Trilingual_Input_and_Children's_Language_Use_in_Trilingual_Families_in_Flanders.

34. Levy, *Baby's First Words in French*, 14.

35. Baker and Wright, *Foundations of Bilingual Education and Bilingualism*, 90–91.

36. Baker and Wright, *Foundations of Bilingual Education and Bilingualism*, 93.

37. Chisato Danjo, "Why It's Okay for Bilingual Children to Mix Languages," *The Conversation*, June 20, 2018, https://theconversation.com/why-its-okay-for-bilingual-children-to-mix-languages-97448.

38. In commenting on the one-person, one-language method, linguist Ingrid Piller writes, "The practices of the well-to-do are a source of linguistic security and a sought after advantage, but the bilingualism of the poor is a source of insecurity and disadvantage," in Ingrid Piller, "Private Language Planning: The Best of Both Worlds?," *Estudios de Sociolingüística* 2, no. 1 (2001): 61–80, where she discusses relative merits and inequities of various bilingualism approaches, https://www.languageonthemove.com/downloads/PDF/piller_2001_private%20lg%20planning.pdf.

39. Baker and Wright, *Foundations of Bilingual Education and Bilingualism*, 92.

40. Beck, *Maximize Your Child's Bilingual Ability*, 123.

41. Grosjean, *Bilingual: Life and Reality*, 207.

42. Baker and Wright, *Foundations of Bilingual Education and Bilingualism*, 94.

43. Baker and Wright, *Foundations of Bilingual Education and Bilingualism*, 94, 92.

44. De Houwer, "Parental Language Input Patterns and Children's Bilingual Use."

45. De Houwer, "Parental Language Input Patterns and Children's Bilingual Use."

46. Code-switching is a part of a larger phenomenon known as *translanguaging*, which describes ways bilingual people use all of their resources to communicate meaningfully. Baker and Wright, *Foundations of Bilingual Education and Bilingualism*, 98–99.

47. Grosjean, *Bilingual: Life and Reality*, 51–57.

48. Shana Poplack, "Sometimes I'll Start a Sentence in Spanish Y Termino en Español": Toward a Typology of Code-Switching," *Linguistics* 18, nos. 7–8 (January 1980): 581–618, https://yorkspace.library.yorku.ca/xmlui/bitstream/handle/10315/2506/CRLC00161.pdf.

49. Ilan Stavans, "In Defense of Spanglish: Low-Bred Languages, the Class Struggle, and Why Amherst College Teaches Spanglish," *The Common Reader*, October 1, 2014, https://commonreader.wustl.edu/c/cervantes-spanglish.

50. Baker and Wright, *Foundations of Bilingual Education and Bilingualism*, 92.

51. De Houwer, "Parental Language Input Patterns and Children's Bilingual Use."

52. Amy Chua, *Battle Hymn of the Tiger Mother* (New York: Penguin, 2011), 18–19.

53. Baker and Wright, *Foundations of Bilingual Education and Bilingualism*, 95.

54. Baker and Wright, *Foundations of Bilingual Education and Bilingualism*, 95, 109.

55. Grosjean, *Bilingual: Life and Reality*, 210–11.

56. Grosjean, *Bilingual: Life and Reality*, 210–11.

57. Baker and Wright, *Foundations of Bilingual Education and Bilingualism*, 91.

CHAPTER 9: NANNIES AND DAYCARES AND GRANDMAS, OH MY!

1. Dinaw Mengestu, "Home at Last," in *Brooklyn Was Mine*, ed. Chris Knutsen and Valerie Steiker (New York: Riverhead Books, 2008), 217.

2. "How to Choose Quality Child Care," Zero to Three, February 8, 2010, https://www.zerotothree.org/resources/84-how-to-choose-quality-child-care.

3. Maki Park, phone interview with author, July 23, 2020.

4. Jessica Glenza, "Why Does It Cost $32,093 Just to Give Birth in America?," *The Guardian*, January 16, 2018, https://www.theguardian.com/us-news/2018/jan/16 /why-does-it-cost-32093-just-to-give-birth-in-america.

5. Taryn Morrissey, "Why Child Care Costs More Than College Tuition—and How to Make It More Affordable," *The Conversation*, March 9, 2018, https://the conversation.com/why-child-care-costs-more-than-college-tuition-and-how-to-make -it-more-affordable-92396.

6. "Net Childcare Costs," *Organisation for Economic Co-operation and Development*, 2019, https://data.oecd.org/benwage/net-childcare-costs.htm.

7. Ajay Chaudry, Taryn Morrissey, Christina Weiland, and Hirokazu Yoshikawa, *Cradle to Kindergarten: A New Plan to Combat Inequality* (New York: Russell Sage Foundation, 2017), 140.

8. Chaudry, Morrissey, Weiland, and Yoshikawa, *Cradle to Kindergarten*, 14, 8.

9. Shelley J. Correll, Stephen Benard, and In Paik, "Getting a Job: Is There a Motherhood Penalty?," *American Journal of Sociology* 112, no. 5 (March 2007): 1297–1338, https://sociology.stanford.edu/sites/g/files/sbiybj9501/f/publications/getting _a_job-_is_there_a_motherhood_penalty.pdf.

10. "Occupational Outlook Handbook: Childcare Workers," US Bureau of Labor Statistics, https://www.bls.gov/ooh/personal-care-and-service/childcare-workers.htm; and "Occupational Employment Statistics: 53-6021 Parking Attendants," US Bureau of Labor Statistics, https://www.bls.gov/oes/current/oes536021.htm.

11. Urban Child Institute, "Baby's Brain Begins Now: Conception to Age 3," http://www.urbanchildinstitute.org/why-0-3/baby-and-brain.

12. Rasheed Malik, Katie Hamm, et al., "America's Child Care Deserts in 2018," Center for American Progress, December 6, 2018, https://www.americanprogress .org/issues/early-childhood/reports.2018/12/06/461643/americas-child-care-deserts -2018.

13. Claudia Dreifus, "The Bilingual Advantage," *New York Times*, May 30, 2011, https://www.nytimes.com/2011/05/31/science/31conversation.html.

14. Jessica Zamberletti, Giulia Cavrini, and Cecilia Tomassini, "Grandparents Providing Childcare in Italy," *European Journal of Ageing* 15, no. 3 (September 2018): 265–75, https://www.ncbi.nlm.nih.gov/pmc/articles/PMC6156721/; and "In China, Childcare Is Truly a Family Affair," *CBS News*, March 7, 2019, https://www.cbsnews .com/news/in-china-childcare-is-truly-a-family-affair.

15. Jessica Mendoza, "More Grandparents Become Caregivers for Grandkids. Is That Good?," *Christian Science Monitor*, February 16, 2016, https://www.csmonitor .com/USA/Society/2016/0216/More-grandparents-become-caregivers-for-grandkids .-Is-that-good.

CHAPTER 10: PROTESTS AND MYTHS

1. Dina Nayeri, *The Ungrateful Refugee* (New York: Catapult, 2019), 12.

2. Kelly Bridges and Erika Hoff, "Older Sibling Influences on the Language Environment and Language Development of Toddlers in Bilingual Homes," *Applied Psycholinguistics* 35, no. 2 (March 2014): 225–41, https://www.ncbi.nlm.nih.gov/pmc /articles/PMC4208071.

3. Bridges and Hoff, "Older Sibling Influences on the Language Environment and Language Development of Toddlers in Bilingual Homes."

4. François Grosjean, "The Languages You Speak to Your Bilingual Child," *Psychology Today*, October 24, 2014, https://www.psychologytoday.com/us/blog/life-bilingual/201410/the-languages-you-speak-your-bilingual-child.

5. Grosjean, *Bilingual: Life and Reality*, 183–84.

6. Levy, *Baby's First Words in French*, 21–22.

7. Levy, *Baby's First Words in French*, 17.

8. Baker and Wright, *Foundations of Bilingual Education and Bilingualism*, 104.

9. Grosjean, *Bilingual: Life and Reality*, 179.

10. Levy, *Baby's First Words in French*, 43.

11. Colin Baker and Sylvia Prys Jones, *Encyclopedia of Bilingualism and Bilingual Education* (Clevedon, UK: Multilingual Matters, 1998), 36.

12. Naomi Steiner, *7 Steps to Raising a Bilingual Child* (New York: AMACOM, 2008), 40–41.

13. Levy, *Baby's First Words in French*, 45.

14. Baker and Prys Jones, *Encyclopedia of Bilingualism and Bilingual Education*, 36–37.

15. "Raising Children Bilingual Offers Surprising Benefits," *Today Show*, October 16, 2013, https://www.today.com/video/raising-children-bilingual-offers-surprising-benefits-54514755730.

16. Kathryn Kohnert, "Bilingual Children with Primary Language Impairment: Issues, Evidence and Implications for Clinical Actions," *Journal of Communication Disorders* 43, no. 6 (November–December 2010): 456–73, https://www.ncbi.nlm.nih.gov/pmc/articles/PMC2900386.

17. "Bilingual Babies: The Roots of Bilingualism in Newborns," *Science Daily*, February 17, 2010, https://www.sciencedaily.com/releases/2010/02/100216142330.htm. The study was conducted by Krista Byers-Heinlein, Tracey C. Burns, and Janet F. Werker and published in *Psychological Science*, January 29, 2010, https://journals.sagepub.com/doi/abs/10.1177/0956797609360758.

18. "Language Development Starts in the Womb," *Science Daily*, July 18, 2017, https://www.sciencedaily.com/releases/2017/07/170718084600.htm. The study was originally conducted by Utako Minai, Kathleen Gustafson, Robert Fiorentino, Allard Jongman, and Joan Sereno at the University of Kansas and published in *NeuroReport* on July 5, 2017, available at https://journals.lww.com/neuroreport/Abstract/2017/08010/Fetal_rhythm_based_language_discrimination__a.4.aspx.

19. Baker and Prys Jones, *Encyclopedia of Bilingualism and Bilingual Education*, 38.

CHAPTER 11: LIVE AND LEARN

1. Viet Thanh Nguyen, "From Here to Home," *New York Times*, November 19, 2019, https://www.nytimes.com/interactive/2019/11/19/opinion/opdocs-immigration.html.

2. Erika Christakis, "The New Preschool Is Crushing Kids," *The Atlantic*, January/February 2016, https://www.theatlantic.com/magazine/archive/2016/01/the-new-preschool-is-crushing-kids/419139.

3. Kasinitz, Mollenkopf, Waters, and Holdaway, *Inheriting the City*, 149.

4. Kasinitz, Mollenkopf, Waters, and Holdaway, *Inheriting the City*, 150.

5. Kasinitz, Mollenkopf, Waters, and Holdaway, *Inheriting the City*, 150. Controlling for age and gender, the research looked at how the children of West Indian

immigrants fared compared to the American Black community, how second-generation Dominicans and South Americans fared compared to the Puerto Rican and "Nuyorican" populations, and how the children of Russian Jewish and Chinese immigrants performed compared to native-born whites. The authors note that the optimistic results may in part be influenced by the fact that most of the respondents' parents had legal status (then or later on), which was easier to obtain at that time than in recent years. Also, their research occurred during a more economically stable time, before the recession of 2007–2009. Finally, the authors note, New York is so culturally diverse that New Yorkers don't perceive themselves to be outsiders as they might in other parts of the country (more on methodology and conclusions on pages 12–15, 23, and 342–43). The authors also note that their research was sensitive to individual variations among the groups they looked at and acknowledged the multiplicity of people's identities and social roles.

6. "Second-Generation Americans: A Portrait of the Adult Children of Immigrants," Social and Demographic Trends, Pew Research Center, February 7, 2013, https://www.pewsocialtrends.org/2013/02/07/second-generation-americans.

7. Kasinitz, Mollenkopf, Waters, and Holdaway, *Inheriting the City*, 20, 354–55.

8. Yalda Modabber, phone and in-person interviews with author, September 20, 2017, and August 6, 2020.

CHAPTER 12: "THEY SAY LITTLE RACIST THINGS"

1. Chua, *Battle Hymn of the Tiger Mother*, 86.

2. Veronika Bondarenko, "Hating Putin and Loving Trump—Why That Makes Sense to Some Russian Americans," *Business Insider*, April 9, 2017, https://www.businessinsider.com/russian-americans-trump-voters-dislike-putin-2017-4; Eliza Willis and Janet A. Seiz, "All Latinos Don't Vote the Same Way—Their Place of Origin Matters," *The Conversation*, March 17, 2020, https://theconversation.com/all-latinos-dont-vote-the-same-way-their-place-of-origin-matters-133600; and Abby Budiman, "Asian Americans Are the Fastest-Growing Racial or Ethnic Group in the U.S. Electorate," Pew Research Center, May 7, 2020, https://www.pewresearch.org/fact-tank/2020/05/07/asian-americans-are-the-fastest-growing-racial-or-ethnic-group-in-the-u-s-electorate.

3. Colorism is tragically endemic in various immigrant communities. In their study of intermarriage and dating patterns among second and 1.5 generation of immigrants in New York, Philip Kasinitz and colleagues found that the same concept of "improving the race" was also a common Latin American expression. *Inheriting the City*, 232.

4. Jill J. Barshay, "Russia's Gay Men Step Out of Soviet-Era Shadows," *New York Times*, February 10, 1993, www.nytimes.com/1993/02/10/world/russia-s-gay-men-step-out-of-soviet-era-shadows.html.

CHAPTER 13: BETWEEN TWO WORLDS

1. Allen Say, *Grandfather's Journey* (Boston: Houghton Mifflin Harcourt, 1993), 31.

2. Richard Gunderman, "Dr. Spock's Timeless Lessons in Parenting," September 6, 2019, *The Conversation*, https://theconversation.com/dr-spocks-timeless-lessons-in-parenting-122377.

3. Pamela Druckerman, *Bringing Up Bébé: One American Mother Discovers the Wisdom of French Parenting* (New York: Penguin Press, 2012), 17.

4. Tiffany De Sousa Machado, Anna Chur-Hansen, and Clemence Due, "First-Time Mothers' Perceptions of Social Support: Recommendations for Best Practice," *Health Psychology Open* 7, no. 1 (January 1, 2020), https://journals.sagepub.com /doi/full/10.1177/2055102919898611.

5. De Sousa Machado, Chur-Hansen, and Due, "First-Time Mothers' Perceptions of Social Support."

6. "Farm Labor," Economic Research Service, United States Department of Agriculture, https://www.ers.usda.gov/topics/farm-economy/farm-labor#demographic. In 2018, only 45 percent of farm laborers, graders, and sorters were born in the US.

7. Julia Higgins, "The Rise and Fall of the American 'Melting Pot,'" *Wilson Quarterly*, December 5, 2015, https://www.wilsonquarterly.com/stories/the-rise -and-fall-of-the-american-melting-pot. The term *melting pot* became popular after Israel Zangwill's 1908 play with the same name, which offered the promise of America: "America is God's Crucible, the great Melting-Pot where all the races of Europe are melting and reforming. . . . Germans and Frenchmen, Irishmen and Englishmen, Jews and Russians—into the Crucible with you all! God is making the American."

8. Susan K. Brown and Frank D. Bean, "Assimilation Models, Old and New: Explaining a Long-Term Process," *Migration Policy Institute*, October 1, 2006, https:// www.migrationpolicy.org/article/assimilation-models-old-and-new-explaining-long -term-process.

9. Elana Firsht, "'Assembly Line Americanization': Henry Ford's Progressive Politics," *Michigan Journal of History*, Fall 2012, https://michiganjournalhistory.files .wordpress.com/2014/02/fall-12-firsht.pdf.

10. Firsht, "'Assembly Line Americanization.'"

11. Brown and Bean, "Assimilation Models, Old and New."

12. Waters and Pineau, "The Integration of Immigrants into American Society," 7.

13. Masha Rumer, "Bilingual Parenting Matters—Even If the White House Says It Doesn't," *SheKnows*, August 21, 2018, https://www.sheknows.com/parenting /articles/1140865/bilingual-parenting-matters. Email interview with author conducted March 12, 2018.

14. John W. Berry, "Immigration, Acculturation, and Adaptation," *Applied Psychology: An International Review* 46, no. 1 (1997): 5–68, https://www.ucd.ie/mcri/resources /Dermot%20Ryan%20Reading.pdf.

15. Berry, "Immigration, Acculturation, and Adaptation."

16. Berry, "Immigration, Acculturation, and Adaptation."

17. Grosjean, *Bilingual: Life and Reality*, 116.

18. Grosjean, *Bilingual: Life and Reality*, 112–13.

19. Grosjean, *Bilingual: Life and Reality*, 111, 117, 120.

20. Grosjean, *Bilingual: Life and Reality*, 104.

21. Grosjean, *Bilingual: Life and Reality*, 115.

22. Anya Dashevsky, phone interview with author, April 19, 2017. Email interview with author, August 12, 2020.

CHAPTER 14: FINDING HOME

    1. Aneta Pavlenko, "Bilingual Selves," chap. 1 in *Bilingual Minds: Emotional Experience, Expression, and Representation*, ed. Aneta Pavlenko (Clevedon, UK: Multilingual Matters, 2006), 29, http://www.anetapavlenko.com/pdf/Bilingual_Selves.pdf.

    2. Mengestu, "Home at Last," 218.

    3. Vanessa Williamson and Isabella Gelfand, "Trump and Racism: What Do the Data Say?," *FixGov* blog, Brookings Institution, August 14, 2019, https://www .brookings.edu/blog/fixgov/2019/08/14/trump-and-racism-what-do-the-data-say.